D

GlassWear

Ursula Ilse-Neuman
Cornelie Holzach
Jutta-Annette Page

GlassWear

Glass in Contemporary Jewelry
Glas im zeitgenössischen Schmuck

ARNOLDSCHE Art Publishers
in collaboration with the Museum of Arts & Design, New York
and the Schmuckmuseum Pforzheim

Authors · Autoren
Ursula Ilse-Neuman,
New York, New York
Cornelie Holzach,
Pforzheim, Germany
Jutta-Annette Page,
Toledo, Ohio

Editing · Lektorat
Nancy Preu, Orono,
Minnesota

Translation · Übersetzung
English-German:
Uta Hasekamp, Bonn,
Germany
Ursula Hundeck-Kemena,
Mainz, Germany
German-English: Joan
Clough, Castallack,
England

Offset-Reproductions
Repromayer, Reutlingen,
Germany

Printing
Leibfarth & Schwarz,
Dettingen/Erms, Germany

Printed on PEFC certified
paper. This certificate
stands throughout Europe
for long-term sustainable
forest management in a
multi-stakeholder process.

**Photo credits ·
Bildnachweis**
See page 209

Every effort has been
made to seek permission
to reproduce the images
and we are grateful to the
individuals and institutions
who have assisted in this
task. Any omissions are
entirely unintentional, and
the details should be
addressed to the publisher.

The excerpt from *Volcano*
that appears on page 118
of this book is printed with
the permission of the current copyright holder from
John Shepley's translation
of Eugène Ionesco's introduction to Maurice and
Katia Krafft's *Volcano,*
with poetry by Max Gérard
(New York: H. N. Abrams,
1975).

The excerpt from *Schnee-
land* by Yasunari Kawabata
on page 130 of this book
is printed with the pub-
lisher's permission from
Yasunari Kawabata,
Schneeland. Roman Aus
dem Japanischen von
Oskar Benl. © 1969 Carl
Hanser Verlag, München –
Wien.

**Cover illustration ·
Titelabbildung**
Tarja Lehtinen, Cameo
Brooches/Kamee-
broschen, 2006, see
page 135

Frontispiece
Thomas Gentille,
brooch/Brosche, 2007,
see page 113

Bibliographic information
published by Die Deutsche
Bibliothek. Die Deutsche
Bibliothek lists this
publication in the Deutsche
Nationalbibliografie;
detailed bibliographic data
is available on the Internet
at http://dnb.ddb.de

ISBN 978-3-89790-274-9
Made in 2007

GlassWear has been made
possible in part through a
generous grant from
The Mondriaan Foundation,
Amsterdam.

Mondriaan Stichting
(Mondriaan Foundation)

Additional support has
been provided by the
Karma Foundation, North
Brunswick, New Jersey,
and Art Alliance for
Contemporary Glass,
Evanston, Illinois.

**Exhibition Schedule ·
Ausstellungsorte**

November 7, 2007 –
January 31, 2008
Glass Pavilion, Toledo
Museum of Art
Toledo, Ohio

March 14, 2008 –
May 25, 2008
Schmuckmuseum
Pforzheim
Pforzheim, Germany

April 18, 2009 –
June 28, 2009
Memorial Art Gallery of
the University of
Rochester, Rochester,
New York

Summer 2009
Museum of Arts & Design
New York, New York

October 2, 2009 –
January 3, 2010
Mobile Museum of Art
Mobile, Alabama

Contents · *Inhalt*

Foreword
Holly Hotchner, Director
Museum of Arts & Design

The Museum of Arts & Design is proud to present *GlassWear*, an exhibition and catalogue of the recent work of sixty leading international jewelry artists whose use of glass in jewelry makes a significant contribution to contemporary visual culture.

The last five decades in the field of art jewelry have been revolutionary as artists have established that ideas and creativity can imbue materials with value that outshines their intrinsic worth. The use of glass in jewelry has been particularly interesting in this regard. Glass is a common material—sand transformed by heat—that acquires value in jewelry only through an artist's concept and mastery. The works in *GlassWear* demonstrate this transformation. Whether fashioned from blown, molded, or flameworked glass, Pyrex, medical vials, antique glass, mirrors, glass beads, optical glass, old bottles, or torched road signs, these "jewels" are tributes to the brilliance of the artists who created them.

The Museum of Arts & Design has long championed contemporary jewelry through its collections, exhibitions, and publications. It has given us great pleasure, therefore, to collaborate on this project with the Schmuckmuseum, Pforzheim, in Germany, a kindred institution dedicated to increasing awareness of the artistic importance of historical and contemporary jewelry. In particular, we extend our thanks to Cornelie Holzach, director of the Schmuckmuseum, Pforzheim, for her enthusiastic participation in the planning of this exhibition and for her perceptive and informative catalogue essay. Jutta-Annette Page, curator of glass at the Toledo Museum of Art, receives our gratitude, as well, for her essay detailing the historical development of the use of glass in jewelry. Among the many individuals on our own staff who worked hard to produce this bi-continental, bi-lingual exhibition and publication, Curator Ursula Ilse-Neuman deserves to be singled out. Her expertise and dedication to the field of art jewelry have made this project a reality. Through her selection of objects for the exhibition and through her insightful essay, she has greatly enriched our understanding of contemporary art jewelry.

Finally, I extend my deepest appreciation to the Mondriaan Foundation, the Karma Foundation, the Art Alliance for Contemporary Glass, and the Museum of Arts & Design's board of trustees for their crucial support for this exhibition and publication.

Vorwort
Holly Hotchner, Direktorin
Museum of Arts & Design

Das Museum of Arts & Design ist stolz darauf, GlassWear zu präsentieren, eine Ausstellung und ein Buch, die die jüngsten Arbeiten von 60 führenden internationalen Schmuckkünstlern zeigen, die mit der Art und Weise, wie sie Glas für Schmuckstücke verwenden, einen entscheidenden Beitrag zur zeitgenössischen Kunst leisten.

In den letzten fünf Jahrzehnten hat es einen großen Umbruch in der Schmuckkunst gegeben. So gelangten Künstler zu der Überzeugung, dass Ideen und Kreativität von einem Material etwas gestalten können, das weit über dessen eigentlichen Wert hinausgeht. In diesem Zusammenhang ist die Verwendung von Glas für Schmuckstücke besonders interessant. Glas ist ein gewöhnliches Material – Sand, der mit Hilfe von Hitze in einen anderen Aggregatzustand übergeht. Es erhält seinen Wert einzig und allein durch die Idee und das Können des Künstlers. Die Arbeiten von GlassWear belegen diese Transformation. Ganz gleich, ob die Werke aus geblasenem, geformtem oder geflammtem Glas, Pyrex, Medizinampullen, antikem Glas, Spiegelglas, Glasperlen, optischem Glas, alten Flaschen oder dem Glas ausgebrannter Ampeln oder Verkehrszeichen geschaffen wurden, all diese „Juwelen" sind ein Tribut an die Brillanz der Künstler, die sie gemacht haben.

Das Museum of Arts & Design setzt sich schon lange mit seinen Sammlungen, Ausstellungen und Publikationen für zeitgenössischen Schmuck ein. Daher war es uns eine große Freude, an diesem Projekt mit dem Schmuckmuseum Pforzheim, einer verwandten Institution in Deutschland, zu arbeiten, die es sich zur Aufgabe gemacht hat, ein größeres Bewusstsein für die künstlerische Bedeutung historischen und zeitgenössischen Schmucks zu schaffen. Insbesondere möchten wir Cornelie Holzach, der Leiterin des Schmuckmuseums Pforzheim, für ihre engagierte Unterstützung bei der Planung der Ausstellung und für ihren scharfsinnigen und informativen Aufsatz für das Buch danken. Auch Jutta-Annette Page, Kuratorin des Toledo Museum of Art, Ohio, Abteilung Glas, möchten wir unseren Dank für ihren Aufsatz aussprechen, in dem sie die historische Entwicklung der Verwendung von Glas im Schmuck darlegt. Unter den zahlreichen Mitgliedern unseres eigenen Personals, die hart an der Umsetzung dieser Ausstellung und Publikation auf zwei Kontinenten und in zwei Sprachen mitgearbeitet haben, verdient unsere Kuratorin, Ursula Ilse-Neuman, besondere Erwähnung. Ohne ihr Fachwissen und ihr Engagement für die Schmuckkunst hätte dieses Projekt nicht Wirklichkeit werden können. Mit der Auswahl der Kunstwerke für die Ausstellung und mit ihrem aufschlussreichen Aufsatz hat sie unser Verständnis für Schmuckkunst einen großen Schritt weiter gebracht.

Schließlich möchte ich auch der Mondriaan Foundation, der Karma-Stiftung, der Art Alliance of Contemporary Glass und dem Aufsichtsrat des Museum of Art & Design für deren entscheidende Unterstützung bei dieser Ausstellung und diesem Buch danken.

To launch an exhibition and a book on this scale—more than sixty artists from all over the world are represented—the assistance and enthusiastic commitment of many people are needed. Collaboration of the kind we have experienced with the Museum of Arts & Design in New York depends first and foremost on all participants working well together. I am overjoyed that little more than two years after Ursula Ilse-Neuman introduced the *GlassWear* project to us, the book and the exhibition have been brought to fruition. This is certainly not something to be taken for granted. Projects that depend on so many participants and require so many partners call for extraordinary powers of persuasion in order to bring everyone on board and make what might first have seemed like a rather vaguely outlined undertaking assume concrete form. It was the enthusiasm and sheer delight with which Ursula Ilse-Neuman presented her *Glass-Wear* project that convinced me at our very first meeting about the exhibition and publication that the Schmuckmuseum Pforzheim should become a partner. The route to realizing the book and exhibition has been a long one, but it has been more than rewarding. Not only has a comprehensive publication emerged, which can justifiably claim to represent the world's cutting-edge art jewelry featuring glass, but, more importantly, the groundwork has been laid for bringing contemporary jewelry to a broader public and encouraging them to learn more about the artists creating it.

A commitment to contemporary jewelry is one of the fundamental goals of the Schmuck-museum Pforzheim. Since we have one of the world's largest collections of post-1950 auteur jewelry, we are challenged daily to make a broad public enthusiastic about this art form, a challenge we gladly accept. We are delighted and proud when we see and hear that we have succeeded in enlisting new friends for modern jewelry. Special exhibitions and publications are valuable contributions to this process since they present the quite divergent yet invariably exciting approaches taken in this new jewelry.

We are particularly indebted to the enormous commitment shown by our colleagues, the staff of the Museum of Art & Design in New York, which will allow *GlassWear* to embark on its transcontinental travels. My particular thanks go to Ursula Ilse-Neuman, whose dedication to the project she initiated has been unswerving, and also to Holly Hotchner, who has made the partnership between New York and Pforzheim possible.

Um ein Ausstellungs- und Buchprojekt in dieser Größenordnung – über sechzig Künstlerinnen und Künstler aus aller Welt sind mit ihren Werken vertreten – auf den Weg zu bringen, bedarf es der Mithilfe und dem freudigen Engagement vieler. Bei Kooperationen, wie wir sie jetzt erstmals mit dem Museum of Arts & Design New York verabreden konnten, ist vor allem das gute Zusammenspiel aller Beteiligten gefordert. Es ist mir eine große Freude, dass – nachdem vor über zwei Jahren Ursula Ilse-Neuman auf uns zukam, um uns das Projekt GlassWear vorzustellen – nun tatsächlich Buch und Ausstellung realisiert werden konnten. Dies ist keineswegs eine Selbstverständlichkeit. Gerade bei Projekten, bei denen es auf viele Beteiligte ankommt, bei denen viele Partner gefragt sind, ist es wohl immer die persönliche Überzeugungskraft, die dann alle mit ins Boot nimmt, um einem anfangs vagen Unternehmen Hand und Fuß zu geben. Es war die Begeisterung und die Freude, mit denen Ursula Ilse-Neuman ihr Projekt GlassWear vermittelte und die mich bei unserem ersten Gespräch über Ausstellung und Publikation überzeugten, dass das Schmuckmuseum Pforzheim sich als Partner engagieren sollte. Der Weg bis zum Buch und zur Ausstellung war lang, aber er hat sich mehr als gelohnt. Es ist nicht nur eine umfangreiche Publikation entstanden, die durchaus den Anspruch für sich erheben kann, heute den internationalen Stand der Schmuckkunst mit Glas zu repräsentieren. Es ist auch ein wichtiger Baustein gelungen, zeitgenössischen Schmuck einem breiten Publikum nahezubringen und die Überzeugungsarbeit zu leisten, dass es spannend und erkenntnisreich ist, sich mit den Schmuckkünstlerinnen und -künstlern der Gegenwart auseinanderzusetzen.

Das Engagement für zeitgenössischen Schmuck ist eine der originären Aufgaben des Schmuckmuseums Pforzheim. Mit einer der größten Sammlungen von Autorenschmuck nach 1950, wobei der Schwerpunkt auf Werken aus Europa liegt, gehört es zu unseren täglichen, gerne angenommenen Herausforderungen, ein breites Publikum für diese Form der Kunst zu begeistern. Es erfüllt uns mit Freude und manchmal ein wenig Stolz, wenn wir hören und sehen, dass wir neue Freunde für modernen Schmuck gewinnen konnten. Sonderausstellungen und Publikationen sind dazu wertvolle Beiträge, die die sehr unterschiedlichen und spannenden Ansätze des neuen Schmucks illustrieren.

Dem großen Engagement vor allem der Kollegen und Mitarbeiter des Museum of Art & Design New York ist es zu verdanken, dass GlassWear nun seine Reise über die Kontinente antreten kann. Mein besonderer Dank gilt Ursula Ilse-Neuman, die sich unermüdlich für ihr Projekt eingesetzt hat, sowie Holly Hotchner, die die Partnerschaft zwischen New York und Pforzheim ermöglicht hat.

Acknowledgments
Ursula Ilse-Neuman, Curator
Museum of Arts & Design

GlassWear has become a reality through the strong support and hard work of a cadre of dedicated individuals. My first acknowledgment goes, deservedly, to Holly Hotchner, director of the Museum of Arts & Design, for her unflagging support of this exhibition and catalogue exploring the importance of contemporary art jewelry.

Cornelie Holzach, director of the Pforzheim Museum, is a jewelry scholar of world renown, and it has been a privilege to work with her on this project from its very inception. I am also indebted to Dirk Allgaier at Arnoldsche Verlagsanstalt, Stuttgart, for his enthusiasm for contemporary jewelry and his expertise in publishing beautiful books, and to Nancy Preu, whose editing of this catalogue sharpened our thinking as well as our prose.

My special gratitude goes to curatorial assistants Jessica Nicewarner and Sara Mandel. Their knowledge and professionalism are admirably complemented by their cheerful demeanor and their unflinching willingness to take on difficult jobs. My appreciation also goes to Steve Mann, traveling exhibitions manager, for the eye-catching promotional material he designed for the exhibition, as well as to registrar Linda Clous and her able staff, Megan Krol and Brian MacElhose. The contributions of many volunteers, summer interns, and part-time assistants were vital to the project's successful completion. In particular, my thanks go to Katherine White Miller, librarian, Toledo Museum of Art, for her generous and unexpected help when it was most needed, and to Jennifer Hinshaw, Michelle Moyal, Sarah Archer, Nora Melendez, and Kally Michalakis. My special appreciation goes to friend and jewelry expert Thomas Gentille, who graciously spent many hours applying his keen artistic eye and vast knowledge of the field for the benefit of this book.

Finally and above all, I want to express my heartfelt thanks to the artists who have contributed to this project. Their insights into jewelry as object and concept have fanned our passion for this lively form of artistic expression and expanded our understanding. I hope we have succeeded in conveying the intelligence and delight they bring to their art.

Danksagung
Ursula Ilse-Neuman, Kuratorin
Museum of Arts & Design

Dass wir GlassWear auf die Beine stellen konnten, verdanken wir der uneingeschränkten Unterstützung und harten Arbeit zahlreicher engagierter Personen. So möchte ich zuallererst Holly Hotchner, der Direktorin des Museum of Arts & Design, meinen Dank für ihren unermüdlichen Einsatz für diese Ausstellung und den Katalog, mit denen wir die Bedeutung zeitgenössischen Schmucks beleuchten wollen, aussprechen.

Cornelie Holzach, Leiterin des Schmuckmuseums Pforzheim, ist eine bekannte Expertin im Bereich Schmuck. Ich habe es als ein besonderes Privileg betrachtet, bei diesem Projekt von Anfang an mit ihr zusammenarbeiten zu können. Des Weiteren bin ich Dirk Allgaier, Arnoldsche Art Publishers, Stuttgart, zu großem Dank verpflichtet. Seine große Begeisterung für zeitgenössischen Schmuck und die Expertise, mit der er wunderschöne Bücher zusammenstellt und veröffentlicht, sind beeindruckend. Ebenso dankbar bin ich Nancy Preu, der Lektorin des Katalogs, die sowohl unseren Gedanken als auch unseren Formulierungen den letzten Schliff gegeben hat.

Mein besonderer Dank gilt den Kurator-Assistentinnen Jessica Nicewarner und Sara Mandel, die neben Wissen und Professionalität eine bewundernswerte Freundlichkeit und eine unermüdliche Bereitschaft zur Übernahme schwieriger Aufgaben an den Tag legten. Des Weiteren möchte ich Steve Mann, Koordinator für Wanderausstellungen, meine Wertschätzung aussprechen für das gelungene Werbematerial, das er für die Ausstellung entworfen hat, sowie der Museums-Registrarin Linda Clous und ihren kompetenten Mitarbeitern Megan Krol und Brian MacElhose. Ohne die wertvollen Beiträge zahlreicher freiwilliger Helfer, Sommerpraktikanten und Teilzeitassistenten hätten wir das Projekt nicht vollenden können. Hierfür möchte ich mich insbesondere bei Katherine White Miller, Bibliothekarin im Toledo Museum of Art, für ihre großzügige und unverhoffte Hilfe zu einem Zeitpunkt, in dem wir der Unterstützung dringend bedurften, bedanken, wie auch bei Jennifer Hinshaw, Michelle Moyal, Sarah Archer, Nora Melendez und Kally Michalakis. Mein besondererer Dank geht an den Schmuck-Künstler und -Experten Thomas Gentille, der liebenswürdigerweise viele Stunden aufwendete, in denen sein waches Auge, sein Sinn für das Künstlerische und sein großes Wissen auf diesem Gebiet diesem Buch zugute kamen.

Zu guter Letzt gilt mein allergrößter Dank den Künstlern, die sich an diesem Projekt beteiligt haben. Ihre Einsichten in Schmuck als Objekt und Konzept haben unsere Begeisterung für diese lebendige Form des künstlerischen Ausdrucks weiter geschürt und größeres Verständnis geschaffen. Ich hoffe, wir können mit der Ausstellung und dem Buch die Gedanken und die Freude, die sie in ihre Werke einfließen lassen, erfolgreich vermitteln.

Ursula Ilse-Neuman

Glass in Contemporary Jewelry
Glas im Schmuck der Gegenwart

Why do jewelry artists choose to use glass in their creations and why do glass artists make jewelry? What forms does glass take in contemporary jewelry? The unique works assembled for *GlassWear,* each imbued with a spirit of exploration, experimentation, and nonconformity, provide answers to these questions.

The sixty artists who created the jewelry in *Glass-Wear* comprise a diverse ensemble. Some are primarily glass artists; most are jewelers who use glass as a featured material. Some employ highly sophisticated glassworking techniques such as blowing, flame-working, casting, cutting, polishing, sandblasting, fusing, coiling, and spinning to realize their ideas; others direct or collaborate with skilled glassmakers to achieve the blown or cast forms they want to create; still others avoid the highly demanding process of glassmaking by assembling their work from beads, tubes, rods, sheets, mirrors, plate glass, and glass objects and fragments that they find in their environment.

Although we refer to glass as if it were a well-defined material, thousands of types of glass are manufactured today for specific applications in industry, engineering, architecture, fiber optics, medicine, and communications, as well as for domestic use. The essential ingredient of all glass is silica, a common mineral composed of silicon and oxygen. Because pure silica melts at exceptionally high temperatures (around 2000°C), it is unsuited for most hand-working processes, and fluxes such as soda, potash,

Warum entscheiden sich Schmuckkünstler, in ihren Arbeiten Glas zu verwenden, und warum schaffen Glaskünstler Schmuck? Welche Formen nimmt Glas im Schmuck der Gegenwart an? Die einzigartigen Werke, die in GlassWear *zusammengetragen wurden, ein jedes vom Geist des Erforschens, Experimentierens und des Individualismus erfüllt, geben Antwort auf diese Fragen.*

Die sechzig Künstler, welche den Schmuck in GlassWear *geschaffen haben, bilden eine breit gefächerte Gruppe. Einige von ihnen sind in erster Linie Glaskünstler, die meisten jedoch sind Schmuckkünstler, für die Glas ein wichtiges Material darstellt. Einige machen sich die äußerst anspruchsvollen Techniken der Glasverarbeitung zunutze, um ihre Ideen umzusetzen, wie die Glasbläserei und die Lampenarbeit, den Glasguss und -schliff, das Polieren, Sandstrahlen, Verschmelzen und Drehen von Glas wie auch das Herstellen von Faserglas. Andere weisen versierte Glashersteller an oder arbeiten mit ihnen zusammen, um die geblasenen oder gegossenen Formen herzustellen, die sie schaffen möchten. Wieder andere umgehen den äußerst aufwendigen Prozess der Glasherstellung, indem sie ihre Arbeiten aus Perlen, Röhren, Stäben, Scheiben, Spiegeln oder Flachglas zusammensetzen oder aus gläsernen Gegenständen und Fragmenten, welche sie in ihrer Umgebung finden.*

Heute werden tausende Arten von Glas für spezielle Anwendungsgebiete hergestellt: Anwendungen in der Industrie, im Ingenieurwesen, der Architektur, der Glasfasertechnik, der Medizin und im Kommunikationsbereich wie auch im Haushalt. Der wesentliche Bestandteil aller Glasarten ist Siliciumdioxid, ein häufig vorkommendes Mineral, das aus Silicium und Sauerstoff besteht. Da der Schmelzpunkt von reinem Siliciumdioxid erst bei außergewöhnlich hohen Temperaturen (um 2000 °C) erreicht wird, ist es für die meisten Arten der

lead, and borax must be added in order to reduce the temperature at which silica fuses or melts. Other substances, as well, are commonly incorporated with silica in order to render it suitable for a particular application. Lime, for example, is commonly added to stabilize the glass used in everyday products such as windowpanes and bottles. Lead oxide, the distinguishing element in lead glass or lead crystal, is added to achieve a denser, clearer, and more brilliant glass that is also softer and easier to cut and engrave. Yet another combination, boric oxide fused with silica, produces a glass that is durable and resistant to heat, corrosion, or breakage. Called borosilicate glass, it enables artists to incorporate thinner yet stronger glass elements into their constructions than had been possible before its relatively recent introduction.

In their freedom to experiment with new materials, techniques, and nontraditional concepts, glass artists and jewelers today benefit from the studio craft movement, a series of revolutionary changes that began in the United States during the post–World War II era and revitalized interest in glass and other craft materials as media for art. Inspired by developments in the fine arts and the desire for individual expression, the movement liberated virtually all craft media—glass, metal, ceramics, fiber, and wood—from traditional practices and more importantly from the constraints of functionality. A key element in studio craft, besides the use and appreciation of undervalued materials, was the realization of a work from

Bearbeitung mit der Hand nicht geeignet. Flussmittel wie Soda, Pottasche, Blei oder Borax müssen hinzugefügt werden, um die Temperatur, bei der Siliciumdioxid (ver)schmilzt, zu senken. Auch werden andere Substanzen häufig zusammen mit Siliciumdioxid verwendet, um es für eine bestimmte Anwendung geeignet zu machen. Beispielsweise wird oft Kalk zugesetzt, um dem Glas für alltägliche Erzeugnisse wie Fensterscheiben oder Flaschen Stabilität zu verleihen. Bleioxid, der besondere Bestandteil von Bleiglas oder -kristall, wird hinzugefügt, um dichteres, klareres und glänzenderes Glas zu erhalten, das zugleich weicher ist und leichter geschliffen oder graviert werden kann. Und eine weitere Zusammensetzung, mit Siliciumdioxid verschmolzenes Boroxid, ergibt ein Glas, das haltbar und gegenüber Hitze, Korrosion oder Bruch widerstandfähig ist. Es wird Borsilikatglas genannt und ermöglicht es Künstlern, dünnere und zugleich stabilere Glaselemente in ihre Werke zu integrieren, als es vor seiner verhältnismäßig kurze Zeit zurückliegenden Einführung möglich war.

Was ihre Freiheit betrifft, mit neuen Materialien, Techniken und nichttraditionellen Konzepten zu experimentieren, profitieren die Glas- und Schmuckkünstler heute vom Studio Craft Movement, einer Anzahl revolutionärer Veränderungen, die in den Vereinigten Staaten in den Jahren nach dem Zweiten Weltkrieg ihren Anfang genommen und das Interesse für Glas und andere im Handwerk verwendete Materialien als künstlerische Medien wiederbelebt haben. Von Entwicklungen in den schönen Künsten angeregt und aus dem Wunsch nach individuellem Ausdruck heraus befreite diese Bewegung praktisch alle handwerklichen Medien – Glas, Metall, Keramik, Textilien und Holz – von den traditionellen Vorgehensweisen und, wichtiger noch, von den Einschränkungen der Funktionalität.

conception to execution by a single artist. The objects that were created through this process were primarily one-of-a-kind and not intended for mass production.

The impact of the studio craft movement on glass was complicated by the fact that hot glass was not a medium that could be worked by an individual. With the exception of creating small pieces by lampworking, fashioning hot glass required large-scale facilities and teams of skilled workers, which at that time in the United States were only available in industrial glass operations. To gain experience working with molten glass, some Americans made pilgrimages to Murano in the 1950s, where they learned from the Italian masters of the centuries-old traditions of glassworking. The development of glass as an artistic medium was given a further boost in 1958 at the Brussels World's Fair, where Westerners were exposed for the first time to highly developed glass art from Czechoslovakia. In 1962, Americans Harvey Littleton, then a professor of ceramics, and Dominick Labino, a renowned glass expert, both of whom were familiar with European methods of making art glass, collaborated to work molten glass with simple equipment in two workshops held at the Museum of Art in Toledo, Ohio. An international community of studio glass artists quickly formed, challenging one another to innovate as they shared new techniques, materials, and concepts. The studio jewelry movement also became increasingly international in the 1960s, as Europeans, primarily in the Netherlands, Germany, and the United Kingdom, overthrew goldsmith

Neben der Verwendung und Wertschätzung gering geschätzter Materialien war die Verwirklichung der Arbeit – von der ersten Idee bis zur Ausführung – durch einen einzigen Künstler ein Grundcharakteristikum der Studio Craft. Die auf diese Weise geschaffenen Objekte waren in erster Linie Unikate und nicht für die Massenproduktion vorgesehen.

Der Einfluss der Studio Craft-Bewegung auf das Glas wurde durch die Tatsache erschwert, dass heiß geblasenes Glas nicht gerade ein Medium ist, das von einer einzelnen Person bearbeitet werden kann. Das Formen von heiß geblasenem Glas erfordert große Einrichtungen und Teams geschulter Arbeiter, die es zu dieser Zeit in den Vereinigten Staaten nur in der industriellen Glasfabrikation gab. Um Erfahrungen mit Schmelzglas zu sammeln, gingen in den 1950er Jahren einige Amerikaner nach Murano, wo sie die jahrhundertealten Traditionen der Glasbearbeitung erlernten. Weiteren Auftrieb erhielt die Entwicklung des Glases als künstlerisches Medium mit der Brüsseler Weltausstellung im Jahr 1958, als die Künstler des Westens zum ersten Mal mit der hochentwickelten Glaskunst der Tschechoslowakei in Berührung kamen. Die Amerikaner Harvey Littleton, damals Professor für Keramik, und Dominick Labino, ein bekannter Glasexperte, waren beide mit den europäischen Methoden der Glasherstellung vertraut. 1962 arbeiteten sie in zwei im Museum of Art in Toledo, Ohio, veranstalteten Workshops zusammen, um mit einfachen Werkzeugen Schmelzglas herzustellen. Schnell bildete sich eine internationale Gemeinschaft von Studio Glass-Künstlern, in welcher der eine den anderen zu Innovationen herausforderte und neuartige Techniken, Materialien und Gedanken miteinander geteilt wurden. Zur selben Zeit wurde auch die Studio Jewelry-Bewegung immer internationaler, als europäische Künstler vor

traditions by featuring non-precious materials and emphasizing the value of concepts over costly metals and gemstones.

Viewing the diversity of jewelry assembled for *GlassWear* is nothing short of a theatrical experience, with glass, the central character, showing off its dramatic abilities to the fullest. The works organize themselves into five different categories according to the principal role glass plays in each artist's creation: "old" glass in a new guise; glass as chameleon; glass as surface and structure; glass as symbol and metaphor; and glass as glass. It must be understood, however, that the creations in *GlassWear* are sophisticated and multi-dimensional, and many of the pieces fit quite comfortably in more than one category.

"Old" Glass in a New Guise

Like actors who take on new roles that depart from their past typecasting, previously "used" glass turns up in new guises in many of the works in *GlassWear*. In this way, old glass objects become part of remarkably precious, even startling, creations; broken fragments and shards coalesce to form abstract compositions; antique glass takes on new life; and industrial products are transfigured as their latent aesthetic properties are animated.

When artists such as Robert Ebendorf and Mieke Groot incorporate familiar objects from daily life into their jewelry in order to trigger responses from the viewer or evoke personal or collective memories, they are linked to a jewelry-making tradition that extends

allem in den Niederlanden, in Deutschland und in Großbritannien die Traditionen der Goldschmiede über Bord warfen, indem sie unedle Materialien verwendeten und den Wert von Ideen über den teurer Metalle und Edelsteine stellten.

Den in GlassWear zusammengetragenen Schmuck in seiner Unterschiedlichkeit zu betrachten, kommt vor allem einem Erlebnis gleich, das an ein Schauspiel erinnert, bei der das Glas seine dramatischen Fähigkeiten voll und ganz präsentiert. Die Arbeiten gruppieren sich in fünf Kategorien, je nach der Hauptrolle, die Glas in den Erzeugnissen eines jeden Künstlers spielt: „altes" Glas in einer neuen Rolle, Glas als Verwandlungskünstler (einem Chamäleon ähnlich), Glas als Oberfläche und Struktur, Glas als Symbol und Glas als Glas. Es ist jedoch wichtig zu verstehen, dass die Arbeiten in GlassWear komplex sind und zahlreiche Dimensionen haben. Viele von ihnen fügen sich ohne Weiteres in mehr als eine Kategorie ein.

„Altes" Glas in einer neuen Rolle

Wie Schauspieler, die neue Rollen annehmen, welche sich von ihrer bisherigen Festlegung auf bestimmte Rollentypen entfernen, erscheint schon einmal verwendetes Glas in vielen der Arbeiten in GlassWear in neuem Gewand. Auf diese Weise wird dieses oder jenes Stück Altglas Bestandteil einer bemerkenswert kostbaren Schöpfung; Fragmente und Scherben fügen sich zu abstrakten Kompositionen zusammen; antikes Glas beginnt ein neues Leben; und industrielle Erzeugnisse werden verwandelt, wenn die in ihnen verborgenen ästhetischen Eigenschaften mit Geist erfüllt werden.

Wenn Künstler wie Robert Ebendorf und Mieke Groot vertraute alltägliche Gegenstände in ihre Schmuckstücke integrieren, um im Betrachter Reaktionen auszulösen oder persön-

back at least thirty thousand years to a time when humans crafted their forms from familiar materials such as carved bones, fish vertebrae, animal teeth, claws, stone beads, and healing herbs.

The American jewelry artist Robert Ebendorf began his groundbreaking work with found glass in the 1960s, and almost fifty years later, glass still fascinates him. A leader in the studio jewelry movement in the United States, he combines traditional goldsmith techniques, collage, and found objects, taking delight in the incongruities between what his jewelry is made from and what it becomes. In *Fragments* (2006), he covers an old photograph with broken glass from vodka and beer bottles to pull a story together out of the cultural associations each fragment carries. Ebendorf's credo that anything can be made into jewelry and that de-valued materials can be reconfigured to endow them with worth is reflected in his brooch.

Dutch artist Mieke Groot's necklaces express cultural interactions in the new global community. In addition to large blown glass bubbles, her *Dieg Bou Diar* necklace (2006) features pieces from a discarded container of the popular Senegalese tomato puree product of the same name. In the Wolof language *Dieg Bou Diar* means "that which you always need," and Groot has appropriated that slogan and its cultural symbolism for her necklace.

Broken glass has an edgy quality that many artists use to energize their jewelry. In *Brooch* (2004), the Austrian artist Peter Skubic sets the random and

liche oder kollektive Erinnerungen hervorzurufen, stehen sie mit einer Tradition der Schmuckherstellung in Verbindung, die mindestens 30.000 Jahre zurückreicht, in eine Zeit, in der die Menschen Formen aus vertrauten Materialien wie geschnitzten Knochen, Wirbelknochen von Fischen, Tierzähnen, Klauen, Steinperlen und Heilkräutern bildeten.

Der amerikanische Schmuckkünstler Robert Ebendorf begann seine wegweisende Arbeit mit gefundenem Glas in den 1960er Jahren, und fast fünfzig Jahre später fasziniert ihn Glas noch immer. Dieser führende Künstler der Studioschmuck-Bewegung in den Vereinigten Staaten kombiniert traditionelle Goldschmiedetechniken, Collagen und Fundobjekte und erfreut sich an den Ungereimtheiten zwischen den Bestandteilen seines Schmucks und dem, zu was diese werden. In Fragmente *(2006) bedeckt er eine alte Fotografie mit Glasscherben von Wodka- und Bierflaschen, um aus den kulturellen Assoziationen, die ein jedes Fragment in sich trägt, eine Geschichte zu ziehen. Ebendorfs Credo, dass alles zu Schmuck verarbeitet werden kann und dass gering geschätzte Materialien neu zusammengestellt werden können, um ihnen Wert zu verleihen, spiegelt sich in seiner Brosche.*

Der Halsschmuck der niederländischen Künstlerin Mieke Groot verleiht den kulturellen Wechselbeziehungen in der neuen globalen Gemeinschaft Ausdruck. Neben großen geblasenen Glaskugeln enthält ihre Halskette Dieg Bou Diar *(2006) Teile einer weggeworfenen Dose des beliebten senegalesischen Tomatenpürees gleichen Namens. „Dieg bou diar" aus der Sprache der Wolof bedeutet „das, was du immer brauchst", und Groot hat sich diesen Slogan und die mit ihm verbundene kulturelle Symbolik für ihren Halsschmuck zu eigen gemacht.*

chaotic patterns of broken window glass underlain and enriched by gold leaf against the symmetry of pyrite that he dug out of a mine in Spain. Skubic sees glass as testimony to man's creativity, and like many *GlassWear* artists, he values displays of creativity more than naturally occurring precious gems. Daniel Kruger is attracted to fragments of broken glass salvaged from bottles, windowpanes, motorcar head-lamps, and functional and decorative glass objects for the home. From these readily available forms of glass, he chooses elements for his jewelry that are transparent or reflective, colorless or colored, matte or shiny. In his *Brooch* (1999), this South African-born artist uses an unremarkable midnight blue glass frag-ment as an armature for five gold balls that seem to emerge from the ocean depths.

The worn-out and abandoned detritus of our waste-ful consumer society—bottles, saw blades, clothes-pins, screws and nails—are the raw materials of Swiss jewelry artist Bernhard Schobinger's work. Ingenious and startling adornments such as *Poison-bottle Bracelet* (2003), in which he gives new life to one of the many poison bottles he has collected, function on several levels, not least of which is pungent social criticism. Schobinger leaves it to the viewer/wearer to decipher the message he creates by sprinkling gold dust on the edge of his green glass bracelet with its leering skull and original chemist's label.

Other artists find quite different ways to resurrect the all-too readily available "used" glass of today's throw-away culture. Finnish artist Tarja Lehtinen

Zerbrochenes Glas hat etwas Scharfkantiges, das sich viele Künstler zunutze machen, um ihren Schmuck mit Energie auf-zuladen. In seiner Brosche (2004) *setzt Peter Skubic die zufäl-ligen und wirren Muster zerbrochenen Fensterglases der Sym-metrie von Pyrit entgegen, den er in einer Mine in Spanien ausgegraben hat. Skubic sieht Glas als Zeugnis für die menschliche Kreativität an, und wie viele der in* GlassWear *vertretenen Künstler schätzt er die Darstellung von Kreativität höher als kostbare Edelsteine. Daniel Kruger ziehen die glä-sernen Bruchstücke an, die er aus Flaschen, Fensterscheiben, Autoscheinwerfern und funktionalen wie dekorativen Glas-gegenständen für den häuslichen Gebrauch geborgen hat. Aus diesen jederzeit erhältlichen Glasarten wählt er für seine Schmuckstücke Elemente aus, die durchsichtig sind oder reflek-tieren, farblos oder farbig, matt oder glänzend sind. In seiner* Brosche (1999) *verwendet er ein unauffälliges mitternachts-blaues Fragment als Verankerung für fünf goldene Bälle, die aus den Tiefen des Meeres aufzutauchen scheinen.*

Der verbrauchte und weggeworfene Müll unserer verschwen-derischen Konsumgesellschaft – Flaschen, Sägeblätter, Wäscheklammern, Schrauben und Nägel – sind das Rohma-terial für die Arbeiten des Schweizer Schmuckkünstlers Bern-hard Schobinger. Erfinderische und erstaunliche Schmuck-stücke wie der Giftflaschen-Armreif (2003), *in dem er den vielen von ihm gesammelten Giftfläschchen neues Leben ver-leiht, wirken auf verschiedenen Ebenen, und scharfe Sozial-kritik ist hierbei nicht die unwichtigste. Schobinger überlässt es dem Betrachter oder Träger, die Nachricht zu entschlüsseln, die er formulierte, indem er Goldstaub auf den Rand des Arm-bandes aus grünem Glas mit seinem grinsenden Totenkopf und dem noch originalen Apothekeretikett streute.*

demonstrates a gentle recycling of empty glass bottles by sandblasting cutout pieces to create a fresh perspective on traditional silhouette portraits in her *Cameo Brooches* (2006). Scouting in a junkyard, American metalsmith Boris Bally spotted old traffic signs. His *Vitrified DPW Brooches, Eye and Ring* (2006) showcase the shimmering beauty of the melded metal, plastic, and glass that had been lost in plain sight.

Historical glass elements appear in the work of several artists. The Italian jeweler Piergiuliano Reveane is attracted to the colors of antique glass and intrigued by the idea that glass was more precious than gold in the ancient world. His remarkable *Vetrata I* bracelet (2004) exploits the subtle colors and density of antique window glass to form a strong counterpoint to the luxurious glow of gold and diamonds. In *Gertrude and Alice (hers-n-hers pendant set)* (2000), American jeweler Sondra Sherman uses Victorian crystal chandelier parts to portray the "male-female" relationship between writer Gertrude Stein and her companion Alice B. Toklas. Czech artist Martina Mináriková found a "big pot of old glass beads" from which she selected the nucleus of her iconic brooch *Atom* (2000). Austrian artist Helfried Kodré enshrines the goddess of love with glass tesserae from a pool on the former site of the ancient Terme Aphrodite on Ischia in his highly geometric *Brooch* (2005). In yet another historical permutation, Australian-born jewelry artist Helen Britton transforms old bits of glass retrieved from a defunct costume

Andere Künstler haben sehr unterschiedliche Wege gefunden, um das nur allzu leicht erhältliche „gebrauchte" Glas der heutigen Wegwerfgesellschaft wieder auferstehen zu lassen. Die finnische Künstlerin Tarja Lehtinen zeigt eine einfühlsame Wiederverwertung leerer Glasflaschen, wenn sie in ihren Kameebroschen *(2006) ausgeschnittene Stücke sandstrahlt, um die traditionelle Porträtsilhouette aus einer neuen Perspektive zu betrachten. Beim Erkunden eines Schrottplatzes machte der amerikanische Metallschmied Boris Bally alte Verkehrsschilder ausfindig. Auge und Ring, verglaste DPW-Broschen (2006) bringt die schimmernde Schönheit von Metall, Plastik und Glas an den Tag, die bei den deutlich sichtbaren Verkehrszeichen verloren gegangen war.*

Bestandteile historischen Glases erscheinen im Werk mehrerer Künstler. Den italienischen Schmuckkünstler Piergiuliano Reveane reizen die Farben von antikem Glas, und er ist fasziniert von der Vorstellung, dass Glas in der Antike wertvoller war als Gold. Sein bemerkenswerter Armschmuck Vetrata I *(2004) macht sich die zarten Farben und die Dichte antiken Fensterglases zunutze, um einen starken Gegensatz zum prächtigen Glanz von Gold und Diamanten zu etablieren. In* Gertrude und Alice („Für sie und sie"-Anhängerset) *(2000) verwendet die amerikanische Schmuckkünstlerin Sondra Sherman Teile viktorianischer Kristallleuchter, um die „männlich-weibliche" Beziehung zwischen der Schriftstellerin Gertrude Stein und ihrer Gefährtin Alice B. Toklas zu porträtieren. Die tschechische Künstlerin Martina Mináriková fand „einen großen Topf voll alter Glasperlen", aus denen sie den Kern für ihr emblematisches* Atom *(2000) aus der Serie* Schöpfung *auswählte. Der österreichische Künstler Helfried Kodré bewahrt in seiner in hohem Maße geometrischen* Brosche *(2005) die*

jewelry factory in Neugablonz in her *Dry Valley* brooch (2006). To Britton, the sense of optimism that prevailed when the costume jewelry industry flourished in postwar Germany no longer exists, so she has recast these carefree glass remnants into a dark and brooding landscape reflective of today's increasingly menacing world.

Glass as Chameleon

The chameleonic mutability of glass allows it to impersonate or stand-in for a variety of substances, from gemstones to flowers and plants to human organs and even tears. Many artists in *GlassWear* prize the innate beauty of glass over gemstones and prefer to let glass speak for itself. In works such as his *Ring* (2004), German artist Karl Fritsch not only breaks with centuries-old jewelry traditions but with contemporary custom regarding the seriousness of what we wear. His dramatic amalgamation of cut and polished glass is supported by a toned-down oxidized silver band that turns the tables on the normal expectations of precious and non-precious, giving glass prominence. Fritsch's pieces are singularly striking in their loud colors and exaggerated forms, and there is an anti-aesthetic element in his unique style that defies the limits of the classically beautiful.

American glass jewelry artist Linda MacNeil's unorthodox treatment of manufactured glass and the formal and technical solutions in her work have been compared to the innovations of René Lalique. Her unique jewelry features carved and polished pâte-de-

Göttin der Liebe in einer Fassung gläserner Mosaiksteinchen aus einem Becken vom ehemaligen Standort der antiken Terme Aphrodite auf Ischia. Und in noch einer weiteren historischen Permutation verwandelt Helen Britton in ihrer Brosche *Ausgetrocknetes Tal* (2006) alte Glasstücke, die sie aus einer stillgelegten Modeschmuckfabrik in Neugablonz rettete. Für Britton existiert der zur Zeit der Blüte der Modeschmuckindustrie im Nachkriegsdeutschland verbreitete Optimismus nicht mehr, und deshalb hat sie die unbekümmerten Überbleibsel aus Glas in einer dunklen Landschaft neu gefasst, welche die heutige, mehr und mehr bedrohliche Welt widerspiegelt.

Glas als Verwandlungskünstler

Die chamäleonhafte Wandlungsfähigkeit von Glas erlaubt es ihm, eine ganze Anzahl von Substanzen zu imitieren oder zu vertreten, von Edelsteinen über Blumen und Pflanzen bis zu menschlichen Organen und sogar Tränen. Viele Künstler in GlassWear schätzen die natürliche Schönheit von Glas mehr als Edelsteine und ziehen es vor, Glas für sich selbst sprechen zu lassen. In Arbeiten wie seinem Ring (2004) bricht Karl Fritsch nicht nur mit jahrhundertealten Schmucktraditionen, sondern auch mit heutigen Gewohnheiten, welche die Ernsthaftigkeit von dem, was wir tragen, betreffen. Seiner dramatischen Vereinigung von geschliffenem und poliertem Glas verleiht ein Band aus mattiertem oxidiertem Silber Stabilität, welches die üblichen Erwartungshaltungen gegenüber dem Wertvollen und dem Nicht-Wertvollen umkehrt und dem Glas den Vorrang einräumt. Mit ihren grellen Farben und übertriebenen Formen sind Fritschs Arbeiten auffällig, und sein einzigartiger Stil birgt eine antiästhetische Komponente, welche sich den Grenzen des klassisch Schönen widersetzt.

verre "gemstones" or cast glass with tiny bubbles that create subtle visual effects. In her elegant and meticulously formed *Elements* necklace (2005), MacNeil uses white diamonds and white gold as supporting players, giving center stage to clear polished glass.

Gemlike qualities are achieved in very different ways by Emiko Oye, Petra Zimmermann, Andreas Eberharter, Joan Parcher, and Monica Backström. Although American artist Emiko Oye works with Pyrex glass pipettes, these laboratory wares take on a jewel-like appearance in her *Craft Tiara* (2006) through the precision and delicacy of their form and the incorporation of precious stones and gold. Swarovski glass crystals are used by the Austrian artists Petra Zimmermann—to provide the glitter for the pinup girl in her *Pin-up VI Brooch* (2004)—and Andreas Eberharter—to enrich his anodized aluminum *Crystal Code Bracelets* (2003).

In her *Phosphene Brooch* (2006), American artist Joan Parcher chooses reflective glass to capture the floating bits of light, the phosphenes, that appear when we close our eyes tightly or rub them. Swedish glass artist Monica Backström has designed the *Halo* series of rings using glass overlays to enhance her colorful and freeform ColorCore gemstones. In his *Neckpiece* (1996), Australian artist Pierre Cavalan also recreates a transient event—wave action on a sandy beach—studding the crinkled silver form with bezel-set colored glass to emulate washed up objects left behind after the tide recedes.

Die unorthodoxe Behandlung industriell hergestellten Glases durch die amerikanische Glasschmuck-Künstlerin Linda MacNeil und die sich in ihren Arbeiten findenden formalen und technischen Lösungen sind mit den Innovationen von René Lalique verglichen worden. Ihr einzigartiger Schmuck enthält geschnittene und polierte „Edelsteine" aus Glaspaste und gegossenes Glas mit winzigen Bläschen, die raffinierte optische Effekte hervorrufen. In ihrem eleganten und mit großer Sorgfalt geformten Halsschmuck der Serie Elemente *(2005) lässt MacNeil weiße Diamanten und Weißgold als Nebendarsteller auftreten und räumt dem durchsichtigen polierten Glas die Hauptrolle ein.*

An Edelsteine erinnernde Charakteristika werden auf sehr unterschiedliche Weise auch von Emiko Oye, Petra Zimmermann, Andreas Eberharter, Joan Parcher und Monica Backström erzielt. Wenn die amerikanische Künstlerin Emiko Oye auch mit Glaspipetten aus Pyrex arbeitet, erhalten diese Laborutensilien in ihrem Handwerks-Diadem (2006) *angesichts der Präzision und Feinheit ihrer Formen und ihrer Verwendung zusammen mit wertvollen Steinen und Gold ein juwelenartiges Erscheinungsbild. Swarovski-Glaskristalle werden von den österreichischen Künstlern Petra Zimmermann und Andreas Eberharter eingesetzt, um dem Pin-up-Girl in Zimmermanns Brosche* Pin-up VI *(2004) den erforderlichen Glamour zu verleihen – ein Kommentar zur penetranten, mit Schmuck behängten modernen Frau auf Zeitschriftentiteln der 1930er Jahre – und um Eberharters* Kristallcode-Armschmuckstücke *(2003) aus anodisiertem Aluminium aufzuwerten.*

Für ihre Lichterscheinungsbrosche (2006) *wählt die amerikanische Künstlerin Joan Parcher Reflexionsglas, mit dem sie die umher schwimmenden Lichtfetzen einfängt, die erscheinen,*

Perhaps the most unusual treatment of glass as gem is Italian artist Annamaria Zanella's *Ring* (1996). The small bundle of gracefully arranged cut plate glass is assembled to exploit the luminosity and subtle color changes of the slightly tinted industrial glass and to highlight its complex reflections and refractions.

Glass also lends itself to the creation of organic forms. American artist Karen Gilbert uses Pyrex glass rods for *Wall Brooches* (2005), a series of fantastic flowers—or are they underwater organisms?—emphasizing the range of glass's seemingly contradictory properties—opacity and transparency, hardness and suppleness, color and colorlessness. Gilbert's otherworldly glass flowers contrast markedly with the flowing blown-glass blossoms in Dutch artist Evert Nijland's *Fiori* necklace (2006), an evocation of traditional delicately blown Venetian glass jewelry that reflects our contemporary nostalgia for a bygone era. Finnish artist Terhi Tolvanen builds fanciful forms using irregular droplets of cast glass whose textures and colors work together to develop an organic feeling that is compatible with the natural wood forms that she incorporates with them. In pronounced contrast, German jewelry artist Georg Dobler emphasizes the rigidity of glass and carries the abstraction of petals to the limit in his *Mechanical Flower Brooch* (2005).

One of the most influential British jewelry artists of the last five decades, Wendy Ramshaw found inspiration in the glass of a Victorian chandelier. In her luxurious *Chain of Glass Tears for Weeping Woman*

wenn wir die Augen zukneifen oder reiben. Die schwedische Glaskünstlerin Monica Backström verwendet in ihrer Ringserie Halo (2002) gläserne Auflagen, um die Wirkung ihrer farbenfreudigen und frei geformten ColorCore-Edelsteine zu verstärken. In seinem Halsschmuck Sieg (1996) erschafft der australische Künstler Pierre Cavalan einen vorübergehenden Moment – die Einwirkung einer Welle auf einen Sandstrand – von Neuem, indem er die gewellte Silberform mit farbigem Glas in Fassungen besetzt, um angespülte Gegenstände nachzuahmen, die nach dem Rückgang der Flut zurückgeblieben sind.

Die vielleicht ungewöhnlichste Art der Behandlung von Glas als edlem Stein findet sich im Ring (1996) der italienischen Künstlerin Annamaria Zanella. Das kleine Bündel aus anmutig zusammengefügtem geschliffenem Flachglas wurde so angeordnet, dass es die Leuchtkraft und die feinen Farbwechsel des leicht getönten Industrieglases bestmöglich einfängt und seine komplexen Spiegelungen und Brechungen betont. Glas eignet sich ebenfalls für die Bildung organischer Formen. Die amerikanische Künstlerin Karen Gilbert verwendet Stäbe aus Pyrex für ihre Wandbroschen (2005), eine Serie phantastischer Blumen – oder handelt es sich um Unterwasser-Organismen? –, wobei sie eine Reihe der scheinbar widersprüchlichen Eigenschaften von Glas betont – Opazität und Transparenz, Härte und Geschmeidigkeit, Farbe und Farblosigkeit. Gilberts der Welt entrückte Glasblumen unterscheiden sich deutlich von den fließenden geblasenen Glasblüten des Halsschmucks Fiori (2006) des niederländischen Künstlers Evert Nijland, eine Evokation des traditionellen, fein geblasenen venezianischen Glasschmucks, in dem sich unsere heutige Sehnsucht nach einem vergangenen Zeitalter widerspiegelt. Die finnische Künstlerin Terhi Tolvanen konstruiert ausge-

from the series *Picasso's Ladies* (1989/1998), she suspends over one hundred luminous blue and green glass droplets, which she conceives of as the symbolic tears of Dora Maar, the photographer and painter who was Picasso's lover and muse.

Glass as Surface and Structure

While most jewelry artists construct their pieces around glass or integrate glass into their compositions, some choose to build with it, transforming light and color from without and within into tangible compositional elements. In his *Brooch* (2004), Czech artist Jiří Šibor incorporates rods of lead glass in a broad range of colors within a stainless steel armature that subtly reflects light and color. In this pristine reduction of color and form, the balance in the brooch's proportion and shape is matched by the balance in the sharply delineated bands of green and yellow.

In his *Trasparenze 1* brooch (2000), Italian jewelry artist Francesco Pavan takes advantage of the transparent qualities of glass, creating open shapes that can be viewed from different viewpoints and that permit the viewer to see into the interior of the object. Pavan transcends the Euclidean understanding of solid geometry and expands our perception of space and volume. Czech artist Martin Papcún draws on the light-bending qualities of glass to contrast reality and illusion. In his *Brooch* (1999), glass appears within and behind its metallic components, expanding the limits of interior and exterior space. Italian jeweler

fallene Formen aus unregelmäßigen Tröpfchen gegossenen Glases, in dessen Zusammenspiel von Texturen und Farben sich etwas Organisches entwickelt, das zu den natürlichen Formen des Holzes passt, in das sie diese Tropfen integriert. In deutlichem Kontrast hierzu betont der deutsche Schmuckkünstler Georg Dobler die Starrheit des Glases und führt die Abstraktheit von Blütenblättern in seiner Brosche Mechanische Blume *(2005) an ihre Grenze.*

Eine der einflussreichsten britischen Schmuckkünstlerinnen, Wendy Ramshaw, ließ sich durch das Glas eines viktorianischen Kronleuchters inspirieren. In ihrer verschwenderischen Kette aus Glastränen der weinenden Frau *(1989/1998) aus der Serie* Picasso's Ladies *hat sie über 100 leuchtend blaue und grüne Glaströpfchen aufgehängt, die sie als die symbolischen Tränen der Fotografin und Malerin Dora Maar auffasst, Geliebte Picassos und seine Muse.*

Glas als Oberfläche und Struktur

Die meisten Schmuckkünstler formen ihre Werke um das Glas herum oder integrieren es in ihre Kompositionen, doch manche entscheiden sich auch dafür, mit ihm zu „bauen", und verwandeln so das Licht und die Farbe in konkrete Elemente der Komposition. In seiner Brosche *(2004) passt der tschechische Künstler Jiří Šibor Stäbe aus Bleiglas in vielen Farben in eine Verankerung aus rostfreiem Stahl ein, welche das Licht und die Farbe raffiniert reflektiert. In dieser makellosen Reduktion von Farbe und Form entspricht die Ausgewogenheit der Proportionen und der Form der Brosche der Ausgewogenheit der klar gezeichneten Bänder in Grün und Gelb.*

In seiner Brosche Trasparenze I *(2000) macht sich der italienische Schmuckkünstler Francesco Pavan die Transparenz*

Stefano Marchetti uses sheets of clear glass in his *Necklace* (2006) to encase metal mosaics in which fragments of gold and silver blend yet maintain their distinctiveness.

During a career spanning over five decades, American jeweler-artist Thomas Gentille has uncovered the essence of his materials, many of which are rarely used for jewelry, including aircraft plywood, crushed pyrite, and eggshell. In his elegant minimalist *Brooch* (2007), a sheet of clear industrial glass with a yellow enameled underside contrasts subtly with the light maple wood in which it is embedded, masterfully bringing color, geometric form, and surface treatment together into dynamic equilibrium.

American jewelry artist Stanley Lechtzin has exchanged hand processes for making jewelry for the latest computer-driven methods. For his bracelet *PusHere* (2006), Lechtzin, with the assistance of Daniella Kerner, uses the Selective Laser Sintering technique (SLS) to fuse finely powdered glass-filled polyamide. The strong but subtle form of the bracelet is built up in thin layers through the rapid-prototyping process. Never touched by the human hand before completion, the bracelet is distinguished by its otherworldly beauty.

American artist Joyce Scott's *Water Coral* (2006) neckpiece and Austrian artist Jacqueline I. Lillie's *Combined Necklace and Bracelet* (2006) are built up from beads, one of the oldest forms of glass. Glass beads offer an endless variety of color and hue that can be combined into compositions featuring

von Glas zunutze und schafft offene Formen, die aus unterschiedlichen Perspektiven gesehen werden können und es dem Betrachter erlauben, in das Innere des Objektes zu blicken. Pavan überschreitet das auf Euklid zurückgehende Verständnis fester geometrischer Formen und erweitert unsere Wahrnehmung von Raum und Körperhaftigkeit. Der tschechische Künstler Martin Papcún schöpft aus der Eigenschaft von Glas, das Licht zu brechen, um Realität und Schein zu kontrastieren. In seiner *Brosche* (1999) erscheint Glas innerhalb von und hinter Metallkomponenten und erweitert so die Grenzen des Raumes. Der italienische Schmuckkünstler Stefano Marchetti verwendet Scheiben aus klarem Glas in seiner *Halskette* (2006), um Mosaiken aus Metall zu umhüllen, in welche sich Fragmente aus Gold und Silber einpassen, den ihnen eigenen Charakter jedoch bewahren.

Im Laufe einer mehr als fünf Jahrzehnte andauernden Karriere hat der amerikanische Schmuckkünstler Thomas Gentille das Wesen der von ihm verwendeten Materialien offengelegt. Viele von ihnen, darunter Flugzeugsperrholz, zerstoßener Pyrit und Eierschale, werden nur selten für Schmuck verwendet. In seiner eleganten und minimalistischen *Brosche* (2007) kontrastiert eine Scheibe aus klarem Industrieglas und einer gelb emaillierten Unterseite raffiniert mit dem hellen Ahornholz, in das sie eingelegt ist. Farbe, geometrische Form und Oberflächenbehandlung werden meisterhaft in einer dynamischen Komposition zusammengeführt.

Der amerikanische Schmuckkünstler Stanley Lechtzin hat die Techniken der manuellen Bearbeitung gegen die neuesten computergestützten Methoden eingetauscht. Für seinen Armreif *Hier drücken* (2006) verwendete Lechtzin, unterstützt von Daniella Kerner, die Selektive Lasersintertechnik (SLS), um

palettes as different as Lillie's modernist abstraction and cool colors and Scott's boisterous celebration of life. Scott adapts a unique African-American quilting stitch—the peyote stitch—to string the beads together into brightly colored sculptural forms that often make a strong social statement.

Glass as Symbol and Metaphor

Glass is rich in metaphoric potential—it can be transparent, opaque, flashy or unfathomable; it can be molded, cast, cut and polished, or fractured—the same expressions we use to describe people. Glass also embodies the paradoxical combination of fragility and hardness that makes it a highly suitable metaphor for artists wanting to comment on the complexity of bodies, structures, society, or even the transience of life itself. Some artists experiment with the medium's suggestive powers in abstract compositions, while others use identifiable forms—looking glass, magnifying glass, hourglass—to create content and symbolic associations.

Like a modern Jonathan Swift, American-born Michael Petry transports us to a world where familiar objects are not so much transformed as revealed. *The Treasure of Memory* (2000), Petry's colossal string of thirty-two colorful blown glass bubbles, is a necklace no longer on a human scale. Inspired by a glass-bead necklace that was buried with its owner in a tomb in Norway one thousand years ago, *The Treasure of Memory* remains a metaphor for both individual and cultural memory. By transforming the familiar

fein pulverisierte, mit Glasfasern verstärkte Polyamide zu verschmelzen. Die robuste, zugleich feine Form des Armschmucks ergibt sich durch ihren Aufbau in dünnen Schichten mittels des Rapid-Prototyping-Verfahrens. Der bis nach seiner Vollendung nie von einer menschlichen Hand berührte Armschmuck zeichnet sich durch seine weltentrückte Schönheit aus.

Der Halsschmuck Wasserkoralle *(2006) der amerikanischen Künstlerin Joyce Scott und der* Kombinierte Hals- und Armschmuck *(2006) der österreichischen Künstlerin Jacqueline I. Lillie sind aus kleinsten Perlen zusammengesetzt worden, einer der ältesten Erscheinungsformen von Glas. Glasperlen bieten eine nicht enden wollende Vielfalt von Farben und Schattierungen; sie können zu Kompositionen zusammengefügt werden, welche so unterschiedliche Farbspektren zeigen wie Lillies moderne Abstraktion in kühlen Farben und Scotts ausgelassene Komposition voller Leben. Scott hat einen nur von Afroamerikanern verwendeten Quiltstich übernommen – den Peyote-Stich –, um die Perlen zu plastischen Formen in leuchtenden Farben zusammenzufädeln. Auf diese Weise ergibt sich häufig eine eindeutige soziale Aussage.*

Glas als Symbol

Glas ist voller Symbolkraft – es kann transparent, undurchsichtig, prahlerisch oder unergründlich sein; es kann geformt, geschliffen oder gebrochen sein –, dieselben Ausdrücke benutzen wir, um Personen und Persönlichkeiten zu beschreiben. Glas steht auch für die paradoxe Kombination von Zerbrechlichkeit und Härte, die es zu einem äußerst geeigneten Symbol für Künstler machen, welche die Komplexität von Körpern, Strukturen, der Gesellschaft oder sogar die Vergänglichkeit des Lebens selbst kommentieren möchten. Einige

necklace form into an oversized object, Petry forces the viewer to rethink the contemporary preconceptions, both personal and cultural, that we routinely apply when we "look at," but often fail to "see," a piece of jewelry for all it can be.

Out-sized proportions also play a major role in the work of Australian-born artist Timothy Horn, who spent months blowing glass in order to create the giant artificial baroque pearls in *Difficult to Swallow (Boy Germs)* (2001). Intended to be hung on a wall, their larger-than-life scale satirizes the lust for precious jewels and more specifically the over-refinement and excessiveness of baroque body ornaments. At the same time *Boy Germs* is a celebration of the fake and the gaudy, with its bulging pearls intended to arouse sexual fantasy.

The symbolic content in other work is more personal and body oriented. Dutch artist Katja Prins encourages the viewer to discover personal associations in her work. She says the glass parts in her *Brooch* (2005) are abstractions of human body parts, but her shapes and materials are never explicit. While her imagery may reflect the rapidly changing view of ourselves that has been brought on by advances in bio-technology, it remains surprisingly human, retaining the softness and sensuality we associate with the body. Brazilian-born Célio Braga's *Fourteen Brooches* from his *Rubros* series (2002–03) also deal with the fragility of the human body and are inspired by blood, open flesh, and organs. Yet the work he has created is sumptuous and extravagant

Künstler experimentieren mit der Suggestivität dieses Mediums in abstrakten Kompositionen, andere wiederum verwenden erkennbare Formen – den gläsernen Spiegel, das Vergrößerungsglas, das Stundenglas –, um inhaltliche Aussagen zu machen und symbolische Assoziationen herzustellen.

Wie ein moderner Jonathan Swift versetzt uns Michael Petry in eine Welt, in der vertraute Gegenstände nicht so sehr verwandelt als vielmehr enthüllt werden. Der Schatz der Erinnerung (2000), Petrys gewaltige Aneinanderreihung von 32 farbenfrohen geblasenen Glaskugeln, ist ein Halsschmuck, der über den menschlichen Maßstab hinausgeht. Von einer Halskette aus Glasperlen inspiriert, die vor mehr als 1000 Jahren mit ihrer Besitzerin in einem Grab in Norwegen bestattet wurde, ist Der Schatz der Erinnerung ein Symbol für die persönliche und auch für die kulturelle Erinnerung. Indem er die vertraute Form der Halskette in ein überdimensionales Objekt verwandelt, zwingt Petry den Betrachter, die heutigen Meinungen zu überdenken, welche wir automatisch anwenden, wenn wir ein Schmuckstück „betrachten" und wenn wir die Bedeutungen, die es annehmen kann, häufig nicht zu „erkennen" vermögen.

Überdimensionierte Proportionen spielen auch im Werk des in Australien geborenen Timothy Horn eine wesentliche Rolle, der Monate beim Glasblasen zubrachte, um die riesigen künstlichen barocken Perlen für Schwer zu schlucken (Bubenkeime) (2001) zu schaffen. Sie sind für die Befestigung an einer Wand vorgesehen, und ihr übergroßer Maßstab macht sich über die Begierde nach kostbaren Juwelen und insbesondere über die übertriebene Eleganz und Exzessivität barocker Schmuckstücke lustig. Gleichzeitig feiert Bubenkeime das Falsche und Protzige, und die sich wölbenden Perlen sollen sexuelle Phantasien hervorrufen.

through his use of handmade felt, silk and cotton fabrics, and tiny red glass beads that he stitches on with "patient labor and obsession." The brooches are intended as a commentary on the transience of life and our attempts to embellish, protect, cure, and save our bodies. In her *Cardiovascular Brooches 1–3* (2006), American artist Patty Cokus uses borosilicate glass tubes to emulate bodily organs down to the cholesterol-clogged arteries. Although she includes a small amount of salted butter in her *Brooches 2: Clogged* (2006), she takes care to ameliorate the pain by including aspirin in *Brooches 1: Pump* (2006). The tiny heads in Dutch jeweler Rian de Jong's brooch *Twice* (2005) seem frail and detached from the real world. De Jong creates a channel to the subconscious through the effects of light on cast glass.

Spanish artist Ramón Puig Cuyàs depends on collage to combine different symbols and transform their meaning. Enigmatic and mysterious, his *Brooch (Ref. no. 601)* (1998) from his *Archipelago* series offers an impressionistic evocation of an island chain. Glass, pebbles, coral, and wood populate this abstract seascape, inviting the viewer to fill in what is unseen and complete the fantasy.

We often pay little notice to the countless things we see behind or under glass in the course of our daily lives. Yet a number of artists in *GlassWear* elevate objects to a symbolic level beyond the commonplace precisely by encapsulating and isolating them in glass. In her necklace *Prudence*, American artist

Der Symbolgehalt anderer Arbeiten ist persönlicher und eher auf den Körper bezogen. Die niederländische Künstlerin Katja Prins ermutigt den Betrachter, in ihrem Werk persönliche Bezüge zu entdecken. Sie sagt, dass die Glasteile in ihrer Brosche *(2005) Abstraktionen menschlicher Körperteile sind, doch werden Formen und Materialien bei ihr niemals explizit. Prins' Bildlichkeit könnte unsere sich schnell verändernden Ansichten über uns selbst widerspiegeln, die auf die Fortschritte in der Biotechnologie zurückzuführen sind, doch bleibt sie überraschend menschlich und bewahrt die Weichheit und Sinnlichkeit, die wir mit dem menschlichen Körper verbinden. Die* Vierzehn Broschen *aus der Serie* Rubros *(2002/03) des aus Brasilien stammenden Célio Braga befassen sich ebenfalls mit der Zerbrechlichkeit des menschlichen Körpers und wurden von Blut, Fleisch und Organen angeregt. Doch sind die von Braga geschaffenen Arbeiten verschwenderisch und extravagant durch seine Verwendung von handgemachtem Filz, Seide und Baumwollstoffen und von winzigen roten Glaskugeln, mit denen er sie „mit geduldiger Mühe und Besessenheit" bestickt. Die Broschen sind als Kommentar zur Vergänglichkeit des Lebens gedacht und zu unseren Versuchen, unseren Körper zu verschönern, zu schützen, zu heilen und zu bewahren. In ihren* Kardiovaskularbroschen 1–3 *(2006) verwendet die amerikanische Künstlerin Patty Cokus Röhren aus Borsilikatglas, um Organe bis hin zu den von Cholesterin verstopften Arterien nachzubilden. Zwar arbeitet sie in* Kardiovaskularbrosche: Verstopft *ein wenig gesalzene Butter ein, doch bemüht sie sich, den Schmerz zu lindern, indem sie in* Kardiovaskularbrosche: Pumpe *Aspirin integriert. Die winzigen Köpfe in der* Brosche Doppelt *(2005) der niederländischen Schmuck-*

Nancy Worden uses Pyrex vials made by a skilled glassmaker, James Minson, to emulate an ancient reliquary and fills them with dried roses to convey the fragility of life. Sandra Enterline's *Souvenirs* (1999) are nine of one thousand necklaces this American artist composed of glass ampoules that hold objects taken out of time and context. The original significance of each object is personal and lost to the viewer, who is left to ponder the mystery of how individual experience can affect our perception of life, from the way in which we view the smallest object to how we perceive the wider metaphysical questions of existence.

Norwegian-born artist Nanna Melland also uses glass to encase yet reveal the essence of substances in her *Fragment of Life 3* (2004). Melland was fascinated by the fact that glass jars gave a poetic beauty to the raw and often repellent body fragments in the laboratory of the Anatomical Institute in Munich, where she was a student. Eager to replicate this transformation, she cast a pig heart in epoxy resin and enclosed it within a glass sphere, giving the organ a new, almost magical presence "as if it existed in a little world of its own."

Dutch jewelry artist Ted Noten has collected precious jewels and treated them as sacred objects, placing them in transparent boxes and urns to preserve them for eternity. By contrast, glass offers only temporary protection in *The Real Love Bracelet* (2005), which focuses on the concept of marriage and marriage itself. The silver bracelet has a glass

künstlerin Rian de Jong scheinen zerbrechlich zu sein und nicht der realen Welt anzugehören. De Jong stellt mittels der Lichteffekte auf gegossenem Glas einen Kanal zum Unterbewusstsein her.

Der spanische Künstler Ramón Puig Cuyàs verlässt sich auf die Technik der Collage, um unterschiedliche Symbole zu vereinen und ihre Bedeutung zu verwandeln. Seine geheimnisvolle Brosche (Ref. No. 601) *(1998) aus der Serie* Archipel *vermittelt Eindrücke, die eine Inselkette hervorrufen. Glas, Kiesel, Korallen und Holz bevölkern diese abstrakte Meereslandschaft und laden den Betrachter ein, das nicht Gesehene einzufügen und das Phantasiebild zu vervollständigen.*

Häufig bringen wir den zahllosen Dingen, die wir in unserem täglichen Leben hinter oder unter Glas sehen, nur wenig Beachtung entgegen. Doch heben in GlassWear *eine Anzahl von Künstlern Gegenstände, gerade durch ihre Einfassung und Absonderung in Glas, auf eine symbolische Ebene jenseits des Alltäglichen. In ihrem Halsschmuck* Umsicht *(2006) verwendet die amerikanische Künstlerin Nancy Worden Ampullen aus Pyrex, die von James Minson, einem versierten Glasmacher, hergestellt wurden, um ein antikes Reliquiar nachzuahmen; sie füllt sie mit getrockneten Rosenblättern, um die Zerbrechlichkeit des Lebens auszudrücken. Sandra Enterlines* Souvenirs *(1999) sind neun von 1000 Anhängern, welche die amerikanische Künstlerin aus Glasampullen zusammenstellte. Sie enthalten Gegenstände, die aus ihrer Zeit und ihrem Zusammenhang entfernt wurden. Die ursprüngliche Bedeutung eines jeden Gegenstandes ist eine persönliche und für den Betrachter verloren; ihm bleibt nichts anderes, als über das Geheimnis nachzusinnen, wie die individuelle Erfahrung unsere Wahrnehmung des Lebens beeinflus-*

ball attached to it, within which are two gold wedding rings that can only be worn when the glass is broken. There are no better words to describe the mystical qualities of glass than those of German artist Marianne Schliwinski, "Glass is more than just a chemical formula. It has a mystique capable of conveying knowledge, truth, and, of course, lucidity." Pieces such as her *Brooch* (2002) provide glimpses, as if through a microscope, of a palpable yet elusive universe beyond our own.

Swiss artist Therese Hilbert has been fascinated by volcanoes for over fifteen years. Her brooch *Glow* (2005) contains the only natural glass in *GlassWear*, a few fragments of obsidian, the volcanic glass that results from rapid cooling. Hilbert's evocative brooch symbolizes the hidden forces in the natural world and in human nature.

Glass is the product of intense heat, and many artists create work that seems to capture and transmit this energy. The inherent ability of glass to amplify, reflect, refract, and convey energy is the subject of Australian glass artist Giselle Courtney's *Like Moths to a Flame* necklace (2006). Noted for her flameworking skill, she uses borosilicate glass for its optical clarity and because it is strong enough to be sculpted with fine detail.

As both a tool and a metaphor, the glass mirror offers unlimited potential for artistic expression. Its ability to throw back reverse images and open up perspectives that allow the viewer to see other and often hidden aspects of objects has fascinated artists

sen kann – von der Art, in der wir das kleinste Objekt sehen, bis zur Frage, wie wir die metaphysischen Fragen der Existenz wahrnehmen.

Auch die aus Norwegen stammende Künstlerin Nanna Melland verwendet Glas, um in Fragment des Lebens *(2004) das Wesen der von ihr verwendeten Substanzen zu umschließen und doch zu enthüllen. Melland ist von der Tatsache fasziniert, dass gerade Glasgefäße den kruden und häufig abstoßenden Körperteilen im Laboratorium des Münchener Anatomischen Institutes, wo sie studierte, eine poetische Schönheit verleihen. Da sie diese Verwandlung gerne nachbilden wollte, goss sie ein Schweineherz in Epoxydharz und schloss es in eine Glaskugel ein, womit sie dem Organ eine neue, fast magische Präsenz verlieh – „als ob es in seiner eigenen kleinen Welt existierte".*

Der niederländische Schmuckkünstler Ted Noten sammelt kostbare Schmuckstücke und verehrt sie wie geheiligte Objekte. Er setzt sie in durchsichtige Kästen und Gefäße, um sie für die Ewigkeit zu bewahren. Im Gegensatz hierzu bietet Glas im Armreif der wahren Liebe *(2005), das den Gedanken an Heirat und das Verheiratetsein selbst in den Mittelpunkt stellt, nur einen vorübergehenden Schutz. An dem silbernen Armschmuck ist ein gläserner Ball befestigt; in ihm befinden sich zwei goldene Eheringe, die nur getragen werden können, wenn das Glas zerbrochen ist.*

Es gibt kaum Worte, welche die mystischen Eigenschaften von Glas besser beschreiben als die der deutschen Künstlerin Marianne Schliwinski: „Glas ist mehr als nur eine chemische Formel. Es hat einen Nimbus, der Wissen, Wahrheit und natürlich auch Klarheit vermitteln kann." Wie durch ein Mikroskop hindurch gewähren Arbeiten wie ihre Brosche *(2002) winzige*

for centuries. As early as 1988, Otto Künzli used the mirror as a symbol of self-discovery, self-knowledge, contemplation, and reflection in his *Ring*. The appearance in the mirror of the eye of the artist, wearer, or viewer recalls the symbol of the "watchful eye," considered in many cultures to be an amulet for combating evil and harm. In *Circumspect* (2003), American jewelry artist Kiff Slemmons frames optical glass and mirrors to surround the wearer with physical and metaphorical possibilities for self-examination and scrutiny by others.

Giampaolo Babetto, one of the world's foremost jewelry artists, is renowned for his superlative craftsmanship and the classic and elegant simplicity of his shapes and gently sinuous surfaces. In recent years this Italian artist has integrated glass and mirrors into masterful compositions that exploit their transparency, color, reflectivity, optical lightness, and disruptive effects on other materials. His *Brooch* (2003) artfully combines disparate elements to take advantage of the optical qualities and interactions of glass and mirrors.

Few artists are as profoundly involved with the mystical aspects of jewelry as Dutch jeweler Ruudt Peters. His *Sefiroth Metatron* (2006), from his recent *Sefiroth* series, is made from blown laboratory glass and shaped like the Tree of Life from the Kabala, an ancient interpretation of the Scriptures by Jewish rabbis. In this context, the *Sefiroth* series is about humankind's ongoing struggle to reach a higher level of self-awareness and self-fulfillment.

Einblicke in ein greifbares, sich uns aber zugleich entziehendes Universum, das jenseits des unsrigen liegt.

Seit über 15 Jahren zeigt sich die Schweizer Künstlerin Therese Hilbert von Vulkanen fasziniert. Ihre Brosche Glut *(2005) enthält das einzige natürliche Glas in* GlassWear, *einige Fragmente Obsidian, das durch schnelle Abkühlung der Lava entstehende vulkanische Glas. Hilberts Brosche symbolisiert die verborgenen Kräfte der Natur und der menschlichen Natur.*

Glas ist ein Erzeugnis, das durch große Hitze entsteht, und viele Künstler schaffen Werke, die diese Energie einzufangen und zu übertragen scheinen. Die im Glas naturgemäß vorhandene Eigenschaft, Energie zu vergrößern, zu reflektieren, zu brechen und zu übermitteln, ist das Thema des Halsschmucks Wie Motten im Licht *(2006) der australischen Glaskünstlerin Giselle Courtney. Sie ist für ihr Geschick in der Lampenarbeit bekannt und verwendet Borsilikatglas aufgrund seiner optischen Klarheit und weil es stabil genug ist, bis ins feine Detail plastisch bearbeitet zu werden.*

Sowohl als Mittel als auch als Symbol bietet der gläserne Spiegel dem künstlerischen Ausdruck unbeschränkte Möglichkeiten. Seine Fähigkeit, umgekehrte Bilder zurückzuwerfen und neue Perspektiven zu eröffnen, welche es dem Betrachter erlauben, häufig verborgene Aspekte von Gegenständen zu sehen, hat Künstler seit Jahrhunderten fasziniert.

Bereits im Jahr 1988 wurde der Spiegel in Otto Künzlis Ring *als Symbol für Selbstfindung, Selbsterkenntnis, Kontemplation und Reflexion verwendet. Das Erscheinen des Auges des Künstlers, Trägers oder Betrachters im Spiegel erinnert an das Symbol des „wachsamen Auges", das in vielen Kulturen als Talisman im Kampf gegen das Böse gilt. In* Circumspect *(2003) rahmt Kiff Slemmons optisches Glas und Spiegel, um*

Glass as Glass

In this final group of works, glass dazzles through its inherent properties—refracted and reflected light, color, and transparency. These creations, to a greater extent than the others in *GlassWear,* are self-referentially about glass and the process of working it. It is perhaps not accidental that this group of artists includes a number who are from the Czech Republic and Italy, countries with long glass traditions.

The earliest work in *GlassWear* is the 1967 *Necklace* by Václav Cigler, the acknowledged leader of the renowned Czech optical school of glass art. Cigler's precise cutting and polishing take full advantage of the internal reflections and refractions of optical glass, extolling its beauty through geometric forms within a deceptively simple spatial composition. In contrast, Jaroslav Kodejš takes a more painterly approach, creating passages of softly modulated light with molten and layered fragments of colored glass in *Brooch* (2000). His colorful abstractions in laminated glass are evocative of moods, experiences, and memories of places, both real and imagined.

Markéta Šílená and Svatopluk Kasalý were both trained in the great Czech glass art tradition. With their superb technical skills, they exploit the qualities of cast and cut glass in abstract forms, setting the translucence and depth of glass against the cold brightness, rigidity, and precision of metal. In her *Brooch* (2005), Šílená uses colorless cast glass that reveals, distorts, or obscures the inner life of the

den Träger des Schmuckstücks mit physischen und symbolischen Möglichkeiten zur Selbstprüfung und zur genauen Untersuchung durch andere zu umgeben.

Giampaolo Babetto, einer der weltweit bedeutendsten Schmuckkünstler, ist für seine überragende Kunstfertigkeit und die klassische und elegante Einfachheit seiner Formen und sanft geschwungenen Oberflächen bekannt. In den letzten Jahren hat der italienische Künstler Glas und Spiegel in meisterhafte Kompositionen integriert, die sich ihre Transparenz und Farbe, ihr Reflexionsvermögen, ihre optische Leichtigkeit und die zerstörerischen Wirkungen, die sie auf andere Materialien ausüben, zunutze machen. Spilla 5 *(2003) vereint gegensätzliche Elemente auf kunstvolle Weise, um die optischen Eigenschaften von und die Wechselwirkungen zwischen Glas und Spiegeln auszunutzen.*

Wenige Künstler sind dem mystischen Aspekt des Schmucks so eng verbunden wie der niederländische Schmuckkünstler Ruudt Peters. Sein Sefiroth Metatron *(2006), aus der kürzlich entstandenen Werkgruppe* Sefiroth, *besteht aus geblasenem Laborglas und ist wie der Baum des Lebens der Kabbala geformt, der uralten Auslegung der Heiligen Schrift durch jüdische Rabbiner. In diesem Zusammenhang geht es in der Sefiroth-Serie um den Kampf der Menschheit, zu einer höheren Ebene der Selbsterkenntnis und Erfüllung zu gelangen.*

Glas als Glas

In dieser letzten Gruppe von Arbeiten blendet uns das Glas durch die ihm eigenen Eigenschaften – gebrochenes und reflektiertes Licht, Farbe und Transparenz. Diese Schöpfungen beziehen sich, in höherem Maße als die anderen Arbeiten in GlassWear, auf das Glas an sich und den Prozess seiner Bear-

piece, depending on how it is animated by light. Šílená ascribes a cerebral quality to glass, through which our minds are opened to other levels of consciousness and imagination. Kasalý's ruby-colored *Neckpiece* (2001) enhances and exults in the beauty of solid glass through precision cutting that contrasts dramatically with areas along the edge of the piece that are left jagged and unfinished. Like many of the works in the exhibition, Kasalý's neckpiece functions as small sculpture when it is off the human body.

A former jewelry designer for the theater, Italian artist Giorgio Vigna takes full advantage of the unsurpassed Italian glassblowing traditions. His dramatic blown glass *Gorgoglio* necklace (2002), created at the renowned Venini glasshouse on Murano, confers energy from the light that is embodied in the glass onto the wearer as well as the viewer. Reflections and refractions ignite the transparent blue glass bubbles, animating this body ornament with flamboyance and vitality that challenge the wearer to match pace.

American jewelry artist Donald Friedlich directs the work of a skilled glassblower to create his initial shapes, which he then cuts and grinds to achieve his final, minimalist form. In his *Brooch* (2004) from the *Translucence* series, Friedlich focuses on the sensual qualities of color and shape, using glass's transparency, translucence, and optical properties to magnify the weave and color of the fabric on which the brooch is worn.

Even though glass has played a minor role in the decorative arts in Japan until recently, Japanese glass

beitung. Es ist vielleicht kein Zufall, dass sich in der entsprechenden Gruppe von Künstlern eine Anzahl von Künstlern aus der Tschechischen Republik und aus Italien befindet – Länder mit weit zurückreichenden Traditionen der Glasherstellung. Das früheste Werk in GlassWear *ist die 1967 entstandene Halskette von Václav Cigler, dem anerkannten Anführer der renommierten optischen Schule der tschechischen Glaskunst. Ciglers präzises Schleifen und Polieren machen sich die inneren Spiegelungen und Brechungen des optischen Glases in vollem Maße zunutze und preisen seine Schönheit mit geometrischen Formen innerhalb einer täuschend einfachen räumlichen Komposition. Im Gegensatz hierzu hat Jaroslav Kodejš einen eher malerischen Ansatz: In* Brosche *(2000) schafft er Durchgänge weich modulierten Lichtes in geschmolzenen und geschichteten Fragmenten farbigen Glases. Seine farbenfrohen Abstraktionen aus laminiertem Glas evozieren Stimmungen, Erlebnisse und Erinnerungen an Orte, welche in der Realität und in der Vorstellung angesiedelt sind.*

Markéta Šílená und Svatopluk Kasalý erhielten beide ihre Ausbildung in der großen tschechischen Tradition der Glaskunst. Mit ihren vorzüglichen technischen Fähigkeiten nutzen sie die Eigenschaften von gegossenem und geschliffenem Glas innerhalb von abstrakten Formen, wobei sie die Durchsichtigkeit und die Tiefe von Glas der kalten Helligkeit, Starrheit und Präzision des Metalls entgegensetzen. In ihrer Brosche *(2005) verwendet Šílená farbloses gegossenes Glas, welches das Innenleben dieser Arbeit enthüllt, verzerrt oder verunklärt – je nachdem, wie sie vom Licht belebt wird. Šílená misst dem Glas eine geistige Dimension zu, durch die unser Verstand anderen Ebenen des Bewusstseins und des Vorstellungsvermögens gegenüber geöffnet wird. Kasalýs rubinroter*

artist Kazuko Mitsushima has helped to move this art form to center stage. In her eloquent and luminous *Will of Glass* neckpiece (2006), she captures the swirls and flow of molten glass and the sharp brilliance of broken, colorless glass, imbuing her compelling collar with the spirit of Japanese ink paintings. Also from Japan and now living in the Netherlands, performance and glass artist Simsa Cho combines his mastery of glassworking techniques and a lifetime pursuit of spiritual awareness in *Akadama* (2003). To Cho, glass resonates with and enhances vibration, light, energy, and emotion. Glass also resonates with the sun's positive energy. *Akadama* was designed to transmit these life-giving forces to the wearer.

The works showcased in *GlassWear* bring together two visually exciting and conceptually provocative art forms—glass and jewelry. Glass jewelry is both ancient—it has been found in early Mesopotamian sites—and up to the minute—it is an expression of artistic, social, political, scientific, and technological forces fueling exploration in the arts today. A wearable art, glass jewelry is a unique reflection of our individual selves, who we think we are and what we have to say about the world and our place in it. The ability for so much to be expressed in such small forms is testimony to the creativity of artists who sense the limitless potential of glass and the unique form of communication that jewelry offers between artist, wearer, and viewer.

Halsschmuck (2001) steigert die Schönheit massiven Glases durch einen Präzisionsschliff, der im auffälligen Gegensatz zu Zonen entlang der Kante der Arbeit steht, die zerklüftet und unvollendet belassen wurden. Wie viele der anderen Arbeiten fungiert Kasalýs Halsschmuck, wenn er nicht mehr am menschlichen Körper getragen wird, als Kleinskulptur.

Der italienische Künstler und ehemalige Designer von Theaterschmuck Giorgio Vigna macht sich die unübertroffene italienische Glasbläsertradition voll und ganz zunutze. Sein dramatischer Halsschmuck Gorgoglio *(2002) aus geblasenem Glas, der in der renommierten Glasmanufaktur Venini auf Murano geschaffen wurde, übermittelt aus dem im Glas verkörperten Licht Energie auf den Träger und auch auf den Betrachter. Spiegelungen und Brechungen entzünden die durchsichtigen blauen Glasblasen und verleihen diesem am Körper zu tragenden Schmuckstück eine Extravaganz und Vitalität, die den Träger herausfordert, Schritt zu halten.*

Der amerikanische Schmuckkünstler Donald Friedlich gibt einem erfahrenen Glasbläser Anweisungen, um das Anfangsstadium seiner Formen zu schaffen, die er dann schleift, um so zu seiner minimalistischen Form zu gelangen. In seiner Brosche *(2004) aus der Serie* Transluzenz *stellt er die sinnlichen Eigenschaften von Farbe und Form in den Mittelpunkt und nutzt die Durchsichtigkeit, Lichtdurchlässigkeit und die optischen Eigenschaften von Glas, um Webart und Farbe des Stoffes hervorzuheben, auf dem die Brosche getragen wird.*

Wenn Glas in den angewandten Künsten Japans bis vor kurzem eine untergeordnete Rolle gespielt hat, hat die japanische Glaskünstlerin Kazuko Mitsushima dazu beigetragen, diese Kunstform ins Rampenlicht zu rücken. In ihrem ausdrucks- und lichtstarken Halsschmuck Wille aus Glas *(2006)*

fängt sie die Wirbel und den Fluss von Schmelzglas ein wie auch die harte Brillanz zerbrochenen farblosen Glases, wobei sie ihren bezwingenden kragenförmigen Halsschmuck mit dem Geist japanischer Tuschemalereien erfüllt. Der ebenfalls aus Japan stammende und nun in den Niederlanden lebende Performance- und Glaskünstler Simsa Cho vereint in Akadama (2003) seine Meisterschaft in den Techniken der Glasbearbeitung mit einer lebenslangen Suche nach spirituellem Bewusstsein. Für Cho ist Glas voll von Schwingungen, Licht, Energie und Emotion, und es intensiviert diese Phänomene zugleich. Glas ist auch mit der positiven Energie der Sonne erfüllt. Akadama wurde geschaffen, um diese Leben spendenden Kräfte dem Träger zu übermitteln.

In den in GlassWear präsentierten Arbeiten vereinen sich zwei visuell erregende und in ihrer Konzeption provokante Kunstformen – Glas und Schmuck. Glasschmuck ist uralt – er wurde in Ausgrabungsstätten der frühen mesopotamischen Kulturen gefunden – und hochaktuell zugleich – er ist ein Ausdruck der künstlerischen, sozialen, politischen, wissenschaftlichen und technischen Kräfte, welche die Entdeckungsreisen in den heutigen Künsten antreiben. Als Kunst, die getragen werden kann, stellt Glasschmuck ein einzigartiges Mittel der Reflexion über unsere eigene Person dar, darüber, was wir denken, was wir sind und was wir über die Welt und unseren Platz in ihr zu sagen haben. Die Tatsache, dass in so kleinen Gebilden so viel ausgesagt werden kann, ist ein Zeugnis für die schöpferische Kraft der Künstler, die das unbegrenzte Potential des Glases erspüren – und für die einzigartige Form der Kommunikation, die Schmuck zwischen dem Künstler, dem Träger und dem Betrachter möglich macht.

Cornelie Holzach
Glass—Art—Jewelry
Glas – Kunst – Schmuck

Art and Jewelry—An Ancient Debate

Contemporary jewelry is a form of fine art that is related both to the human body and to space. Since jewelry artists have been moving further and further away from traditional goldsmithing, they have invariably been subjected to discussion of whether their home is "art" or the "applied arts." Often enough this discussion of how their work should be classified has taken place amongst the artists themselves, naturally without coming to a definitive conclusion. Ultimately each artist has devised his or her own justification—or rather—explanatory paradigm.

We assume that contemporary jewelry is a special form of artistic expression that exists in a more or less obvious relationship to both the fine arts, such as painting or sculpture, and the applied arts, although it cannot be unequivocally assigned to either of the two extremes. On the contrary, such jewelry is an expression of both the fine arts and the applied arts in varying degrees of intensity—depending on how artists define themselves and on the system, structure, and concept that are dominant in their work. This can be manifest either in an intensive preoccupation with the past and the professional traditions of goldsmithing and craftsmanship or in a focus on very abstract concepts that at first seem to have little or nothing at all to do with the actual subject of "jewelry." In principle, they approach their subject matter with the same working methods as those used by "practitioners of the fine arts."

The phrase *working methods* is not used here to refer to the specific craft techniques employed by an

Schmuck und Kunst – eine alte Debatte

Zeitgenössischer Schmuck ist eine Form der freien Künste, die sich sowohl auf den menschlichen Körper als auch auf den Raum bezieht. Seit sich Künstler, die Schmuck als ihre Ausdrucksform wählten, mehr und mehr vom traditionellen Goldschmiedehandwerk entfernten, haben sie sich immer mit der Diskussion, ob sie in der „Kunst" beheimatet sind oder doch eher den „angewandten Künsten" zugerechnet werden sollen, ausgesetzt gesehen.

Oft genug haben sie diese Debatte um die Zuordnung selbst geführt, freilich ohne zu einem endgültigen Ergebnis zu gelangen. Letztendlich hat sich jeder ein eigenes System – oder besser – Erklärungsmuster angeeignet.

Wir gehen davon aus, dass zeitgenössischer Schmuck, wie er hier gezeigt wird, eine ganz besondere Form des künstlerischen Ausdrucks ist, der zur freien Kunst, wie Malerei oder Plastik, ebenso wie zur angewandten Kunst in einem mehr oder weniger deutlichen Spannungsverhältnis steht und keinem der beiden Pole eindeutig zuzuordnen ist. Vielmehr ist er beiden in unterschiedlicher Intensität zugehörig – je nachdem, wie sich der Künstler/die Künstlerin selbst definiert und welche Systematik, Struktur und Konzeption dem Werk eigen ist. Dies kann sich sowohl in einer intensiven Auseinandersetzung mit der Vergangenheit und den Traditionen der Profession der Goldschmiede- und Schmuckhandwerker manifestieren als auch in sehr abstrakten Fragestellungen, die zunächst wenig oder gar nichts mit dem eigentlichen Thema „Schmuck" zu tun haben. Es sind prinzipiell die gleichen Arbeitsmethoden, mit denen sich der als „freier Künstler" Bezeichnete seiner Thematik nähert.

Mit „Arbeitsmethoden" sind dabei nicht die handwerklichen Techniken gemeint, sondern der künstlerische Ansatz. Dies

artist but rather to the attitude with which an artist sets about working. It is necessary to point this out because in the applied arts —especially in jewelry making because the tradition of goldsmithing goes back so far—it is often assumed that strong emphasis should be placed on workmanship and technique. Too often misunderstanding arises from this assumption; it is not only jewelry artists who give priority to craftsmanship or view it as at least of almost equal value to the content of art, but viewers who do so as well.

It is an unspoken fact that as soon as an object is classified as belonging to the applied arts, craftsmanship is given more weight than is the case in the fine arts. Content, rather than craftsmanship, is the sole criterion by which art is evaluated. Apart from workmanship, function is addressed in the applied arts. After all, function runs like a leit-motif through the applied arts.

In contemporary jewelry, on the other hand, the threads of this line of reasoning run very thin. There has always been and continues to be room for debating the main purpose of jewelry. This is not the place to discuss yet again the multilayered reasons for adorning oneself—beginning with the definitely dubious notion that human beings have a "primal urge" to adorn themselves and progressing on to the explanation of jewelry as a sign of belonging to a group while demarcating oneself from others and to jewelry's being a code denoting status within a group. In modern society all these explanatory paradigms are valid only to a limited extent since they originated, after all, in

zu betonen ist notwendig, da gerade in den den angewandten Künsten verwandten Ausdrucksformen – insbesondere im Schmuck, bedingt durch die so weit zurückreichende Goldschmiedekunst – eine starke Betonung des Handwerks und der technischen Umsetzung angenommen werden kann. Oft genug ergibt sich daraus ein Missverständnis, denn es ist nicht der Künstler, der Schmuck macht, der die handwerklichen Fertigkeiten in den Vordergrund stellt oder zumindest nahezu gleichwertig mit dem künstlerischen Gehalt ansieht, sondern der interessierte Betrachter der Schmuckobjekte.

Es scheint eine unausgesprochene Selbstverständlichkeit zu sein, dass, sobald ein Objekt dem Angewandten zugerechnet wird, dieser Aspekt mehr Gewicht bekommt als es in den freien Künsten der Fall ist. Kunst wird nicht nach diesem Gesichtspunkt bewertet, sondern ausschließlich nach dem künstlerischen Gehalt. Neben der Handwerklichkeit ist es im Bereich des Angewandten auch die Funktionalität, die angesprochen wird, zieht sie sich doch, durchaus berechtigt, wie ein roter Faden durch die angewandten Künste.

Beim zeitgenössischen Schmuck allerdings, bleibt man bei diesem Bild, wird der Faden dieser Argumentation hauchdünn. Es war und ist immer noch ein Feld der Rechtfertigung, wozu Schmuck notwendig ist. Es sollen hier nicht noch einmal die vielschichtigen Aspekte des sich Schmückens diskutiert werden – angefangen vom durchaus fragwürdigen Begriff des „Urtriebs" des Menschen, sich zu schmücken, über den Schmuck als Zeichen der Gruppenzugehörigkeit und zugleich Abgrenzung zu anderen bis zur Chiffre der Rangordnung innerhalb einer Gruppe. In einer modernen Gesellschaft greifen all diese Erklärungsmuster nur bedingt und lassen sich keineswegs eindeutig zuschreiben, gingen sie doch von ganz

cultures that were unlike those that exist today and in societies that were ordered in entirely different ways.

In addition, jewelry has constantly been forced to defend itself against the stigma of being devoid of function, of being a luxury, of being nothing but useless trinkets. No other area of applied arts has been attacked as strongly as jewelry in this regard, which leads jewelry artists to assume defensive postures ranging from more or less casual to irate.

Since the Renaissance at the latest, when art and artists became emancipated, the concept of art has developed, to the greatest extent imaginable, within societal consensus. The often very conflicting and heatedly disputed views on what is and isn't art are neither here nor there, since art is autonomous, with no obligations other than to itself and the artist.

When we speak of jewelry as art, we find ourselves caught on the horns of a dilemma: on the one hand jewelry purports to be autonomous according to the criteria applied to art; on the other, however, the characteristics of the applied arts cannot be overlooked. Further, except where highly conceptual approaches are concerned, jewelry relates directly to the human body and/or to a person as a personality. This represents both a limitation and a challenge. In the best examples of jewelry, we see as if through a powerful lens the thought that has been lavished on these small objects, and this opens up the potential for experiences similar to those that can be had through outstanding works of art—regardless of genre. Workmanship and function, then, play a very subordinate

anderen Gesellschaftsordnungen und kulturellen Befindlichkeiten aus, als wir sie heute vorfinden.

Hinzu kommt, dass Schmuck sich immer wieder dem Stigma der Funktionslosigkeit, des Luxus, des nutzlosen Tands erwehren muss. Kein anderer Bereich der angewandten Künste sieht sich so stark wie Schmuck diesem Gemeinplatz ausgesetzt, der zu einer mehr oder weniger gelassenen bis zornigen Verteidigungshaltung der Protagonisten führt.

Spätestens seit der Renaissance, als sich Kunst und Künstler emanzipierten, entwickelte sich, weitestgehend im gesellschaftlichen Konsens, der Begriff von Kunst. Die im Detail oft sehr konträren und heiß diskutierten Auffassungen widersprechen dem nicht, basieren sie doch letztendlich auf dem Verständnis der Autonomie der Kunst, die nichts und niemandem verpflichtet ist außer der Kunst und dem Künstler.

Wenn wir nun von Schmuck als einer Form der Kunst sprechen, befinden wir uns in eben dem Zwiespalt: Einerseits will Schmuck nach den Kriterien der Kunst autonom sein, andererseits aber sind die Charakteristika der angewandten Kunst nicht zu übersehen. Hinzu kommt, dass Schmuck sich, auch wenn es sich um äußerst konzeptuelle Ansätze handelt, sehr direkt auf den menschlichen Körper und/oder auf den Menschen als Persönlichkeit bezieht. Dies ist zum einen Einschränkung, zum anderen aber auch Herausforderung. Bei wirklich guten Schmuckstücken sehen wir wie im Brennpunkt einer Linse die Konzentration, die auf dieses kleine Objekt verwandt wurde, und es eröffnet uns Erfahrungen, die wir bei herausragenden Kunstwerken – welcher Gattung auch immer – machen können. Handwerk und Funktion spielen dann eine sehr untergeordnete, eine dienende Rolle. Es wäre allerdings ein Fehler, nun anzunehmen, man könne beides vernachläs-

role. It would be wrong, however, to assume one might neglect both with impunity. On the contrary, what is important to realize is that knowledge or mastery of techniques considerably facilitates the realization of ideas. A freedom of art that is often registered in jewelry is choosing not to use techniques one has at one's disposal. One need only look at the contemporary example of Hermann Jünger to understand how an excellent goldsmith bends wires with the simplest of means to produce pieces of jewelry that have exerted a substantial influence on developments in recent jewelry history. Other artists from recent decades might also be mentioned who have made clear that what counts most of all in jewelry is the artistic idea rather than consummate craftsmanship. The dubious yet often quoted saying "art comes from artifice" might be interpreted to mean that art doesn't require the input of the artist. However, the artist does have to contribute both technical and artistic inspiration—art doesn't make itself—and real artifice is expressed in deciding whether artifice should be employed or not.

Material and Jewelry—A New View of Things

Today the question of artifice or not must be supplemented or rather expanded. We are at a point in contemporary art where strict boundaries between fields of art and between fine art and the applied arts, such as architecture, design, and jewelry, in fact, no longer exist. Examples from recent art history furnish evidence that artists are increasingly moving beyond the classic boundaries in what they are producing and that strict

sigen. Vielmehr gilt hier: Die Kenntnis über oder das Beherrschen von Techniken erleichtert die Umsetzung von Ideen ungemein. Gerade das nicht Anwenden von Techniken, über die man verfügt, ist eine der Freiheiten der Kunst, die im Schmuck vielfach dokumentiert wird. Man betrachte nur aus der Geschichte des zeitgenössischen Schmucks am Beispiel Herrmann Jüngers, wie ein exzellenter Goldschmied mit einfachsten Mitteln Drähte biegt und zu Schmuckstücken macht, die ganz wesentlichen Einfluss auf die Entwicklung der neueren Schmuckgeschichte haben. Es ließen sich noch einige Künstler der letzten Jahrzehnte nennen, die mit dieser Methode deutlich machen, dass es im Schmuck in erster Linie um die künstlerische Idee und nicht um die handwerklichen Fertigkeiten geht. Die durchaus fragwürdige und vielfach zitierte Aussage „Kunst kommt von Können…" ließe sich dahingehend interpretieren, dass etwas nicht getan werden muss, auch wenn es gekonnt wird, und dass es sich gerade dann um wirkliches Können handelt, wenn es entscheidungsabhängig ist, ob dieses – das Können – eingesetzt wird oder eben nicht.

Material und Schmuck – eine neue Sicht der Dinge
Heute muss die Frage nach dem Können beziehungsweise Nicht-Können ergänzt oder besser erweitert werden. Wir befinden uns in der zeitgenössischen Kunst an einem Punkt, an dem die rigide Abgrenzung der Sparten in der Kunst selbst als auch zu den angewandten Künsten wie Architektur, Design und auch zum Schmuck nicht mehr gültig ist. Beispiele aus der neuesten Kunstgeschichte belegen, dass sich immer mehr Künstler mit ihren Werken jenseits der klassischen Grenzziehungen bewegen, dass diese bei vielen Werken nicht mehr eingesetzt werden können. Damit wird auch ein Bestehen

separation no longer exists. Consequently, insisting on skills in a particular field (painting, for instance) becomes ever more questionable because artists use all sorts of techniques, some of which can only be executed by specialists. Therefore, it is utterly impossible to expect that artists must be conversant from a technical standpoint with all transformations of materials. The venerable image of the painter at his easel is still with us (and will continue to be so), yet it is being increasingly complemented by new ways of making art.

Something else can also be illustrated using the Damien Hirst work *For the Love of God* (2007), a life-size platinum cast of a human skull covered with diamonds that weigh in total 1,106.8 carats. To make this work, which was the focal point of the Hirst show at the White Cube Gallery in London, classic goldsmithing techniques and materials were used. To call this work jewelry, however, would be wrong. Aside from two of its components—technique and materials—it has nothing to do with jewelry. On the contrary, the artist has made use of the craft of goldsmithing in order to transport artistic content. It is, therefore, neither techniques nor materials that make jewelry jewelry, even though in contemporary jewelry the classic materials such as noble metals and precious stones are also used—albeit often in the form of an ironic allusion to what are known as jewels.

Since the 1970s especially, auteur jewelry has changed completely. Although it was still common then for artists such as Reinhold Reiling and Hermann Jünger to be adept in goldsmithing techniques, the

auf den Fertigkeiten einer bestimmten Sparte (zum Beispiel Malerei) immer fragwürdiger, denn Künstler bedienen sich der unterschiedlichsten, zum Teil nur durch Spezialisten auszuführenden Techniken. Es ist daher gänzlich unmöglich zu erwarten, dass Künstler sich auf die technische Umsetzung verstehen müssen. Das schöne Bild des Malers an der Staffelei gibt es noch (und wird es auch weiterhin geben), doch es wird mehr und mehr durch neue Formen der Kunstherstellung ergänzt.

Am Beispiel von Damien Hirsts Werk *For the Love of God*, des lebensgroßen Platinschädels, der mit über 1000-Karat-Diamanten versehen ist, lässt sich noch etwas anderes zeigen. In dieser Arbeit von 2007, die das Kernstück seiner Ausstellung in der Londoner Galerie White Cube bildete, werden klassische Goldschmiedetechniken und Materialien verwendet. Dieses Werk aber Schmuck zuzurechnen, ist ein Irrtum, es hat außer diesen beiden Komponenten – Technik und Material – nichts damit zu tun. Vielmehr macht sich ein Künstler die Goldschmiedekunst zunutze, um den künstlerischen Inhalt umzusetzen. Es sind also nicht die Techniken und Materialien, die Schmuck zu Schmuck machen, auch wenn im zeitgenössischen Schmuck die klassischen Werkstoffe wie Edelmetalle und Edelsteine zu finden sind – letztere allerdings häufig in Form von ironischer Anspielung auf den sogenannten Juwelenschmuck.

Vor allem seit den 1970er Jahren hat sich der Autorenschmuck grundlegend gewandelt. War es bis dahin für Künstler wie Reinhold Reiling oder Hermann Jünger noch ganz selbstverständlich, sich in der Tradition der Goldschmiedekunst zu verstehen, stellte die damals junge Generation eben diese Tradition grundsätzlich in Frage. Dies äußerte sich nicht

younger generation was questioning the basic assumptions of that tradition. This was demonstrated primarily through their use of all sorts of materials that until then had been reserved at best for models of jewelry but not for the actual pieces. Nowadays one can no longer imagine how charged with emotion the discussion of which materials were suitable for jewelry once was. The belief in commitment to a tradition that was thousands of years old collided with an attitude that called it into question and oriented itself instead to 1960s and 1970s art in Europe and the United States. The increasing politicization and socially critical attitude in art during those years did not bypass jewelry. Plastic was used and not just because of its physical properties. It also conveyed a specific message: modernity coupled with defiant rejection of traditional goldsmithing materials.

Nowadays, materials are no longer an issue for those who have anything to do with contemporary jewelry. Whatever has shown itself to be adequate as a vehicle for content is used. But daily experience in museums shows that there is still a considerable need for explaining that the use of these "non-goldsmithing" materials is justified. It is not easy to get across to visitors that contemporary jewelry need not continually invoke the classic jewelry tradition of gold, silver, and precious stones. It is probably the firmly rooted notions that jewelry must be timeless, ornamental, and at the same time—as far as the material is concerned—of lasting market value that still, again and again, must be called into question. These

zuletzt in dem Einsatz der unterschiedlichsten Materialien, die bis dahin höchstens für Modelle von Schmuckstücken verwendete wurden, nicht aber für ein Schmuckstück selbst. Es ist heute kaum mehr vorstellbar, wie emotionsgeladen die Auseinandersetzung über das für Schmuck angemessene Material geführt wurde. Hier stieß das Selbstverständnis des Kunsthandwerkers, der sich einer jahrtausendealten Tradition verpflichtet fühlt, auf eine Haltung, die dies alles in Frage stellte und sich sehr viel mehr an der Kunst der 1960er und 1970er Jahre in Europa und den USA orientierte. Eine zunehmende Politisierung und gesellschaftskritische Haltung der Kunst in diesen Jahren machte auch vor der Schmuckkunst nicht Halt. Kunststoff wurde nicht nur wegen seiner Materialeigenschaften verwendet, sondern stand auch für eine bestimmte Aussage: Modernität einerseits, aber auch bewusste Abgrenzung zu den traditionellen Materialien der Goldschmiede.

Inzwischen ist die „Materialfrage" für alle, die mit zeitgenössischem Schmuck zu tun haben, sich mit ihm beschäftigen, ob als Sammler, Träger oder Macher, ein weitgehend sekundäres Thema. Man setzt das ein, was sich zur Beförderung der Inhalte als adäquat erweist. Aber die tägliche Erfahrung im Museum zeigt, dass noch immer ein erheblicher Erläuterungsbedarf besteht, dass diese „nicht-goldschmiedischen" Werkstoffe ihre Berechtigung haben. Es ist nicht einfach zu vermitteln, dass zeitgenössischer Schmuck lebendiges Schmuckschaffen bedeutet, welches sich gerade nicht ständig auf die Tradition des klassischen Schmucks aus Gold, Silber und Edelsteinen berufen muss. Es sind wohl diese fest verankerten Vorstellungen, dass Schmuck zeitlos, dekorativ und zugleich – im Material – wertbeständig sein muss, die immer noch und immer wieder in Frage gestellt werden

assumptions are what make it necessary to explain the relationship between jewelry and art.

Glass as a Material—In Jewelry, Too

An exhibition and a publication devoted to contemporary jewelry serve as vehicles for supporting this type of art. To gain access to an unfamiliar subject matter, it is helpful to approach it through a well-defined route. Approaching contemporary jewelry via a particular material, in our case, glass, makes the special features and differences in contemporary jewelry understandable through a material everyone is familiar with. At the same time, contemporary jewelry as an autonomous art form can be understood through the questions touched on above. The manifold ways in which glass is used and the way its form is related to the way it is worked—we are not concerned here with analyzing and researching individual works and approaches— make it clear to the viewer how multifaceted and rich modern jewelry can be.

Just being aware of the numerous design possibilities subsumed in a single object can be rewarding for interested viewers. Such awareness can lead to increased knowledge, followed by a growing receptivity to the sophistication and content of art jewelry. Thus, although being limited to a single material might at first seem restrictive, at second glance it can be seen to provide a useful scope for learning more about contemporary jewelry.

Glass as a jewelry material provides a means to experience contemporary jewelry. Glass is a material

müssen und die es notwendig machen, die Beziehung des Schmucks zur Kunst darzustellen.

Glas als Material – auch im Schmuck

Eine Ausstellung und Publikation zum zeitgenössischen Schmuck dienen stets auch dazu, diese Art des Kunstschaffens zu vermitteln. Um einen Weg aufzuzeigen, wie ein Zugang geschaffen werden kann, ist es durchaus hilfreich, sich über ein definiertes Thema zu nähren. Die Hinführung über ein Material, in unserem Falle Glas, birgt die Möglichkeit, durch einen jedermann bekannten und im Alltag ständig gegenwärtigen Stoff die Besonderheiten und Unterschiedlichkeiten im zeitgenössischen Schmuck verständlich zu machen. Zugleich kann über die oben angesprochene Frage nach den Materialien im Schmuck die eigenständige Kunstform des zeitgenössischen Schmucks geklärt werden. Dabei ist es schon allein die Verschiedenartigkeit von Form und Zustand, wie das Material eingesetzt wird, die für den Betrachter – es geht nicht um die Analyse und Erforschung einzelner Arbeiten und Ansätze – deutlich macht, wie vielfältig und reichhaltig moderner Schmuck ist.

Schon allein diese Tatsache, das einfache zur Kenntnisnehmen dieser Gestaltungsvielfalt zu einem Thema, kann für den interessierten Betrachter zu dem Erkenntnisgewinn führen, der im Weiteren mehr und mehr die Vielschichtigkeit und den Gehalt der Schmuckkunst erschließen kann. So ist die zunächst als Einschränkung zu vermutende Restriktion auf ein Material beim zweiten Hinsehen eine Erweiterung der Möglichkeit, mehr über zeitgenössischen Schmuck zu erfahren.

Mit Glas als Material im Schmuck wurde ein Thema gewählt, das viele Chancen bietet, sich auf Schmuck einzulassen. Glas ist ein Stoff, der uns ständig umgibt, uns überall begegnet.

that is all around us, that we encounter everywhere. We even see the world through glass—that may sound like overstatement but on closer scrutiny it is not. Glass substantially shapes our everyday lives. With a touch of bathos one might even put it as follows: we perceive the world through glass. That does not mean in the way that those who wear glasses see their surroundings. Instead it refers to the fact that glass is used as a material almost everywhere: in the manufacture of technology, for utilitarian objects, in architecture, and in the applied and fine arts.

Architecture particularly illustrates our dependence on glass and its importance. In former times glass was rare and expensive. Techniques for making it were not so highly developed that large areas could be spanned with glass. Moreover, unlike masonry, glass could not be used as effective insulation material that would protect sufficiently from heat and cold. Even nowadays traditional architecture in southern countries—thick walls and just a few windows and small ones at that—confirms that this is so. The desire for a view of the world (just for the pleasure of it), of the natural environment, the sea, or the mountains, is a relatively recent desire that has influenced developments in architecture. In fact, such a desire could only be realized through large spans of glass that offer protection against prevailing weather conditions.

Whether we see our surroundings through an invisible protective wall of glass and, therefore, like a vast painting before our eyes, or whether we are exposed to wind and rain, heat, and cold is crucial to the way

Wir sehen die Welt durch Glas – das mag übertrieben erscheinen, ist es bei näherem Hinsehen aber nicht. Der Werkstoff Glas bestimmt ganz wesentlich unseren Alltag. Etwas pathetisch könnte man auch formulieren: Wir nehmen die Welt durch Glas wahr. Damit ist nicht – zumindest nicht zuerst – die Sichtweise der Brillenträger auf ihre Umgebung gemeint, sondern der Umstand, dass Glas als Werkstoff fast überall eingesetzt wird: in der Produktion von technischen Gütern, bei Gebrauchsgegenständen, in der Architektur und in der angewandten und freien Kunst.

Besonders in der Architektur lässt sich die Abhängigkeit und die Bedeutung von Glas deutlich machen. Früher war Glas ein knappes und teures Gut, die Technik der Fertigung noch nicht so weit entwickelt, dass große Glasflächen hergestellt werden konnten. Zudem konnten im Gegensatz zum Mauerwerk mit den Gläsern keine Dämmwerte erreicht werden, die ausreichend vor Kälte und Hitze schützten. Noch heute zeigt uns traditionelle Architektur in südlichen Ländern dieses Faktum – starke Wände und wenige kleine Fenster. Der Wunsch nach dem Blick (aus Vergnügen) in die Natur, auf das Meer oder in die Berge ist eine neue – und auch relativ junge – Sicht auf die Welt und beeinflusste die Entwicklung der Architektur. Er konnte in der Weise nur durch große Gläser als Schutz vor Witterung realisiert werden.

Es ist für die Art der Wahrnehmung des Außen entscheidend, ob wir unsere Umgebung durch die unsichtbare Schutzwand des Glases erfahren und sie also wie ein riesiges Gemälde vor uns sehen oder ob wir Wind und Regen, Hitze und Kälte ausgesetzt sind. Die Außenwelt wird durch Glas ein Stück weit künstlich, wenn eben diese natürlichen Einflüsse ausgeschaltet oder eingedämmt werden. Die Fortführung dieser Künst-

we perceive what is outside. The external world becomes quite artificial when these natural influences are eliminated or checked. Perceiving the world through the glass television screen simply marks a further development of this artificiality: reality has been entirely eliminated; all that remains is a prepared simulacrum.

Glass in architecture has an ambivalent status that depends on the viewer's vantage-point: if the viewer is in a room, that is, behind the glass pane, it is best if glass is as close to invisible as possible to permit an unobstructed or defined view of what is outside. If a building made of glass is viewed from the outside, the glass surfaces precisely describe the contours of the spatial body, changing it depending on whether it is seen in daylight or at night, when it is illuminated from within.

The protective function of glass becomes especially obvious in conservatories and greenhouses of the kind that have existed since the seventeenth century—at which time they were magnificent orangeries owned by rich royal families and the nobility. By the mid-nineteenth century, the many types of greenhouses as we know them today were in existence. This is not the place to go into the social and economic repercussions they had other than to say that they offered a way to protect staple food commodities from the vagaries of the weather.

Apart from their practical uses, glasshouses induced people to express euphoric remarks. When the vast Glass Palace was built in Hyde Park in London in 1851, thousands of people thronged to it to admire the awe-

lichkeit ist die Wahrnehmung der Welt durch die Glasscheibe des Fernsehers: die gänzliche Ausschaltung der Wirklichkeit, es ist nur mehr ihr aufbereitetes Abbild.

Glas hat hier eine ambivalente Stellung je nach Position des Betrachters: Befindet er sich im Raum, also hinter der Glasscheibe, ist die beste Eigenschaft des Glases, möglichst unsichtbar zu sein, um den ungehinderten beziehungsweise definierten Blick nach Außen zuzulassen. Betrachtet man ein Gebäude aus und mit Glas von außen, zeichnen die Glasflächen exakt die Konturen des Raumkörpers, verwandeln ihn je nachdem, ob wir ihn im Tageslicht oder in der Nacht und von Innen beleuchtet sehen.

Die schützende Funktion von Glas wird besonders in den Wintergärten und Glashäusern sichtbar, wie sie seit dem 17. Jahrhundert – damals waren es die prächtigen Orangerien der reichen Herrscher- und Adelshäuser – entstanden. Schon Mitte des 19. Jahrhunderts gab es alle auch heute noch gebräuchlichen Arten von Gewächshäusern. Es würde zu weit führen, hier auf die sozialen und ökonomischen Auswirkungen einzugehen, die die vor der Unbill des Wetters geschützte Produktion von Lebensmitteln hatte.

Abgesehen von ihrem praktischen Nutzen, verführten die Glashäuser zu euphorischen und überschwänglichen Äußerungen. Als 1851 der große Glaspalast im Hydepark erbaut wurde, strömten die Menschen zu Tausenden dorthin und bewunderten die eindrucksvolle Wirkung des Glasgebäudes. Theodor Fontane schildert diesen Glaspalast in seinen Wanderungen durch England und Schottland von 1852: „[U]nter dem Strahlenstrom (der Mittagssonne) glühte die ferne Kuppel des Kristallhauses wie ein ‚Berg des Lichts‘, wie der echte und einzige Kohinoor [ein knapp 110-karätiger

inspiring sight. Theodor Fontane described the wonder in *Wanderungen durch England und Schottland* (1852): "[U]nder the flood of light rays (from the midday sun), the distant dome of the Crystal House glowed like a 'mountain of light,' like the genuine one and only Kohinoor."[1] While Fontane resorted to poetic language to capture a functional glass building, Bruno Taut translated this fascination with glass buildings into reality in 1914. His Glass Pavilion created for the first large Werkbund exhibition in Cologne was an architectural paean to glass. In conception and composition, it was a world-class glass building. Boasting glass staircases, walls of glass stones, ornamental prisms, some stained glass, and glass backed with colored foil, Taut's creation was a construction of glowing, shimmering colors whose interior and exterior captivated visitors. These two examples from the infancy of building with glass should suffice to convince us that the power of glass transcends its technical function in architecture and, therefore, in our daily lives, and that even twentieth-century buildings are based on our enthusiasm for transparency and light.

If we consider glass in the fine arts, and look to the past, we can admire the incredible effects achieved with Gothic cathedral windows, which made light and color come alive in a peerless hymn to God. The intention informing them cannot be compared to current artistic concepts, but they have helped to shape the way we visualize glass in art. Gerhard Richter has facilitated the transition from Gothic to modern with his new stained-glass window for the south transept of Cologne

Diamant]."[1] *Wenn hier ein Funktionsbau aus Glas so poetisch beschrieben wird, setzte Bruno Taut diese Faszination 1914 um. Sein Glashaus, für die erste große Werkbundausstellung in Köln erbaut, ist eine architektonische Hymne an das Glas. Es war in seiner Konzeption und Komposition ein gläsernes Weltgebäude. Mit gläsernen Treppen, Wänden aus Glassteinen, ornamentalen, teils durchgefärbten, teils farbig hinterlegten Prismengläsern schuf Taut ein leuchtendes, in allen Farben schimmerndes Gebäude, das den Besucher sowohl im Innern als auch von außen in seinen Bann schlug. Diese beiden Beispiele aus den Anfängen des Glasbaus sollen genügen, die weit über seine technische Funktion hinausreichende Überzeugungskraft von Glas in der Architektur und damit in unserem täglichen Leben zu beschreiben. Auch Gebäude des 21. Jahrhunderts fußen auf dieser Begeisterung für Transparenz und Licht.*

Wenn wir das Glas in der Kunst betrachten, so sehen wir in der Vergangenheit die unglaubliche Wirkung gotischer Kirchenfenster, die Licht und Farbe durch Glas lebendig werden lassen und eine einzige Lobpreisung Gottes sind. In ihrer Intention mit unserem Begriff von Kunst in der Gegenwart nicht mehr vergleichbar, haben sie doch unser Bild von Glas in der Kunst mitgeprägt. Eine Brücke schlug Gerhard Richter mit dem neuen Kirchenfenster für die Südquerhausfassade des Kölner Doms. Farbige Gläser wurden mit Hilfe eines Zufallsgenerators angeordnet, ihre Größe entspricht den Maßen, die notwendig sind, um kein Flimmern oder Verschwimmen zu erzeugen. Die so entstehenden farbigen Lichtstrahlen tauchen das Kircheninnere in einen fast mystischen Raum. Die Nähe zur Raumwirkung der Gotik ist dabei nicht zu übersehen.

Cathedral. With the aid of an aleatoric algorithm, stained glass panes have been sized and arranged in such a way that there is a flickering and dissolving of light and a fusion of color and light that transforms the interior of the church into an almost mystical space. The affinities of the spatial effects thus created with those of Gothic architecture are unmistakable.

For contemporary artists, glass is just one of the materials they use in their work. They are interested in specific properties of glass, for instance, the virtual invisibility of its physical substance, its "fluidity," its fragility, or again its mundane qualities and its exquisiteness. Only a few artists work solely in glass.

In the fine arts in general, we become aware of how much we are influenced by what glass can be. Most people associate broken glass panes with danger, fear, and destruction. When these mental images surface in art, they plunge us into a palpable state of fear. We feel threatened even though we know that the exhibition space or the museum in which we are viewing the art is a safe place. In the 1960s the mania for destruction at "happenings" and "performance" events was so overwhelming that in some cases vast quantities of glass were provided just to be broken.

How menacing, wounding, and repellent glass can be, and, on the other hand, how delicate, fragile, gentle, and alluring. Whisper-thin blown-glass bodies recalling the receptacles used in science laboratories, configurations of transparent glass that look like ice, or smooth-surfaced blocks of glass recalling deep, still waters are ways of giving glass *qua* material a

Für zeitgenössische Künstler ist Glas nur eines der Materialien, mit denen sie arbeiten. Sie interessieren sich dabei für ganz bestimmte Eigenschaften von Glas, wie zum Beispiel seine nahezu unsichtbare Materialität, seine „Flüssigkeit", seine Zerbrechlichkeit oder seine Alltäglichkeit und Kostbarkeit. Nur wenige arbeiten ausschließlich mit Glas, die Besonderheit des Studioglases wird in dieser Publikation an anderer Stelle beschrieben.

In den Kunstwerken zeigt sich, was uns beeinflusst und wie stark wir von Vorstellungen und Bildern von Glas geprägt sind. Zerbrochene Glasscheiben verbinden die meisten Menschen mit Gefahr, Angst und Zerstörung. Sobald sie in der Kunst auftauchen, werden diese Bilder wach und versetzen uns in einen körperlich spürbaren Zustand des Bedrohtseins, auch wenn wir wissen, dass die Ausstellungshalle oder das Museum ein sicherer Ort sind. In den 1960er Jahren war die Zerstörungswut in den Happenings und Aktionen besonders groß, dort wurden zum Teil Unmengen zu Bruch gehendes Glas eingesetzt.

So bedrohlich, verletzend und abstoßend auf der einen Seite, so zart, fragil, weich und anziehend kann Glas andererseits sein. Hauchdünn geblasene Glaskörper, die an naturwissenschaftliche Behälter erinnern, Glasgebilde, die wie klar gefrorenes Eis wirken, oder Glasblöcke, deren absolut glatte Oberfläche an tief stehende Gewässer erinnern, sind Wege, dem Material Glas Gesicht und Geschichte zu geben, die unterschiedlicher nicht sein können. Gewiss kann man einwenden, dass auch Stein oder Metall diese Eigenschaften zur Veränderung haben, aber im Gegensatz zu deren „schwerfälliger" Materialität vermittelt Glas den Eindruck von Leichtigkeit und Wandelbarkeit, die wir keiner anderen Materie zutrauen.

face and history, ways that could not be more diverse. Admittedly, one might object that stone or metal also have this capacity for transformation, but unlike their "more ponderous" physical substance, glass conveys an impression of lightness and mutability that we do not impute to any other material.

One cannot write about glass without mentioning the craft of the glassblower. The craftsmen of Murano, the "glass island" off Venice, perpetuate a local tradition that has been shown to go back to the first century B.C. Glassblowing exploits specific physical properties of glass. Since glass, unlike metals, for instance, does not have a definable melting point (one speaks instead of the glass transition temperature) and the viscosity of glass increases as it cools down, it can be shaped as desired in this amorphous, viscous state without surface tension and gravity causing the piece to dissolve at once. Not always artistically compelling and quite often kitsch, vases and objects from Murano nevertheless attest to the enormous skill, knowledge of the material, and experience needed to make glass so diverse in appearance. Good, ambitious works demonstrate the range that is possible in glass design, from whisper-thin and translucent through vibrantly glowing, glittering, and reflecting to matte, rough-textured, and entirely opaque bodies. No other material permits this diversity of appearance except plastic, which since the 1960s has increasingly replaced glass in the field of utilitarian housewares.

The "studio glass" movement, which has been active since the early 1960s, mainly in the United States, was

Man kann nicht über Glas schreiben, ohne das Handwerk der Glasbläserkunst zu erwähnen. Sinnbild für deren bis in das 1. Jahrhundert v. Chr. nachweisbare Tradition sind die Kunsthandwerker der „Glasinsel" Murano bei Venedig. Es sind die besonderen physikalischen Eigenschaften von Glas, die sich die Glasbläserei zunutze macht. Da Glas nicht, wie zum Beispiel Metalle, einen definierten Schmelzpunkt besitzt, vielmehr die Zähflüssigkeit im Laufe der Abkühlung zunimmt – man spricht vom Transformationsbereich –, erlaubt es eine beliebige Verformung in diesem amorphen, zähflüssigen Zustand, ohne dass Oberflächenspannung und Gravitation das Werkstück sofort zerfließen lassen. Nicht immer künstlerisch überzeugend und leider oft genug kitschig, beweisen dennoch die Vasen und Objekte aus Murano, welch enorme Kunstfertigkeit, Kenntnis des Materials und Erfahrung notwendig ist, Glas das unterschiedlichste Aussehen zu geben. Die guten und anspruchsvollen Arbeiten belegen, welche Bandbreite in der Gestaltung von Glas möglich ist: Von hauchdünn durchscheinend über kraftvoll leuchtend, glitzernd und spiegelnd zu matten, rauen und völlig undurchsichtigen Körpern reicht sie. Kein anderes Material – außer Kunststoff, der Glas ab den 1960er Jahren aus dem Bereich der Gebrauchsgüter mehr und mehr verdrängte – lässt diese Vielfalt der Erscheinungsformen zu.

Auch die „Studioglas"-Bewegung, die, vor allem in den USA, seit den frühen 1960er Jahren aktiv ist, war gerade in ihren Anfängen von den viskosen, d.h. zähflüssigen, Eigenschaften beeindruckt, ließen sie doch ein spontanes Eingehen auf die Formen des weichen Glases zu. Der Zufall wurde in das künstlerische Konzept einbezogen, ähnlich wie im zeitgleichen Action Painting. Aus dem Zufall entwickelte sich in den folgenden Jahren eine Perfektion, die es den Studioglaskünst-

in its infancy particularly enamored of the viscosity of glass. Artists advocated spontaneous development of forms from molten glass. Accidental shaping was part of the artistic concept, just as it was in Action Painting, a parallel movement in the fine arts of the day. In the following years, the accident developed into technical perfection, which enabled studio glass artists to stain, paint, etch, or engrave glass without losing the spontaneity of shaping it.

The history of glass as and in jewelry is discussed elsewhere in the present publication; consequently, only a few phenomena are to be touched on here that are also relevant to contemporary glass jewelry. Glass has been very popular as jewelry material from time immemorial. Even when it was not yet possible to make glass, natural glass was worked into pieces of jewelry. This is known from prehistoric and protohistoric finds. The ability to make glass and the continuing development of glassmaking techniques and technologies meant that there were no limits to the designs possible with glass. Its similarity—after processing—to precious stones caused it to be used very early on as a substitute material for them. Soon a hierarchy was created between precious stones as valuable by virtue of being rare, and glass, which could be made in any quantity desired. In eras in which precious stones were especially prized in jewelry, the technique was perfected of making cut stones of glass that were almost indistinguishable from genuine precious stones. The best known example of this is probably the invention of strass, usually known in the United States as rhinestones, simulat-

ler möglich macht, das Glas zu färben, zu bemalen, zu ätzen oder zu gravieren, ohne dadurch die Leichtigkeit einer spontanen Formgebung zu verlieren.

Die Geschichte von Glas als und im Schmuck wird an anderer Stelle in dieser Publikation ausführlich dargestellt, daher soll hier nur auf einige Phänomene eingegangen werden, die auch für den zeitgenössischen Schmuck mit Glas von Relevanz sind. Glas war als Schmuckmaterial seit alters her sehr beliebt, sogar verehrt. Schon als noch keine Glasherstellung möglich war, wurden natürliche Gläser zu Schmuckstücken verarbeitet. Dies belegen vor- und frühgeschichtliche Funde. Mit der Herstellung von Glas und der immer weiter entwickelten Technik waren dem Aussehen und der Gestaltung kaum Grenzen gesetzt. Durch seine – nach der entsprechenden Verarbeitung – Ähnlichkeit mit Edelsteinen wurde Glas schon sehr früh als eine Art Ersatzmaterial eingesetzt. Es entstand bald eine Hierarchie zwischen den wertvollen, weil seltenen Edelsteinen und dem in beliebiger Menge herzustellenden Glas. Besonders in Epochen, in denen im Schmuck Edelsteine eine hohe Wertschätzung genossen und sie ausgesprochen in Mode waren, wurde die Technik, aus Glas geschliffene Steine herzustellen, die von echten Edelsteinen kaum zu unterscheiden waren, perfektioniert. Das bekannteste Beispiel dafür ist wohl die Erfindung des Strass, ein stark bleihaltiges Glas, das in Diamantschliffen bearbeitet Diamanten imitierte. Benannt wurde Strass nach einem seiner Erfinder, dem französischen Juwelier G. F. Strass. Er bot im 18. Jahrhundert zu dem ungemein begehrten weißen Diamanten eine erschwingliche Alternative. In der zweiten Hälfte des 20. Jahrhunderts taucht dann im Modeschmuck vermehrt das gläserne Gegenstück zu Edelsteinen auf, hier allerdings schon eindeutig als

ed diamond or colored stones made of glass with a high lead content that could be given diamond cuts. It was named after its inventor, the French jeweler G. F. Strass. In the eighteenth century, he offered an afford-able alternative to the white diamonds that have always been so highly prized. In the latter half of the twentieth century, costume jewelry began to feature glass as an alternative to precious stones, but by then identifiable as "faux." In this instance glass was viewed as a substi-tute material for something more valuable, but in Jugendstil/art nouveau it became the "genuine," extraordinary material out of which jewelry was made. René Lalique is the leading representative of that peri-od. He composed jewelry concoctions of glass, pre-cious stones, ivory, horn, tortoiseshell, precious metals, and pearls. Glass had attained a status equal to that of many other materials. Lalique's career, which would lead him to devote himself almost exclusively to making objects of glass, shows how interested he was in glass.

These two extremes inherent in glass as a material for jewelry, the quality of being both "faux" and "genuine," that is, simulating more valuable materials but also being usable as a material in its own right, are probably unique and provide contemporary jewelry artists with something that is stimulating to experi-ment with. These particular qualities make glass something very special for jewelry.

[1] Quoted in: Wolfgang Becker (ed.), *Broken Glass—Glas in Kunst und Architektur*, Cologne 2005, p. 99. At l05 carats, the Kohinoor was the world's largest diamond when it was taken to England in 1849.

"nicht echt" zu identifizieren. Ist in diesem Zusammenhang Glas als Ersatzmaterial für etwas Wertvolleres zu sehen, wurde es im Jugendstil zu einem "echten", außergewöhnlich verar-beiteten Schmuckmaterial. René Lalique ist der wichtigste Vertreter dieser Epoche, der kongenial Glas, Edelsteine, Elfen-bein, Horn, Schildpatt, Edelmetalle und Perlen zu Schmuck-stücken komponierte. Jetzt erfuhr Glas eine ebenbürtige Anerkennung neben sehr viel wertvolleren Materialien. Laliques Werdegang, der ihn in späteren Jahren fast ausschließlich zur Herstellung von Glasobjekten führte, zeigt sein besonderes Interesse an Glas.

Diese beiden Pole, die Glas im Schmuck innewohnen, sowohl "echt" als auch "unecht" sein zu können, also als Imitat von wertvolleren Materialien und auch als eigenständiges Material eingesetzt werden zu können, sind wohl einzigartig und bieten zeitgenössischen Schmuckkünstlern eine reizvolle Auseinandersetzung. Es ist tatsächlich eine Besonderheit, die in dieser Ausprägung nur im Glas für Schmuck zu finden ist.

[1] Wolfgang Becker (Hrsg.), Broken Glass – Glas in Kunst und Architektur, *Köln 2005, S. 99.*

Jutta-Annette Page

Glass as Jewels: An Uneasy Relationship
Glas als Schmuck: Eine schwierige Beziehung

Glass is one of the earliest man-made materials, and one of its first significant functions was as personal adornment. Glassy substances also occur in nature in the form of fulgurites, tektites, and obsidian. Especially the latter, because of its shiny dark green to black color, was used by ancient civilizations for making amulets, beads, and carved sculptures.[1] The oldest known man-made glass body ornaments are modest monochromatic beads produced in Mesopotamia in the second half of the third millennium B.C.[2] Humble though the pioneering technology used to produce them was, it provided the foundation on which the development of larger glass ornaments and vessels would be based and revealed the tantalizing promise of glass's shimmering translucency and brilliant color. Through history, these characteristics have supported the close aesthetic comparison of glass with semiprecious stones and gems. It is an uneasy association, one that has often driven the technological development of glass but just as often impeded glass's reception as an artistic medium. Through time, glass emerged as a material of lesser intrinsic value; this hierarchy of glass and gems was not perceivable, however, in the dawn of glass history.

As glassmaking and glass-working capabilities progressed in the Bronze Age, ornaments became more figurative and increased in scale. By the sixteenth century B.C., sculptural pendants modeled after contemporaneous representations of gods and goddesses were cast in relief (fig. 1). Also in the second millennium B.C, small pendant vessels emulating metal prototypes were formed of crushed glass that was applied and fired over a

Glas ist eines der ältesten vom Menschen hergestellten Materialien, und eine seiner ersten wichtigen Funktionen war die des persönlichen Schmucks. Glasartige Substanzen treten auch in der Natur auf, in der Form von Fulguriten, Tektiten und Obsidian. Aufgrund seiner glänzenden dunkelgrünen bis schwarzen Farbe wurde insbesondere Letzterer von frühen und antiken Kulturen für Amulette, Perlen und gemeißelte Skulpturen verwendet.[1] Die ältesten bekannten künstlichen Schmuckobjekte für den menschlichen Körper sind schlichte einfarbige Perlen, die in der zweiten Hälfte des 3. Jahrtausends v. Chr. in Mesopotamien hergestellt wurden.[2] Wenn die Technik ihrer Produktion auch eine sehr bescheidene war, stellte sie die Grundlage für die Entwicklung größerer gläserner Gegenstände mit Schmuckfunktion und Gefäße dar und zeigte sich in ihr verheißungsvoll die glänzende Durchsichtigkeit und leuchtende Farbigkeit von Glas. In der Geschichte haben diese Merkmale stets die enge ästhetische In-Beziehung-Setzung von Glas mit Halbedelsteinen und Edelsteinen begünstigt. Es ist eine schwierige Beziehung, eine, welche die technische Entwicklung von Glas häufig vorangebracht, ebenso oft aber seine Rezeption als künstlerisches Medium behindert hat. Im Laufe der Zeit wurde Glas zu einem weniger kostbaren Material; diese Rangfolge von Glas und Edelsteinen ist für die Frühzeit der Glasgeschichte jedoch nicht zu erkennen.

Da die Fähigkeiten der Glasherstellung und -bearbeitung in der Bronzezeit Fortschritte machten, wurden die Schmuckstücke gegenständlicher und größer. Spätestens im 16. Jahrhundert v. Chr. wurden skulpturhafte Anhänger, die nach zeitgenössischen Darstellungen von Göttern und Göttinnen

removable core. These served as portable containers for scented oils or as amulets providing a form of communication between individuals and supernatural powers. Apotropaic notions were never far from this ancient jewelry —the images of stylized heads, faces, masks and symbols, formed on rods and stamped on pendant disks, can be counted among the protective devices averting the evil eye from their wearer (fig. 2).

By the Late Bronze Age, about 1500–1200 B.C., glass bead workshops in the Near East were supplying local jewelers working in precious metals with glass beads that could be combined with gold elements to create colorful necklaces. Complex gold ear ornaments found at Megiddo in Israel and in tombs at Tell el-Ajjul in the Gaza Strip were probably made in Palestine in the Late Bronze Age and attest to Near Eastern jewelers' early familiarity with glass as ornamental inlays.[3] These ear ornaments are composed of clusters of gold disks with bezel settings into which molten glass has been trailed to form colorful inlays. Ancient glass ornaments often echo popular metal beads of the time; melon and pomegranate shapes, for instance, are common in both materials. Another practice was to cover solid glass spacers of pyramidal shape with gold foil in order to create an ornament with the appearance of solid gold. Ancient glassworkers also fused gold leaf onto the surfaces of shimmering and translucent glass beads. By the second century B.C., Central European jewelers linked small glass rings with gold wire hoops of equal size in order to form colorful chains.[4]

Wrist and ankle bangles were made since the second millennium B.C., and indeed colorful glass bangles worn

geformt sind, in Reliefform gegossen (Abb. 1). Ebenfalls im 2. Jahrtausend v. Chr. wurden kleine Anhänger in Gefäßform, die Vorbilder aus Metall nachahmten, aus zerstoßenem Glas geformt, welches auf einen entfernbaren Kern aufgetragen und auf ihm geschmolzen wurde. Sie dienten als tragbare Behälter für parfümierte Öle oder als Amulette, die eine Art Kommunikation zwischen dem menschlichen Individuum und übernatürlichen Mächten etablierten. Der Gedanke des Glücksbringers oder die Vorstellung, damit Unheil abzuwenden, war von diesem uralten Schmuck nie weit entfernt – die Darstellungen stilisierter Köpfe, Gesichter, Masken und Symbole zum Beispiel, die aus dünnen Glasstäben modelliert oder auf scheibenförmige Anhänger eingeprägt wurden, kann man zu den Schutzvorrichtungen zählen, die den bösen Blick vom Träger abwendeten (Abb. 2).

Von etwa 1500–1200 v. Chr. belieferten Glasperlen-Werkstätten des Nahen Ostens einheimische Schmuckkünstler, die Edelmetalle mit Glasperlen verarbeiteten, welche mit Goldelementen zu buntem Halsschmuck kombiniert werden konnten. Der aufwendige goldene Ohrzierrat, der im israelischen Megiddo und in Gräbern in Tell el-Ajjul im Gazastreifen gefunden wurde, ist wahrscheinlich in der späten Bronzezeit in Palästina hergestellt worden und bezeugt die frühe Vertrautheit der Schmuckkünstler des Nahen Ostens mit Glas als Bestandteil ornamentaler Einlegearbeit.[3] Diese Ohrschmuckstücke bestehen aus Bündeln von Goldscheiben mit Stegfassungen, in die geschmolzenes Glas gegossen wurde, um farbenfrohe Einsätze zu bilden. Die alten Schmuckstücke aus Glas ahmen häufig auch die in dieser Zeit beliebten Metallperlen

in multiples were a widespread ornament in the ancient world from the Roman period onward. Some of the more remarkable glass bracelets were worn by Celtic women in the third and second century B.C. These bangles of local production were usually bright blue or translucent green with applied trails in contrasting colors of white or yellow and with tooled relief decorations. Their seamless construction is of a technical complexity that is not completely understood today.[5] As a type, simpler mono-chromatic versions, as well as bangles decorated with twisted multicolored rods, remained prolific for centuries around the Mediterranean and in the ancient Near East (fig. 3). The practice of wearing glass bangles faded in post-Roman Europe but reappeared in medieval times when fashionable bracelet ornamentation was created through enameling, gilding, and sculpted figurative motifs.

Sound was a significant aspect of ancient (and ethnic) jewelry. In addition to clanking bangles, little glass bells and ring pendants were worn to attract the attention of others and to keep away evil spirits.

One-piece glass finger rings are known to have been made as early as the second millennium B.C. in Egypt but are comparatively rare. The most accomplished rings of nearly modern appearance, with a prominent gem and continuous shank, date to the Hellenistic period (323–146 B.C.) and were primarily made around the Aegean and on Cyprus.[6] They are most frequently cast of transparent, nearly colorless glass and have been finished by cold-working techniques similar to those used to finish their gemstone counterparts. Some are mounted with a

nach; beispielsweise finden sich häufig Melonen- und Granatapfelformen in beiden Materialien. Ein anderes Ver-fahren war es, pyramidenförmige Abstandselemente aus Glas mit Blattgold zu bedecken, um ein Schmuckstück zu schaffen, das aussah, als wäre es aus massivem Gold. Die frühen Glashandwerker der Antike schmolzen Blatt-gold auch auf die Oberflächen von glänzenden und durch-sichtigen Glasperlen auf. Spätestens im 2. Jahrhundert v. Chr. verbanden Schmuckkünstler in Mitteleuropa kleine Glasringe mit gleich großen Reifen aus Golddraht und bildeten so bunte Ketten.[4]

Arm- und Fußreifen wurden seit dem zweiten vorchrist-lichen Jahrtausend hergestellt, und tatsächlich waren farbenfreudige Glasreifen, von denen mehrere gleichzeitig getragen wurden, in der Antike von der römischen Zeit an ein weit verbreiteter Schmuck. Recht außergewöhnlicher Armschmuck aus Glas wurde von keltischen Frauen im 2. und 3. Jahrhundert v. Chr. getragen. Diese Armreifen aus lokaler Produktion waren üblicherweise hellblau oder durchscheinend grün, und auf sie waren Glasfäden in kontrastierenden Farben wie Weiß oder Gelb und durch Werkzeuge bearbeitete Reliefornamente aufgesetzt worden. Ihre nahtlose Konstruktionsweise ist technisch so komplex, dass sie selbst heute nicht gänzlich nachvollzogen werden kann.[5]

Was den Typus angeht, waren die einfarbigen Varianten und auch Armreifen, die mit gedrehten vielfarbigen Stäb-chen verziert waren, im Mittelmeerraum und Nahen Osten für Jahrhunderte sehr erfolgreich (Abb. 3). Der Brauch, gläserne Armreifen zu tragen, ging im Europa der nachrömi-schen Zeit zurück, trat im Mittelalter aber erneut auf. In

dieser Zeit wurden modische Armreifornamente durch Emaillieren, Vergolden und geformte gegenständliche Motive geschaffen.

Klang war ein wichtiger Aspekt des antiken (und des volkstümlichen) Schmucks. Außer klirrenden Armreifen trug man kleine Glasglocken und ringförmige Anhänger, um die Aufmerksamkeit anderer zu erregen und böse Geister fernzuhalten.

Es ist bekannt, dass Fingerringe aus einem einzigen Stück Glas bereits im Ägypten des 2. Jahrtausends v. Chr. hergestellt wurden, sie sind jedoch vergleichsweise selten. Äußerst vollendete, beinahe modern anmutende Ringe mit einem auffälligen Edelstein und einem durchgehenden Reif datieren aus der hellenistischen Zeit (336–30 v. Chr.) und wurden in erster Linie im ägäischen Raum und auf Zypern hergestellt.[6] Sie sind zumeist aus durchsichtigem, fast farblosem Glas gegossen und wurden durch Kaltbearbeitungs-Techniken, welche den Techniken für ihre Gegenstücke aus Edelstein ähnelten, abschließend bearbeitet. Auf einigen der Ringe wurde ein Schmuckstein aus Glas befestigt, der mit an seiner Rückseite aufgebrachtem Blattgold dekoriert wurde. Angesichts ihrer Größe wurden diese Ringe wahrscheinlich nicht am Finger getragen, sondern hingen an einer Schnur um den Hals.

Im Laufe der Zeit wurden die Attraktivität gläserner Gegenstände und die künstlerischen Fähigkeiten, die in ihnen zutage traten, wichtiger als ihr eigentlicher Materialwert – eine Entwicklung, die dazu beitrug, dass Glasschmuck, sogar als er für eine breitere Verbraucherschicht leichter erhältlich und erschwinglich wurde, auch in den oberen Schichten der antiken Kulturen aktuell blieb. Die nubische

glass gem that has been painted or decorated with gold foil applied to the back. Because of their size, these rings were probably not worn on the finger but suspended from a string around the neck.

Through time, the aesthetic appeal and artistic capabilities represented in glass objects became more important than their intrinsic material value, a development that helped to ensure that glass jewelry remained fashionable with the ancient upper classes even as it became more readily available and affordable to a broader consumer base. The Nubian queen Amanishakheto (ruled first century B.C.) was entombed in Meroe (northern Sudan) with rich gold and glass jewelry that is believed to have been worn by her during her lifetime and was not made specifically for burial purposes, as was presumed earlier.[7]

The potential of glass to assume the appearance of gemstones remains one of this material's most desirable aesthetic characteristics. Throughout history, glass-makers have explored this quality to enhance the appeal of their product, sometimes exploiting the potential with the intent to deceive. The Roman scholar Pliny the Elder (ca. A.D. 23–79) described Indian methods of producing simulated precious gems and urged his contemporaries to employ methods that he delineated for distinguishing real stones from fake gems made of fused glass paste.[8] He also noted that the appearance of both genuine gems and glass imitations was sometimes enhanced by backing them with metal foil.[9] During his lifetime, glass was also used for special Roman military parade decorations, so-called *dona militaria*. Sets of nine circular glass medallions were officially awarded for distinction in battle

Königin Amanishakheto (die im 1. Jahrhundert v. Chr. regierte) ist in Meroe (im Norden des heutigen Sudan) bestattet worden – zusammen mit prachtvollem Schmuck aus Glas und Gold, von dem man glaubt, dass er zu ihren Lebzeiten von ihr getragen und nicht, wie früher angenommen, eigens für Begräbniszwecke hergestellt wurde.[7]

Das Vermögen von Glas, das Aussehen von Edelsteinen anzunehmen, ist noch immer eines der meistgewünschten ästhetischen Merkmale dieses Materials. Schon immer haben Glaskünstler diese Eigenschaft genutzt, um die Attraktivität ihres Produkts zu steigern, manchmal haben sie diese auch ausgenutzt, um zu täuschen. Der römische Gelehrte Plinius der Ältere (ca. 23–79 n. Chr.) beschrieb indische Techniken, wertvolle Edelsteine zu imitieren, und drängte seine Zeitgenossen, von ihm beschriebene Methoden anzuwenden, echte Steine von gefälschten Edelsteinen aus geschmolzener Glaspaste zu unterscheiden.[8] Er vermerkte zudem, dass das Aussehen sowohl von echten Edelsteinen als auch von Glasimitationen manchmal verbessert würde, wenn diese mit Metallfolie unterlegt wurden.[9] Zu seinen Lebzeiten verwandte man Glas auch für spezielle Ehrenzeichen auf römischen Militärparaden, die sogenannten Dona militaria. Ein Satz von neun runden Glasmedaillons wurde offiziell an Soldaten verliehen, die sich im Kampf ausgezeichnet hatten und die Medaillons dann stolz auf ihren Brustpanzern zur Schau stellten. Die zumeist blauen Glasmedaillons imitierten wahrscheinlich gemeißelten Lapislazuli und waren in glänzende Bronze gefasst. Sie zeigten üblicherweise Porträt-reliefs von Mitgliedern des julisch-claudischen Kaiserhauses. Wenn sie auch aus einem weniger wertvollen Material als

to soldiers who proudly displayed them attached to the fronts of their armored breastplates. The mostly blue glass medallions presumably imitating carved lapis lazuli were mounted in shiny bronze fittings and usually featured relief portraits of members of the imperial Julio-Claudian household. Although made from a material of lesser intrinsic value than the more desirable (and rarer) silver versions, they represented an attractive and desirable mark of personal distinction.[10]

The use of glass in jewelry made of precious metal continued in glassmaking centers founded during Roman times, such as those in the Rhineland in Germany,[11] even after the collapse of Roman imperial power. During the centuries following the Migration period (500–800 A.D.), as in other periods of decline, it was mostly the production of small-scale works such as beads and inlays that kept the industry alive. The most elaborate jewelry with glass at this time featured transparent copper red glass that was used as inlays in similar fashion to the preferred semi-precious stone, almandine garnet.[12]

Technical treatises on the production of glass were preserved by medieval monks as custodians of historical knowledge. These texts repeated and expanded on Pliny's writings. It has been pointed out that the perceptions of glass in art historical and archaeological discussions differ markedly from those in technical publications, where the interdependence of the development of working gems and working glass is consistently noted.[13] In Medieval technical treatises, the production of glass and the production of gems were discussed together because gem-cutters and glasscutters used the same tools and

die begehrteren (und selteneren) Versionen aus Silber bestanden, waren sie doch eine ansprechende und erstrebenswerte persönliche Auszeichnung.[10]

Die Verwendung von Glas in Schmuckstücken aus Edelmetall setzte sich in den zur römischen Zeit gegründeten Zentren der Glasverarbeitung auch nach dem Zusammenbruch des römischen Kaiserreiches fort, wie beispielsweise im deutschen Rheinland.[11] Zur Zeit der Völkerwanderung (500–800 n. Chr.) erhielt, wie in anderen Perioden des Verfalls, hauptsächlich die Herstellung von Arbeiten kleinen Maßstabs wie von Perlen und Glaseinsätzen den Wirtschaftszweig am Leben. Der aufwendigste Schmuck dieser Zeit, in dem auch Glas verwendet wurde, zeigt durchsichtiges kupferrotes Glas, das, ähnlich wie der bevorzugte Halbedelstein, der Granat Almandin, als Material für Einsätze diente.[12]

Technisch orientierte Abhandlungen über die Glasherstellung wurden von den Mönchen des Mittelalters, den Hütern des alten Wissens, bewahrt. Diese Texte wiederholten und erweiterten die Schriften des Plinius. Man hat hervorgehoben, dass sich die Wahrnehmungsweisen von Glas in der kunsthistorischen und archäologischen Diskussion wesentlich von denen technischer Publikationen unterscheiden, in denen durchgehend auf die wechselseitige Abhängigkeit der Entwicklung der Edelstein- und der Glasbearbeitung hingewiesen wird.[13] In frühen technischen Traktaten wurden die Glas- und die Edelsteinerzeugung zusammen abgehandelt, da Steinschleifer und Glasschleifer dieselben Werkzeuge benutzten und häufig auch mit beiden Materialien arbeiteten.[14] Diese Verknüpfung des Schleifens von Edelsteinen und der Glasherstellung setzte sich in der

often worked in both materials.[14] This association of gem cutting and glassmaking continued in the Renaissance, which, with its keen interest in the exploration of nature, brought forth a new attitude toward design and craftsmanship. Venice became the premier center not only for luxury glass production but also for the European gem trade. As early as 1233, making and selling glass gemstones with the intent to deceive was prohibited, as was mounting them in gold or silver. Transgressions were severely punished by loss of the right hand, banishment into exile, and confiscation of the merchandise.[15] Starting in the thirteenth century, the guild system enforced quality controls, mostly to protect the Venetian republic's competitive edge in the luxury market. In 1502, similar laws were enacted for the manufacture and trade of fake pearls, since their prolific production had a serious impact on the sale of the genuine article.[16] Although curbed and regulated, their production continued: the wardrobe accounts of Elizabeth I from 1566 indicate that she purchased 520 false (glass) pearls to be used for dress trimmings, in keeping with the prevalent fashion of the period (fig. 4).[17]

The only exceptions to the Venetian rules were fake gems in the possession of the church, allegedly because they remained outside the mercantile world. It may have been irrelevant for the function of ecclesiastical vessels and ornaments whether they were set with genuine stones or not. Inventories of cloisters often include reliquaries set with glass gems. Christian reliquary containers such as those enshrined in churches to keep sacred objects safe as well as visually accessible to the faithful were also

Renaissance fort, die mit ihrem lebhaften Interesse an der Erforschung der Natur eine neue Einstellung zum künstlerischen Entwurf und zur Handwerkskunst an den Tag legte. Venedig wurde zum Hauptzentrum nicht allein für die Produktion von Luxusglas, sondern auch für den europäischen Edelsteinhandel. Bereits 1233 war dort das Herstellen und der Vertrieb von Glasedelsteinen in täuscherischer Absicht verboten worden und auch, sie in Gold oder Silber zu fassen. Zuwiderhandlungen wurden streng bestraft – durch den Verlust der rechten Hand, Verbannung und Beschlagnahmung des Handelsgutes.[15] Vom 13. Jahrhundert an hatte das venezianische Zunftsystem Qualitätskontrollen durchgesetzt, hauptsächlich, um den Wettbewerbsvorteil der Republik Venedig im Luxusgüter-Markt zu bewahren. 1502 wurden ähnliche Gesetze für die Produktion und den Handel falscher Perlen erlassen, da ihre Herstellung in großen Mengen ernste Auswirkungen auf den Verkauf des echten Produktes hatte.[16] Trotz aller Einschränkungen und Regulationen stellte man sie weiterhin her: Die die Ausgaben für die königliche Garderobe verzeichnenden Wardrobe accounts von Elizabeth I. aus dem Jahr 1566 zeigen, dass diese 520 falsche (gläserne) Perlen für den Besatz ihrer Kleider erwarb – im Einklang mit der zu dieser Zeit aktuellen Mode (Abb. 4).[17]

Die einzigen Ausnahmen zu den in Venedig aufgestellten Regeln bildeten die falschen Edelsteine, die sich in kirchlichem Besitz befanden, angeblich, weil diese außerhalb der Welt des Handels verblieben. Es mag für die Funktion kirchlicher Gefäße und Schmuckgegenstände nicht relevant gewesen sein, ob sie mit echten Steinen besetzt waren oder nicht. Klosterinventare verzeichnen häufig mit gläsernen

produced on a smaller, more portable, and personal scale. Lockets encapsulating sacred objects, such as a blessed host or a relic acquired on a pilgrimage, were frequently fitted on the front with a transparent domed window of rock crystal or glass that provided an enlarged view of the precious object within.[18]

Accounts of pageants performed to celebrate great princely occasions such as weddings and state visits also note the use of glass ornaments in themed costumes, allowing for close color-coordination of jewelry and fabric. The Florentine historian Pierfrancesco Giambullari (1495–1555) described a pageant of the muses performed on the occasion of Cosimo I de' Medici's wedding to Eleonora de Toledo in July 1539, noting that the Muse Euterpe wore a greenish-yellow dress and glass beads of the same color.[19]

At the time, the main suppliers for such ornaments were the *perleri* in Venice, who created a large variety of glass beads, buttons, figurines, and jewelry in small family-owned workshops. These ornaments were formed from glass rods that were heated over a small oil or paraffin lamp, its flame increased by a foot-powered bellows. The Venetian lamp-working industry played an artistically subordinate but economically important role in the production of glass beads made for export, especially for trade on the African continent; however, the most talented lamp-workers reached new artistic heights, and their skillful creations were sought by the European courts. These included glass feathers, flowers, and figural ornaments for personal adornment. Fragile and ephemeral in nature, little of this production has survived, which has led to the

Steinen besetzte Reliquiare. Behältnisse für christliche Reliquien – wie die, welche in Kirchen verehrt wurden und die Sicherheit heiliger Gegenstände wie auch ihre für die Gläubigen wichtige Sichtbarkeit gewährleisteten – wurden auch in kleinerem Maßstab hergestellt, sie waren so leichter zu transportieren und hatten einen persönlicheren Charakter. Medaillons, die heilige Gegenstände wie eine geweihte Hostie oder eine auf einer Pilgerfahrt erworbene Reliquie in einer Kapsel aufbewahrten, waren häufig an ihrer Vorderseite mit einem durchsichtigen gewölbten Fenster aus Bergkristall oder Glas versehen, welches das kostbare Objekt im Inneren optisch vergrößerte.[18]

Berichte über Festumzüge zu bedeutenden höfischen Anlässen wie Hochzeiten und Staatsbesuchen vermerken ebenfalls die Verwendung von Glasschmuck in den einem bestimmten Thema gewidmeten Kostümen, was eine genau farbliche Abstimmung von Schmuck und Kleiderstoff möglich machte. Der Florentiner Historiker Pierfrancesco Giambullari (1495–1555) beschrieb einen Festzug der Musen, der im Juli 1539 anlässlich der Vermählung von Cosimo I. de' Medici mit Eleonora von Toledo aufgeführt wurde, und stellte fest, dass die Muse Euterpe ein grüngelbes Kleid und Glasperlen in der gleichen Farbe trug.[19]

Zu dieser Zeit waren die wichtigsten Lieferanten für solche Schmuckstücke die venezianischen Perleri, die in kleinen Familienbetrieben eine große Vielfalt von Glasperlen, Knöpfen, Figurinen und Schmuckstücken schufen. Diese wurden aus Glasstäben geformt, welche über einer kleinen Öl- oder Petroleumlampe erhitzt wurden, wobei die Flamme mittels eines fußbetriebenen Blasebalgs vergrö-

Figure 4 Portrait of Elizabeth I,
Anonymous, Britain, ca. 1588.
Oil on canvas, 30×25 in. Toledo
Museum of Art, Toledo, Ohio
(1953.94).
Photo: Toni Marie Gonzalez

*Abbildung 4 Bildnis Elizabeth I.,
anonymer Künstler, Großbritannien,
ca. 1588. Öl auf Leinwand,
76,2×63,5 cm. Toledo Museum
of Art, Toledo, Ohio (1953.94).
Foto: Toni Marie Gonzalez*

ßert wurde. Die Branche der venezianischen Lampenhersteller spielte eine künstlerisch untergeordnete, aber wirtschaftlich wichtige Rolle, was die Herstellung von Glasperlen für den Export, insbesondere für den Handel auf dem afrikanischen Kontinent, anging; allerdings erzielten die talentiertesten Lampenmacher neue künstlerische Höhen, und ihre kunstvollen Schöpfungen waren an den europäischen Höfen gefragt. Zu diesen zählten für den persönlichen Gebrauch bestimmte Schmuckstücke in Form von gläsernen Federn, Blumen und Figuren. Von diesen naturgemäß zerbrechlichen und vergänglichen Erzeugnissen hat sich nur wenig erhalten, was zu der Ansicht geführt hat, dass solcher Glasschmuck nie getragen werden sollte. Berichte aus dieser Zeit deuten jedoch darauf hin, dass diese Stücke sowohl als Sammlerstücke als auch als tragbare Schmuckstücke angesehen wurden.

Aus dem 16. Jahrhundert werden ganze Schmuckgarnituren aus Glas auf Schloss Ambras in Österreich aufbewahrt, in der Kunstkammer Erzherzog Ferdinands II. (1529–1596), eines wichtigen Mitglieds der Familie der Habsburger. Schwarzer, aus Böhmen importierter Gagat-Schmuck war bei den europäischen Eliten dieser Zeit sehr beliebt. Er wurde vor allem von den geschmacklich den Ton angebenden Damen am Hof der spanischen Habsburger für ihre Halsketten und Rosenkränze bevorzugt, und es dauerte nicht lange, bis die venezianischen Lampenmacher diesen in schwarzem Glas kopierten.[20] Solche Schmuckneuigkeiten entsprachen ganz dem ausgefallenen und exotischen Geschmack der europäischen Auftraggeber, die sich an dem sich auf die ganze Welt vergrößernden Materialkosmos des 16. und 17. Jahrhunderts erfreuten.

suggestion that such glass jewelry was never meant to be worn. However, accounts of the period indicate that these pieces were viewed as both collectible and wearable ornament.

Entire ensembles of glass jewelry from the sixteenth century have been preserved at Ambras Castle in Austria in the *Kunst- und Wunderkammer* of Archduke Ferdinand II (1529–1595), a prominent member of the Hapsburg family. Black jewelry made of jet imported from Bohemia was very popular with European elites in the sixteenth century. It was especially favored by the taste-making ladies at the Iberian Hapsburg Court for their necklaces and rosaries, and Venetian lamp-workers quickly copied them in black, sometimes combined with contrasting white glass.[20] Such novelty ornaments appealed to the unusual and exotic tastes of European patrons who delighted in the globally expanding material universe of the sixteenth and seventeenth centuries.

From the fringes of the world colonized by Europeans has survived an equally exotic personal ornament of a very different nature. An Iroquois Indian grave dating to about 1662 in Seneca Falls, New York, yielded a multi-chain necklace with a pendant consisting of the stem and base fragment of a green glass *roemer*, a drinking glass with a prunted stem and trailed foot. The fragment, worthless to the Dutch settlers who probably imported the glass to the colonies, received new cultural significance from its Native American owner, who elevated it to a jewel—maybe due to its color, form, or rarity, and possibly also as a symbol of the significant circumstances (now unknown) under which it was obtained.

Vom Rand der von den Europäern kolonialisierten Welt hat sich ein nicht weniger exotisches Schmuckstück ganz anderer Art erhalten. Ein etwa auf das Jahr 1662 zu datierendes Irokesengrab in Seneca Falls, New York, gab einen aus vielen Ketten bestehenden Halsschmuck frei, mit einem Anhänger in Form eines grünen Glasfragments aus Schaft und Fuß eines Römers, eines Trinkglases mit nuppenbesetztem Schaft und geripptem Fuß. Die für die holländischen Siedler, die das Glas wahrscheinlich in die Kolonien importiert hatten, wertlose Scherbe erhielt von ihrem neuem Besitzer, einem amerikanischen Ureinwohner, eine neue kulturelle Bedeutung. Er erhob es zum Schmuckstück – vielleicht aufgrund seiner Farbe, seiner Form oder seines Seltenheitswertes und vielleicht auch aufgrund seiner Symbolhaftigkeit für die (heute unbekannten) bedeutungsvollen Umstände, unter denen er es erlangt hatte.

Bis zum Ende des 19. Jahrhunderts vollzog sich die Produktion von Schmuck mit Bestandteilen aus Glas im Gleichschritt mit Verbesserungen, welche Glas in Form von Schmucksteinen attraktiver machten. Tiefrotes, dem Feuer von Rubinen ähnelndes Glas erfreute sich stets besonderer Wertschätzung. Ein in Deutschland hergestellter, herrlicher frühbarocker Anhänger aus vergoldetem Kupfer und Email, der in seiner Mitte einen großen geschliffenen Stein aus durchsichtigem roten Glas zeigt (Abb. 5), kündet die Vorliebe für rubinrotes Glas der folgenden Jahrhunderte an. Zwischen 1678 und 1683 konnte der hessische Chemiker und Glasmacher Johann Kunckel (geb. zwischen 1632 und 1637, gest. 1703) ältere europäische Rezepturen für Goldrubinglas untersuchen und verbessern. Die hoch begehrte, tief blaurote Farbe von Goldrubinglas wird

Until the end of the nineteenth century, the production of jewelry with glass elements continued in lockstep with improvements that enhanced the appeal of glass as a gem. Glass with a rich red color resembling the fire of rubies was always held in great esteem. A splendid early baroque pendant made in Germany of gilded copper and enamel and featuring a large, central, faceted gem of transparent red glass (fig. 5) heralds the penchant for ruby-red glass in the following centuries. Between 1678 and 1683, the Hessian chemist and glassmaker Johann Kunckel (b. 1632–37, d. 1703) was able to investigate and improve earlier European recipes for gold-ruby glass. The highly desirable deep bluish red color of gold-ruby glass is achieved by adding colloidal gold to colorless molten glass. Kunckel's gold-ruby glass was sought after for luxury tableware and ornaments. The manufacturing process was complicated, however, and the use of gold-ruby glass remains limited to this day to a small market of luxury goods.

Rock crystal and diamonds were the preferred models for colorless glass. In the late seventeenth century, the quest for heavy, crystal-clear glass tableware and sparkling lighting devices resulted in new glass formulas. These recipes relied on either lead or chalk as additives to improve transparency and refractive qualities. During the early Restoration in England, the Royal Society encouraged English glassmakers to make use of several groundbreaking publications describing new technological developments, and this led to further dramatic improvements.[21] In 1674, the merchant George Ravenscroft obtained the first patent to produce lead glass at his

erzielt, indem man kolloidales Gold der farblosen Glasschmelze hinzufügt. Kunckels Goldrubinglas war für luxuriöses gläsernes Tischgeschirr und luxuriöse Schmuckobjekte sehr gefragt. Der Herstellungsprozess war jedoch kompliziert, und noch heute beschränkt sich die Verwendung von Goldrubinglas auf einen kleinen Markt von Luxusgütern.

Bergkristall und Diamanten waren die beliebtesten Vorbilder für farbloses Glas. Im späten 17. Jahrhundert führte die Suche nach kristallklarem gläsernem Tischgeschirr und funkelnden Beleuchtungsvorrichtungen zu neuen Glasrezepturen. Als Zusatzstoffe, um die Durchsichtigkeit und die Lichtbrechungsfähigkeit zu verbessern, waren entweder Blei oder Kalk notwendig. In den Jahren nach der englischen Restauration ermutigte die Royal Society die englischen Glasmacher, sich eine Anzahl von bahnbrechenden Publikationen zunutze zu machen, welche neue technische Entwicklungen beschrieben, und dies führte zu weiteren wesentlichen Verbesserungen.[21] 1674 erhielt der Kaufmann George Ravenscroft als Erster die Lizenz, in seiner Glashütte im Londoner Savoy-Bezirk Bleiglas herzustellen. Als Vertriebspartner sicherte er sich die einflussreiche London Glass-Sellers' Company. Seit langem wird er als einziger „Erfinder" dieser Glasart in England angesehen. Allerdings wurden etwa zur selben Zeit Experimente mit Bleiglasrezepturen in den Niederlanden, an anderen Orten in England und in Irland durchgeführt.[22] Auf dem europäischen Festland entwickelten in den 1670er Jahren böhmische Glasmacher eine Rezeptur aus Pottasche und gebranntem Kalk, die aus Gründen der Stabilität einen hohen Anteil Kalk (Calciumcarbonat) enthielt. Das neue

glasshouse in the Savoy district of London. He secured the powerful London Glass-Sellers' Company as a distributor and has long been regarded as the sole "inventor" of such glass in England. However, experiments with lead glass formulae were pursued at roughly the same time in the Netherlands, elsewhere in England, and in Ireland.[22] On the Continent in the 1670s, Bohemian glassmakers developed a potash-lime formula that included a considerable quantity of chalk (carbonate of lime) to provide stability. The new glass was clearer and more brilliant than Venetian *cristallo*, and because it was also harder than English lead glass, it was eminently suited for decorations executed in deeply modeled relief by gem cutters. Innovative grinding and setting techniques appropriate for the new materials were developed, which brought about general improvements in working precious and semi-precious gems.

Before the eighteenth century, wearing jewelry was a symbol of status limited to a large extent to the courts for their ceremonies, but gradually jewelry became available to the general public and gained footing as a mere decorative ornament.[23] The appearance of the rhinestone played a major part in this phenomenon. A glass imitation of transparent precious gems (especially diamonds), it emerged as a collective European development in the seventeenth century and increased in popularity with industrialization.[24] About 1775, Monsieur Ganchez, jeweler to Marie-Antoinette, advertised ornaments set with rhinestones from England. At the time, a French jeweler working in precious metal and gems who also employed fashionable false gems and other materials (ivory, coral,

Glas war klarer und leuchtender als das venezianische Cristallo, und weil es auch härter als das englische Bleiglas war, eignete es sich vorzüglich für tief eingeschnittene Ornamente, die von Steinschleifern eingearbeitet wurden. Für die neuen Materialien wurden Techniken des Schleifens und Fassens entwickelt, welche generelle Verbesserungen für die Arbeit mit Edelsteinen und Halbedelsteinen nach sich zogen.

Vor dem 18. Jahrhundert war das Tragen von Schmuck ein Statussymbol, das zu einem guten Teil auf die Zeremonien der Fürstenhöfe beschränkt war, doch nach und nach wurde Schmuck auch für die Allgemeinheit verfügbar und gewann als bloßes Ornament an Bedeutung.[23] Dieses Phänomen ist zu einem Großteil durch das Auftreten von sogenanntem Strass bedingt. Diese gläserne Imitation von durchsichtigen, kostbaren Edelsteinen (insbesondere von Diamanten) trat im 17. Jahrhundert als allgemeineuropäische Entwicklung auf und wurde im Zeitalter der Industrialisierung immer beliebter.[24] Um 1775 warb Monsieur Ganchez, Juwelier der französischen Königin Marie-Antoinette, für strassbesetzte Schmuckstücke aus England. In dieser Zeit wurden französische Schmuckkünstler, die mit kostbaren Metallen und Steinen arbeiteten, in ihre Arbeiten aber auch modische falsche Steine und andere Materialien (wie Elfenbein, Koralle, Horn) einsetzten, eher den Bijoutiers als den Joailliers zugeordnet, welche in erster Linie kostbare Steine verwendeten. (Beide wiederum sind von den Orfèvres, den Erzeugern silberner und goldener Gefäße, zu unterscheiden.) Die wichtigsten Schmuckkünstler der Zeit überschritten die Grenzen zu allen drei Produktionsbereichen. In den englischsprachigen Ländern gab es diese strenge

Figure 6 Brooch with miniature of female eye, probably England, about 1815. Watercolor and body-color on ivory, gold-plated brooch with convex glass, 1 3/4 × 7/8 in., length x width. Gift of Mr. and Mrs. John Starr, 973.51.2, courtesy of the Royal Ontario Museum

Abbildung 6 Brosche mit Miniatur eines weiblichen Auges, wahrscheinlich England, um 1815. Wasserfarbe und Deckfarbe auf Elfenbein, vergoldete Brosche mit Konvexglas, Länge 3,8 cm, Breite 2,4 cm. Schenkung von Mr. und Mrs. John Starr, 973.51.2, mit freundlicher Genehmigung des Royal Ontario Museum

Figure 7 Model of the Koh-i-Noor and two other Indian diamonds, in fitted case, Apsley Pellat, Falcon Glass Works, England, 1850–51. Mold-cast lead glass, cut and polished, 4 1/2 × 2 1/2 in., length × width (fitted case). Toledo Museum of Art, Toledo, Ohio, purchased with funds from the Libbey Endowment, Gift of Edward Drummond Libbey (2006.171).
Photo: Toni Marie Gonzalez

*Abbildung 7 Nachbildung des Koh-i-Noor und zweier weiterer indischer Diamanten, in eigens angefertigter Schatulle, Apsley Pellat, Falcon Glass Works, England, 1850/51. Formgegossenes Bleiglas, geschliffen und poliert, Schatulle 11,5 Länge, 6,5 cm Breite. Toledo Museum of Art, Toledo, Ohio, erworben mit Mitteln der Libbey-Schenkung, Geschenk von Edward Drummond Libbey (2006.171).
Foto: Toni Marie Gonzalez*

horn, etc.) in his designs was classed among the *bijoutiers* rather than among the *joailliers*, who predominantly used precious gems (both, in turn, are distinguished from the *orfèvres*, the producers of silver and gold vessels). The premier jewelers of the day crossed into all three areas of production. This rigid categorization of jewelers and metalworkers was absent in English-speaking countries, where jewelers and metalsmiths working with precious and non-precious materials formed a united trade. The French classification posed a particular problem during the world's fairs in the nineteenth century, since the borders between the categories are in reality rather fluid. During the 1851 Crystal Palace Exposition in London, displays were unified, highlighting jewelry made of precious

Kategorisierung von Schmuckproduzenten und Metall-handwerkern nicht, dort vereinten sich Schmuckkünstler und Metallschmiede, die mit wertvollen oder weniger wertvollen Materialien arbeiteten, in einem einzigen Hand-werkszweig. Die französische Eingruppierung stellte während der Weltausstellungen des 19. Jahrhunderts ein besonderes Problem dar, da die Grenzen zwischen den einzelnen Kategorien in der Praxis fließend sind. Während der Ausstellung im Londoner Crystal Palace im Jahr 1851 wurden die präsentierten Objekte zusammengefasst und Schmuckstücke aus kostbaren wie auch aus weniger kostbaren Materialien hervorgehoben. Eine der besonders beliebten Attraktionen dieser Weltausstellung war ein ungefasster Edelstein aus Indien, der gefeierte Koh-i-Noor

materials as well as semi-precious jewelry. One of the more popular attractions at the fair was an unmounted gem, the celebrated Indian Koh-i-Noor (Mountain of Light) diamond, then the largest known diamond in the world, which had been presented to Queen Victoria as a spoil of war by the British East India Company the year before. Also on view at the fair, at the display of the London firm Falcon Glass Works owned by Apsley Pellat IV, was a remarkable glass copy of the Koh-i-Noor diamond that was acclaimed for its brilliance and flawlessness. The Apsley Pellat IV (1791–1863) copy is appreciated today for preserving the gem's original size and Indian cut (fig. 7).

During the Victorian period, the ritualization of mourning, especially in English society, promoted a large range of somber jewelry appropriate to signify the depth of one's emotional loss. After the death of her uncle William IV in 1837, newly crowned Queen Victoria demonstrated a particular fondness for old-fashioned mourning jewelry. Among the types she adored were miniature eye portraits, a curious type of sentimental token fashionable from the late 1780s to about 1830. These were painted by miniaturists on a variety of materials (including glass) after the life model and were mounted in pins or brooches or set in rings or bracelet clasps, their delicate painted surfaces protected by convex glass covers, the shiny surfaces of which enforced the appearance of human eyes (fig. 6).[25] These personal ornaments were exchanged as gifts between lovers, friends, and relatives, particularly between female friends, sisters, or mothers and daughters,[26] and could serve later to commemorate deceased loved ones. After the death of Prince Consort Albert in

(Berg des Lichts), der damals der größte bekannte Diamant überhaupt und im Jahr zuvor von der Britischen Ostindien-Kompanie Königin Victoria als Kriegsbeute überreicht worden war. Auf der Weltausstellung, am Stand der Londoner Firma Falcon Glass Works von Apsley Pellat IV. war zudem eine bemerkenswerte gläserne Kopie des Koh-i-Noor-Diamanten zu besichtigen, welche für ihre Leuchtkraft und Makellosigkeit gerühmt wurde. Die Kopie von Apsley Pellat IV. (1791–1863) schätzt man heute, weil sich mit ihr die Originalgröße und der indische Schliff des Edelsteins erhalten haben (Abb. 7).

Im viktorianischen Zeitalter förderte die Ritualisierung der Trauer vor allem innerhalb der englischen Gesellschaft die Entstehung eines ganzen Spektrums von unauffälligem Schmuck, welcher in angemessener Weise die Tiefe des erlittenen Verlustes kundtat. Nach dem Tod ihres Onkels William IV. im Jahr 1837 legte die gerade gekrönte Königin Victoria eine besondere Vorliebe für altmodischen Trauerschmuck an den Tag. Zu den Typen, die sie über alles liebte, zählten miniaturartige Augenporträts, eine eigentümliche Spielart des empfindsamen Andenkens, das vom Ende der 1780er Jahre bis etwa 1830 in Mode gewesen war. Diese Porträts wurden nach dem lebenden Modell von Miniaturmalern auf eine ganze Anzahl von Bildträgern (darunter auch Glas) gemalt und auf Anstecknadeln oder Broschen befestigt oder in Ringe oder Armbandspangen eingesetzt. Ihre empfindlichen gemalten Oberflächen wurden durch konvexe Glasdeckel geschützt, deren Glanz wiederum den Eindruck verstärkte, dass es sich um menschliche Augen handelte (Abb. 6).[25] Diese persönlichen Schmuckstücke wurden zwischen Geliebten, Freunden

Figure 8 Neck ornament in the form of a snake, Boucheron, France, 1885. Gold, silver, glass gems, 28 in., length. Toledo Museum of Art, Toledo, Ohio, Purchased with funds from the Florence Scott Libbey bequest in memory of her father, Maurice A. Scott (1998.9). Photo: Tim Thayer

Abbildung 8 Halsschmuck in Form einer Schlange, Boucheron, Frankreich, 1885. Gold, Silber, Glassteine, Länge 71 cm. Toledo Museum of Art, Toledo, Ohio, erworben mit Mitteln des Florence Scott Libbey-Nachlasses im Gedenken an ihren Vater Maurice A. Scott (1998.9). Foto: Tim Thayer

1861, the Victorian court sank into a nearly permanent state of mourning, with black jet as the only ornamental gem acceptable to be worn at court. The desirable British jet from Whitby was comparatively light in weight and could be carved into designs of grand scale, including large pendant earrings. Cheaper and heavier black glass versions of this jewelry, known as French jet, were cast, cut, and often matt-polished in order to resemble more closely the appearance of natural jet.

In France, in the second half of the nineteenth century, glass gems were primarily found in lower-grade jewelry, although even the best jewelry houses continued to utilize glass in fashionable *joaillerie* designs. At the Paris Exposition of 1867, the French organizers insisted that *joaillerie*, *bijouterie*, and *orfèvrerie* be displayed separately, which enforced the underlying tendencies of the traditional *joailliers* to regard *bijouterie* as unwelcome competition, tasteless, and crude.[27] Traditional jewelers (*joailliers*) such as the venerable House of Boucheron relied on glass gems only for mock-ups employed to work out the design details of significant commissions. Such was the case with an elaborate snake neck ornament that was commissioned in 1885 by an anonymous French princess. Set with cut glass stones, Boucheron's gold mock-up of the piece displays a complex hinged body with a spring-loaded tongue (now missing) that pops out when the creature's jaw is made to drop (fig. 8).

The work of René Lalique (1860–1945) emerged in the late 1880s in stark contrast to these rigid conventions. A *bijoutier artistique* and leading jeweler of the belle epoque who discovered glass as an artistic medium late

und Verwandten und vor allem zwischen Freundinnen, Schwestern oder Müttern und Töchtern als Geschenke ausgetauscht[26] und konnten später dazu dienen, die geliebten Verstorbenen in der Erinnerung zu bewahren. Nach dem Tod des Prinzgemahls Albert im Jahr 1861 fiel der Hof Queen Victorias in einen Zustand nahezu immerwährender Trauer, und schwarzer Gagat war der einzige Schmuckstein, der bei Hof getragen werden konnte. Der begehrte britische Gagat aus Whitby war verhältnismäßig leicht und konnte zu Objekten eindrucksvoller Größe geschnitten werden, zu denen auch große Ohrgehänge zählten. Preiswertere und schwerere schwarze Glasversionen solcher Schmuckstücke waren als „French jet" (französischer Gagat) bekannt, sie wurden gegossen, geschliffen und häufig matt poliert, um echtem Gagat stärker zu ähneln.

In Frankreich fand man in der zweiten Hälfte des 19. Jahrhunderts Glassteine hauptsächlich in weniger qualitätvollem Schmuck, wenn auch einige der renommiertesten Schmuckhäuser weiterhin Glas in modischen Joaillerie-Stücken verwendeten. Auf der Pariser Weltausstellung 1867 bestanden die französischen Organisatoren darauf, dass Joaillerie, Bijouterie und Orfèvrerie getrennt ausgestellt wurden, was die schon vorhandenen Tendenzen der Joailliers, die Bijouterie als unwillkommene Konkurrenz, geschmacklos und kunstlos anzusehen, verstärkte.[27] Die traditionsbewussten Juweliere (Joailliers) wie die altehrwürdige Firma Boucheron verwandten Glassteine lediglich in Modellen, an denen sie die Details der Entwürfe für bedeutende Aufträge ausarbeiteten. Dies geschah im Fall eines aufwendigen Schlangen-Halsschmucks, der 1885

in his life, Lalique introduced jewelry in the art nouveau style. Using precious materials alongside non-precious ones such as horn and glass, he subordinated all materials equally to his overall aesthetic idea. His works obliterated the boundaries between jewelry and sculpture and between applied and fine art. Inspired by Japanese art, he observed nature, from its humblest plants to insects, and distilled its aesthetic essence. He arranged a poppy with petals of cast and carved translucent glass into a florid gold construction enhanced by enamel and set with diamonds (fig. 9). Most of the larger, solid glass components were cast in molds and finished with cold-working techniques. He was particularly fond of the delicate *pâte-de-verre* (glass paste) technique for creating complex opaque designs. Pioneered by nineteenth-century French artist Henri Cros (1840–1907), the technique involves fusing powdered glass with a fluxing medium in molds. The careful layering of different hues of powder in the mold allows for greater control of the color range and shading within the cast piece. For insect wings and leaves executed in the art nouveau style, Lalique used the *plique-à-jour*, or "window enamel," technique. Many among Lalique's contemporaries, including George Auger and Lucien Gaillard, became proponents of the *genre Lalique*.

American Louis Comfort Tiffany (1848–1933), whose company had strong ties to Paris, also explored glass in his art nouveau jewelry designs. He preferred true gemstones, whether opaque or translucent, to glass, but turned to enameling techniques to create the desired color and translucency in some of his creations. His use of large solid, gem-like glass elements in jewelry was

von einer nicht namentlich bekannten französischen Prinzessin in Auftrag gegeben wurde. Das goldene Modell des Schmuckstücks von Boucheron ist mit geschliffenen Glassteinen besetzt, es hat einen aus Gelenkstücken kompliziert zusammengesetzten Körper und eine Zunge mit einer Sprungfeder (die heute fehlt), welche herausschnellte, wenn der Unterkiefer des Tieres nach unten bewegt wurde (Abb. 8).

In den späten 1880er Jahren entwickelte sich das Werk von René Lalique (1860–1945) im deutlichen Gegensatz zu diesen strengen Konventionen. Lalique, *Bijoutier artistique* und führender Schmuckkünstler der Belle Époque, entdeckte Glas erst spät in seinem Leben als künstlerisches Medium. Er führte Schmuckstücke im Stil des Art Nouveau ein. Indem er wertvolle Materialien neben weniger kostbaren wie Horn und Glas verwendete, ordnete er alle Materialien ohne Unterschied einer übergreifenden ästhetischen Konzeption unter. Seine Arbeiten verwischten die Grenzen zwischen Schmuck und Skulptur wie auch die zwischen angewandter und schöner Kunst. Angeregt von der japanischen Kunst beobachtete er die Natur, von den bescheidensten Pflanzen bis zu Insekten, und kristallisierte ihr ästhetisches Wesen heraus. Er fügte eine Mohnblume mit Blütenblättern aus gegossenem und geschliffenem durchsichtigem Glas in eine reich verzierte Goldarbeit ein, die durch Emailarbeit und Diamantenbesatz noch prächtiger wirkte (Abb. 9). Viele der größeren, massiven Glaskomponenten seiner Arbeiten wurden in Formen gegossen und durch Kaltbearbeitungs-Techniken abschließend bearbeitet. Besonders liebte er die feine Pâte-de-verre- oder Glaspaste-Technik, um komplizierte Entwürfe aus

Figure 9 Necklace with a pendant in the form of a poppy, René Lalique, France, ca. 1900–03. Patinated glass, enamel, gold, rose-cut diamonds, 2 ⅞ in., height. Toledo Museum of Art, Toledo, Ohio, Mr. and Mrs. George M. Jones, Jr., Fund (1995.13). Photo: Tim Thayer

Abbildung 9 Halsschmuck mit einem Anhänger in Form einer Mohnblüte, René Lalique, Frankreich, ca. 1900–1903. Patiniertes Glas, Email, Gold, Diamanten mit Rosettenschliff, Höhe 7,4 cm. Toledo Museum of Art, Toledo, Ohio, Mr. and Mrs. George M. Jones, Jr., Fund (1995.13). Foto: Tim Thayer

Figure 10 Beetle necklace, Louis Comfort Tiffany, Tiffany Studios, United States, ca. 1911. Gold, favrile glass, 16 ⅛ in., length. Greco Corporation, Nagoya, Japan. Photo: Janet Zapata

Abbildung 10 Käfer-Halsschmuck, Louis Comfort Tiffany, Tiffany Studios, Vereinigte Staaten, ca. 1911. Gold, Favrile-Glas, Länge 41,15 cm. Greco Corporation, Nagoya, Japan. Foto: Janet Zapata

Figure 11 Brooch, Raymond Templier, France, ca. 1934. White gold, lapis lazuli, blue glass, 1 $^{10}/_{16}$ × 1 $^{9}/_{16}$ in., height × width. Victoria and Albert Museum, London, England (M.18–1979). Photo: ©V&A Images/Victoria and Albert Museum, London

Abbildung 11 Brosche, Raymond Templier, Frankreich, ca. 1934. Weißgold, Lapislazuli, blaues Glas, Höhe 4,3, Breite 4,2 cm. Victoria and Albert Museum, London (M.18–1979). Foto: ©V&A Images/Victoria and Albert Museum, London

Figure 12 Necklace and pendant, Naum Slutzky, Germany, ca. 1930. Chrome, glass insert, 2 $^{1}/_{5}$ × 2 in., height × width of pendant. Museum für Kunst und Gewerbe Hamburg, Germany (Inv.-Nr. 1932/276). Photo: Museum für Kunst und Gewerbe, Hamburg

Abbildung 12 Halsschmuck und Anhänger, Naum Slutzky, Deutschland, ca. 1930. Chrom, Glaseinsatz, Höhe des Anhängers 5,6 cm, Breite 5 cm. Museum für Kunst und Gewerbe Hamburg (1932/276). Foto: Museum für Kunst und Gewerbe, Hamburg

limited to his settings of iridescent favrile glass beetles dating from about 1910 and later. For these designs, a large circular metal die cut with beetles in different sizes was stamped into a molten disk of red or blue favrile glass.[28] Removed from the cooled glass disk, the beetles were mounted in fully backed metal bezel settings and applied to a large variety of jewelry for men and women (fig. 10). The necklaces especially were probably inspired by ancient Egyptian originals set with dried scarabs, an example of which he owned.

The popularity of art nouveau jewelry percolated into designs for cheap industrial jewelry, causing those on the cutting edge to seek new aesthetic directions. High-end avant-garde jewelers such as Georges Fouquet, Gérard Sandoz, Jean Puifurcat, Raymond Templier, and Jean Després began using glass and ceramic in geometric and stereometric shapes set into cool metals such as platinum, white gold, and silver (fig. 11). Their ideas, characteristic of the art deco period, were quickly translated into custom jewelry production made of chrome and nickel. Such cheaper but fashionable and innovative ornaments made a spectacular appearance in 1925 at the Exposition Internationale des Arts Décoratifs et Industriels Modernes in Paris, where more than forty firms presented their work.

The most radical jewelry designs from 1919 to 1933 emerged from the Bauhaus school operating in Weimar and Dessau, Germany. The school's aesthetic mandate required works to display high quality craftsmanship and thorough understanding of the selected material and to rely on pure functional forms that required no ornament. Form and material were to speak for themselves.

opakem Glas auszuführen. Diese im 19. Jahrhundert von dem französischen Künstler Henri Cros (1840–1907) wiederentdeckte und weiterentwickelte Technik versintert in Gussformen pulverisiertes Glas mit einem Bindemittel. Die vorsichtige Schichtung der verschiedenfarbigen Pulver in der Form erlaubt es, das Spektrum der Farben und ihre Übergänge im gegossenen Stück bis zu einem gewissen Grade zu kontrollieren. Für Insektenflügel und Blätter im Stil des Art Nouveau verwendete Lalique die Plique-à-jour- oder Fensteremail-Technik. Viele von Laliques Zeitgenossen, darunter George Auger und Lucien Gaillard, wurden zu Befürwortern des Genre Lalique.

Auch der Amerikaner Louis Comfort Tiffany (1848–1933), dessen Firma enge Verbindungen nach Paris hatte, untersuchte die Verwendung von Glas in seinen Art-Nouveau-Schmuckstücken. Zwar zog er wirkliche Edelsteine, ob sie nun opak oder durchsichtig waren, dem Glas vor, doch nutzte er Emailtechniken, um einigen seiner Schöpfungen die erwünschte Farbe und Lichtdurchlässigkeit zu verleihen. Seine Verwendung großer, massiver, edelsteinartiger Glaselemente in Schmuckstücken beschränkte sich auf gefasste Käfer aus irisierendem Favrile-Glas, die um 1910 und später entstanden. Für ihre Herstellung wurde ein großer runder Prägestempel, in den Käfer unterschiedlicher Größe geschnitten worden waren, in eine Schmelzglas-Scheibe aus rotem oder blauem Favrile-Glas gedrückt.[28] Nachdem sie aus der erkalteten Glasscheibe herausgelöst worden waren, wurden die Käfer in mit einer Rückseite versehene Stegfassungen aus Metall eingesetzt und auf zahlreichen unterschiedlichen Schmuckstücken für Herren und Damen angebracht (Abb. 10). Insbesondere die

Ukranian-born Naum Slutzky (1894–1965), one of the leading Bauhaus metalwork and jewelry designers, was attracted to glass as a man-made material. He adapted elements of industrial production methods and materials for his simple jewelry constructions (fig. 12). Slutzky still employed polished geometric glass shapes like jewels in his ornaments made of non-precious metals, but this and the work of his contemporaries solidified the aesthetic and conceptual foundation for the following generations of contemporary artists creating ornaments for the human body. Today, there exists an unprecedented artistic freedom among jewelers to explore glass as a medium for expression, including using it as a comment on the traditional perceptions of glass as a mere surrogate for precious gems in jewelry.

[1] Fulgurite, a tube-like formation of glassy silica mineral in sand or rock, is caused by a lightning strike. Tektites are created by terrestrial impact. Obsidian is produced when molten lava cools rapidly through the glass transition temperature and freezes without sufficient time for crystal growth. Because of the lack of crystal structure, obsidian blade edges can reach almost molecular thinness. Obsidian was explored by ancient civilizations for use in cutting tools and weapons, and it is still used today as blades in scalpels, especially for delicate eye surgery.
[2] Maud Spaer, introduction to *Ancient Glass in the Israel Museum: Beads and Other Small Objects* (Jerusalem: The Israel Museum, 2001).
[3] Christine Lilyquist, "Granulation and Glass: Chronological and Stylistic Investigations at Selected Sites, ca. 2500–1400 B.C.E," *Bulletin of the American Schools of Oriental Research* 290–1 (1993), 524.
[4] Spaer, 74, no. 43; 337, pl. 4.
[5] Felix Müller, *Das Keltische Schatzkästlein* (Bern: Historisches Museum, 1999), 51–2.
[6] *Greek Jewelry: 6000 Years of Tradition* (Athens: Ministry of Culture, 1997), no. 141.
[7] K. H. Priese, *The Gold of Meroe* (New York: Metropolitan Museum of Art, 1993), 16, 22, fig. 12.
[8] Pliny, *Historia Naturalis*, Jones, trans. W. H. S. [William Henry Samuel] (Cambridge : Harvard University Press, 1942), bk. 37, pp. 22, 26, 44.

Halsketten waren wahrscheinlich von antiken ägyptischen Originalen inspiriert worden, die mit getrockneten Scarabaeus-Käfern besetzt waren; Tiffany besaß ein solches Schmuckstück.

Die Beliebtheit des Art-Nouveau-Schmucks schlug sich auch in den Entwürfen für preiswerten, industriell hergestellten Schmuck nieder, was dazu führte, dass innovative Künstler nach neuen Ausdrucksformen suchten. Der Avantgarde angehörende Spitzenjuweliere wie George Fouquet, Gérard Sandoz, Jean Puifurcat, Raymond Templier und Jean Després fingen an, Glas und Keramik in zwei- oder dreidimensionalen geometrischen Formen zu verwenden, die sie in kühl anmutende Metalle wie Platin, Weißgold und Silber fassten (Abb. 11). Ihre für das Art Déco typischen Ideen wurden bald auf die Herstellung von Modeschmuck übertragen, der aus Chrom und Nickel hergestellt wurde. Diese preiswerteren, aber modischen und neuartigen Schmuckstücke hatten 1925 auf der Exposition internationale des arts décoratifs et industriels modernes in Paris, auf der mehr als vierzig Firmen ihre Erzeugnisse präsentierten, ihren großen Auftritt.

Die revolutionärsten Schmuckentwürfe aus den Jahren 1919 bis 1933 gingen aus dem Bauhaus, zuerst in Weimar, ab 1925 in Dessau, hervor. Der ästhetische Auftrag der Schule erforderte es, dass die Arbeiten großes kunsthandwerkliches Können und genaue Kenntnis des gewählten Materials zeigten und auf reine, funktionale Formen, die kein Ornament erforderten, zurückgriffen. Form und Material sollten für sich selbst sprechen. Den in der Ukraine geborenen Naum Slutzky (1894–1965), einer der führenden Schmuck- und Metalldesigner des Bauhauses, reizte

[9] Pliny, bk. 37, pp. 31, 42.

[10] David Frederick Grose, *Early Ancient Glass: Core-formed, Rod-formed, and Cast Vessels and Objects from the Late Bronze Age to the Early Roman Empire, 1600 B.C. to A.D. 50* (New York: Hudson Hills Press in association with the Toledo Museum of Art, 1989), 359.

[11] Christina Schroeter, *Schmuckstücke Antike bis Jugendstil* (Frankfurt: Museum für Kunsthandwerk, 1991), 29, no. 17.

[12] W. A. von Jenny and W. F. Volbach, *Germanischer Schmuck des frühen Mittelalters* (Berlin: Verlag für Kunstwissenschaft, 1933).

[13] Theo Jülich, "Gemmenkreuze. Die Farbigkeit ihres Edelsteinbesatzes bis zum 12. Jahrhundert," *Aachener Kunstblätter* 54/55 (1986): 110.

[14] See Isidor von Sevilla, *Etymologiarium*, book 16, ed. José O. Reta, vol. 2 (Madrid: Editorial Católica, 1983), 183, and Theophilus Presbyter, *On divers arts: the foremost medieval treatise on painting, glassmaking, and metalwork*, trans. John G. Hawthorne and Cyril Stanley Smith (New York: Dover Publications, 1979), 3, 95.

[15] G. Giamo, "Il lusso, leggi moderatrici, pietre e perle false," *Nuovo Archivio Veneto*, n.s., 16 (1908): 112.

[16] Ibid., 113.

[17] *Princely Magnificence: Court Jewels of the Renaissance, 1500–1630* (London: Debrett's Peerage Ltd. and the Victoria and Albert Museum, 1980), 66, no. 57.

[18] Schroeter, 38–9, no. 29.

[19] Giambullari's letter to Giovanni Bandini, Florentine ambassador to Charles V: "Apparato e feste nelle noze dello Illustrissimo Signor Duca di Firenze, e della Duchessa sua Consorte, con le Stanze, Madriali, Comedia, e Intermedii, in quelle recitati," Florence, 1539. Cited in Claudia Rousseau, "The Pageant of the Muses at the Medici wedding of 1539," in *Theatrical Spectacle and Spectacular Theatre: Papers in Art History from The Pennsylvania State University, Department of Art History VI* (University Park, Penn.: Pennsylvania State University, 1990), 2: 419.

[20] See a chain composed of multiple strands of black and white glass rings: Veronika Sandbichler, "Glaskette," in: Wilfried Seipel, ed. *Alle Wunder dieser Welt. Die kostbarsten Kunstwerke aus der Sammlung Erzherzog Ferdinands II. (1529–1595).* Exhibition catalogue. Kunsthistorisches Museum Sammlungen Schloss Ambras, 30 June–31 October 2001 (Vienna: Kunsthistorisches Museum, 2001), 82–83, no. 47.

[21] The German alchemist Johann Glauber published his *Furni novi philosophici* in Amsterdam in 1651. The new furnace had vents for temperature control that allowed a high temperature for refining and a lower temperature for working. The Florentine priest Antonio Neri's book *L'arte vetraria* (1612), including a (difficult to work) recipe for lead glass, was translated into English by Merrit in 1662 and published in Amsterdam in 1669.

[22] In 1665, three glassmakers worked on the development of a lead glass formula in Nijmegen, in eastern Holland: John Barrowmont da Costa, Dr. Jean Guillaume

Glas als künstlich hergestelltes Material. Er adaptierte industrielle Materialien und Produktionsmethoden für seine einfach konstruierten Schmuckstücke (Abb. 12). Slutzky verwendete polierte geometrische Glasformen noch wie Edelsteine in seinen Schmuckstücken aus unedlen Metallen, doch festigte sich hierdurch und durch die Arbeit seiner Zeitgenossen die ästhetische und konzeptuelle Basis für die folgenden Generationen moderner Künstler, die Schmuckstücke für den menschlichen Körper schaffen. Heute genießen Schmuckkünstler eine nie zuvor gekannte künstlerische Freiheit, Glas als Medium für den bildnerischen Ausdruck zu erkunden, wozu auch zählt, dass sie durch die Wahl dieses Materials die traditionelle Wahrnehmung von Glas als bloßen Ersatz für kostbare Schmucksteine kommentieren.

[1] *Fulgurit, eine röhrenförmige Formation aus glasartigem Siliciumdioxid in Sand oder Stein, entsteht durch einen Blitzeinschlag, Tektite entstehen durch Einschläge auf der Erdoberfläche. Obsidian bildet sich, wenn flüssige Lava durch schnelle Abkühlung die Glasübergangstemperatur erreicht und erstarrt, bevor sich Kristall bilden kann. Aufgrund des Fehlens von Kristallstrukturen können die Schneiden von Klingen aus Obsidian fast molekular dünn sein. Obsidian wurde in frühen Kulturen häufig für Werkzeuge und Waffen verwendet, und noch heute wird es für Skalpellklingen, insbesondere für viel Feingefühl erfordernde Augenoperationen, eingesetzt.*

[2] *Maud Spaer, Einführung zu:* Ancient Glass in the Israel Museum: Beads and Other Small Objects, *Jerusalem: The Israel Museum 2000.*

[3] *Christine Lilyquist, „Granulation and Glass: Chronological and Stylistic Investigations at Selected Sites, ca. 2500–1400 B. C. E.", in:* Bulletin of the American Schools of Oriental Research, *Nr. 290/291, 1993, S. 524.*

[4] *Spaer (wie Anm. 2), S. 74, Nr. 43; S. 337, Tafel 4.*

[5] *Felix Müller, Das keltische Schatzkästlein. Schmuck als Zier und Zeichen (Glanzlichter aus dem Bernischen Historischen Museum, 1), Zürich: Chronos-Verlag 1999, S. 51 f.*

[6] *Greek Jewelry: 6000 Years of Tradition, Athen: Kulturministerium 1997, Nr. 141.*

Reinier, who made lead glass in Sweden by 1675, and John Odacio Formica, who obtained a fourteen-year patent in Ireland in 1675 (Peter Francis, "The Development of Lead Glass: The European Connection," *Apollo* 151 (February 2000): 47 and n. 3.

23 Gabriele Greindl, *Gems of Costume Jewelry*, trans. Laura Lindgren (New York: Abbeville Press, 1991), 10.

24 The material known in English as rhinestone, strass, or paste (French *pierres de Stras*) was not the original invention of the Parisian master goldsmith and court jeweler Georges Frédéric Stras, who experimented extensively with glass and specialized in the production of artificial stone to imitate diamonds.

25 Gisela Zick, *Gedenke mein: Freundschafts- und Memorialschmuck 1770–1870* (Dortmund: Harenberg, 1980), 167. The eye perceived as personal commemoration differs from the more general ancient Egyptian Wedjat (The Sound One) eye imagery on inlays and amulets or the all-seeing eye of god in Christian iconography, which have a primarily regenerative and protective notion.

26 Queen Victoria commissioned several eyes from her court miniaturist Sir William Ross in the 1840s and 1850s. See Hanneke Grootenboer, "Treasuring the Gaze: Eye Miniature Portraits and the Intimacy of Vision," *Art Bulletin*, September 2006, 496–507.

27 Michael Koch, "Bijoutier, joaillier, orfèvre: Bemerkungen zum Erscheinungsbild der Pariser Goldschmiede und Juweliere auf den Weltausstellungen," in *Pariser Schmuck* (Munich: Hirmer Verlag,1989), 13.

28 Janet Zapata, *The Jewelry and Enamel of Louis Comfort Tiffany* (New York: Abrams, 1993), 103–6.

7 *Karl-Heinz Priese, The Gold of Meroe, Ausst.-Kat. Metropolitan Museum of Art, New York, Mainz: Zabern 1993, S. 16, S. 22, Abb. 12 (deutsche Ausgabe unter dem Titel: Das Gold von Meroe, Ausst.-Kat. Staatliche Museen zu Berlin – Preußischer Kulturbesitz, Ägyptisches Museum, Mainz: Zabern 1992).*

8 *Pliny, Historia Naturalis, übersetzt von W. H. S. [William Henry Samuel], Cambridge: Harvard University Press 1942, Buch 37, S. 22, 26, 44.*

9 *Ebenda, Buch 37, S. 31, 42.*

10 *David Frederick Grose, Early Ancient Glass: Core-formed, Rod-formed, and Cast Vessels and Objects from the Late Bronze Age to the Early Roman Empire, 1600 B. C. to A. D. 50, New York: Hudson Hill Press in association with the Toledo Museum of Art 1989, S. 359.*

11 *Christina Schroeter, Schmuckstücke – Antike bis Jugendstil, Frankfurt: Museum für Kunsthandwerk 1991, S. 29, Nr. 17.*

12 *Wilhelm Albert von Jenny und Wolfgang Fritz Volbach, Germanischer Schmuck des frühen Mittelalters, Berlin: Verlag für Kunstwissenschaft 1933.*

13 *Theo Jülich, „Gemmenkreuze: Die Farbigkeit ihres Edelsteinbesatzes bis zum 12. Jahrhundert", in: Aachener Kunstblätter, Nr. 54/55, 1986, S. 110.*

14 *Siehe Isidoro de Sevilla, Etymologiarum, hrsg. von José O. Reta, Madrid: Editorial Católica 1983, Buch 16, Bd. 2, S. 183, und Theophilus Presbyter, On divers arts: the foremost medieval treatise on painting, glassmaking, and metalwork, übersetzt von John G. Hawthorne und Cyril Stanley Smith, New York: Dover Publications 1979, S. 3, 95.*

15 *G. Giamo, „Il lusso, leggi moderatrici, pietre e perle false", in: Nuovo Archivio Veneto, Neue Folge, Nr. 16, 1908, S. 112.*

16 *Ebenda, S. 113.*

17 *Princely Magnificence: Court Jewels of the Renaissance, 1500–1630, Ausst.-Kat. Victoria and Albert Museum London, London: Debrett's Peerage Ltd. and the Victoria and Albert Museum 1980, S. 66, Nr. 57.*

18 *Schroeter (wie Anm. 11), S. 38 f., Nr. 29.*

19 *Giambullari in seinem Brief an Giovanni Bandini, Botschafter der Republik Florenz am Hof Kaiser Karls V.: „Apparato e feste nelle noze dello Illustrissimo Signor Duca di Firenze, et della Duchessa sua Consorte, con le Stanze, Madriali, Comedia, e Intermedii, in quelle recitati", Florenz 1539. Zitiert nach Claudia Rousseau, „The Pageant of the Muses at the Medici wedding of 1539", in: Theatrical Spectacle and Spectacular Theatre (Papers in Art History from The Pennsylvania State University, Department of Art History VI), University Park, Pennsylvania: Pennsylvania State University, Bd. 2, S. 419.*

20 *Siehe auch eine aus mehreren Reihen schwarzer und weißer Glasringe zusammengesetzte Kette: Veronika Sandbichler, „Glaskette", in: Wilfried Seipel (Hg.), Alle Wunder dieser Welt. Die kostbarsten Kunstwerke aus der Sammlung Erzherzog Ferdinands II. (1529–1595), Ausst.-Kat. Kunsthistorisches Museum Sammlungen Schloss Ambras, 30. Juni–31. Oktober 2001, Wien: Kunsthistorisches Museum, 2001, S. 82–83 f., Nr. 47.*

[21] *Der deutsche Alchemist Johann Glauber publizierte 1651 in Amsterdam sein Werk* Furni novi philosophici. *Der „neue Ofen" hatte der Temperaturkontrolle dienende Lüftungsschlitze, die hohe Temperaturen für die Veredelung und niedrigere für die Bearbeitung ermöglichten. Das Buch des Florentiner Priesters Antonio Neri* L'arte vetraria (1612), *das eine (schwer umzusetzende) Rezeptur für Bleiglas enthält, wurde von Merrit 1662 ins Englische übersetzt und 1669 in Amsterdam veröffentlicht.*

[22] *1665 arbeiteten im ostniederländischen Nijmegen drei Glasmacher an der Entwicklung einer Rezeptur für Bleiglas: John Barrowmont da Costa, Dr. Jean Guillaume Reinier, der spätestens 1675 in Schweden Bleiglas herstellte, und John Odacio Formica, der 1675 in Irland eine 14 Jahre gültige Lizenz erhielt. Siehe Peter Francis, „The Development of Lead Glass: The European Connection", in:* Apollo, *Nr. 151, Februar 2000, S. 47 und Anm. 3.*

[23] *Gabriele Greindl,* Gems of Costume Jewelry, *übersetzt von Laura Lindgren, New York: Abbeville Press 1991, S. 10 (Titel der deutschen Originalausgabe:* Strass. Glitzer, Glanz und Glamour. Modeschmuck aus zwei Jahrhunderten, *München 1990).*

[24] *Das im Deutschen als Strass bekannte Material (französisch: pierres de Strass) entspricht nicht der ursprünglichen Erfindung des Pariser Meistergoldschmieds und Hofjuweliers Georges Frédéric Strass, der zahlreiche Experimente mit Glas durchführte und sich auf die Herstellung künstlicher Steine spezialisiert hatte, welche Diamanten imitierten.*

[25] *Gisela Zick,* Gedenke mein. Freundschafts- und Memorialschmuck 1770–1870, *Dortmund: Harenberg 1980, S. 167. Das als persönliche Erinnerung verstandene Auge unterscheidet sich von der allgemeineren Augen-Symbolik der altägyptischen Göttin Wadjet auf Einlegearbeiten und Amuletten oder dem allessehenden Auge Gottes der christlichen Ikonographie, mit denen sich vorrangig Vorstellungen der Erneuerung und des Schutzes verbinden.*

[26] *Königin Victoria gab bei ihrem Hofminiaturmaler Sir William Ross in den 1840er und 1850er Jahren mehrere Augenbilder in Auftrag. Siehe Hanneke Grootenboer, „Treasuring the Gaze: Eye Miniature Portraits and the Intimacy of Vision", in:* Art Bulletin, *September 2006, S. 496–507.*

[27] *Michael Koch, „Bijoutier, joiallier, orfèvre: Bemerkungen zum Erscheinungsbild der Pariser Goldschmiede und Juweliere auf den Weltausstellungen", in:* Pariser Schmuck. Vom 2. Kaiserreich zur Belle Époque, *Ausst.-Kat. Bayerisches National-museum, München 1989/90, München: Hirmer 1989, S. 13.*

[28] *Janet Zapata,* The Jewelry and Enamels of Louis Comfort Tiffany, *New York: Abrams 1993, S. 103–106.*

Catalogue
Katalog

Giampaolo Babetto
Arquà Petrarca, Italy
Born: 1947, Padua, Italy

Education · Ausbildung
Accademia di Belle Arti, Venice, Italy, 1966–68; Istituto d'Arte Pietro Selvatico, Padua, Italy, 1963–66

Selected Collections · Sammlungen (Auswahl)
Art Gallery of Western Australia, Perth, Australia; Grassimuseum, Leipzig, Germany; Kunstgewerbemuseum, Berlin, Germany; Musée d'Art Moderne et d'Art Contemporain, Nice, France; Musée des Arts Décoratifs, Paris, France; Museo degli Argenti, Florence, Italy; Museum für Angewandte Kunst, Frankfurt, Germany; Museum für Konkrete Kunst, Ingolstadt, Germany; Museum für Kunst und Gewerbe, Hamburg, Germany; Museu Textil i d'Indumentaria, Barcelona, Spain; National Gallery of Australia, Canberra, Australia; Die Neue Sammlung, Staatliches Museum für Angewandte Kunst, Design in der Pinakothek der Moderne, on permanent loan from the Danner Foundation, Munich, Germany; Nordenfjeldske Kunstindustrimuseum, Trondheim, Norway; Rhode Island School of Design Museum, Providence, Rhode Island; Schmuckmuseum Pforzheim, Pforzheim, Germany; Victoria and Albert Museum, London, England

"Transparency, color, reflections, separation of images, disruption of geometry, imperceptibility, and optical lightness—it is for these qualities and effects that at certain creative moments I choose to use glass and mirrors." ▪ *„Transparenz, Farbe, Reflexion, die Auflösung von Bildern, ein Bruch in der geometrischen Form, Nichtwahrnehmbarkeit und optische Leichtigkeit – diese Eigenschaften und Effekte sind es, die mich in bestimmten kreativen Momenten veranlassen, Glas und Spiegel als Material zu wählen."*

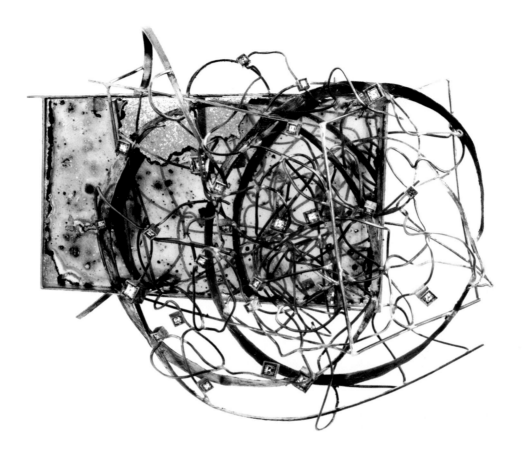

Spilla 5 (brooch)
2003, mirror, white gold,
pigment, diamonds,
4 3/8 × 3 × 1 1/2 in.
Collection of the artist

Spilla 5 (Brosche)
2003, Spiegelglas, Weißgold,
Pigmentfarbe, Diamanten,
11 × 7,6 × 3,5 cm
Sammlung des Künstlers

Monica Backström
Kalmar, Sweden
Born: 1939, Stockholm,
Sweden

Education · Ausbildung
Konstfackskolan, Reklam- och
bokhantverk, HKS Konstfackskolan, Metall- och industri-
formgivning, Stockholm,
Sweden, 1959–64

**Selected Collections ·
Sammlungen (Auswahl)**
Cooper-Hewitt, National Design
Museum, Smithsonian Institu-
tion, New York, New York;
Corning Museum of Glass,
Corning, New York; Glas-
museet Ebeltoft, Ebeltoft,
Denmark; Kunstindustrimuseet,
Oslo, Norway; Malmö Museum,
Malmö, Sweden; Museum of
Arts & Design, New York,
New York; Nationalmuseum,
Stockholm, Sweden; Röhsska
Museet för Konsthantverk
och Design, Gothenburg,
Sweden; Småland Museum,
Växjö, Sweden; Victoria and
Albert Museum, London,
England

"The combination of metal and glass has always fascinated me and has been the source of much of my inspiration. Reflections, mirrored and refracted, interact strikingly with one another." ▪ *„Die Kombination von Metall und Glas hat mich schon immer fasziniert und ist eine reiche Quelle der Inspiration für mich. Widergespiegelte und gebrochene Reflexionen zeigen hier ein beeindruckendes Zusammenspiel."*

**Rings from the Halo series
for Kosta Boda**
2002, cut and sandblasted
glass, silver, approx. 1–2 in.
Collection of Kosta Boda

*Ringe aus der Halo-Serie
für Kosta Boda*
*2002, geschnittenes und
sandgestrahltes Glas,
Silber, ca. 3–5 cm
Sammlung Kosta Boda*

Boris Bally
Providence, Rhode Island
Born: 1961, Chicago, Illinois

Education · Ausbildung
Carnegie Mellon University,
Pittsburgh, Pennsylvania, 1984,
B.F.A.; Tyler School of Art,
Temple University, Elkins Park,
Pennsylvania, 1980–82

**Selected Collections ·
Sammlungen (Auswahl)**
Brooklyn Museum of Art,
Brooklyn, New York; Carnegie
Museum of Art, Pittsburgh,
Pennsylvania; Cooper-Hewitt,
National Design Museum,
Smithsonian Institution, New
York, New York; Mint Museum
of Craft + Design, Charlotte,
North Carolina; Museum of
Arts & Design, New York, New
York; Smithsonian American
Art Museum, Renwick Gallery,
Washington, D.C.; Victoria
and Albert Museum, London,
England

"While experimenting with discarded traffic signs that were lying around the studio, I became fascinated by their ominously reflective, graphic-laden, weatherworn qualities. I also noticed that several signs at my local scrap yard had been cut by oxyacetylene torch. The scorch marks and molten metal were intriguing, but far more exciting was the effect upon the signage coating: the glass melted beautifully into the plastic finish, creating a rich organic surface. These brooches are part of a body of work that illustrates my initial attempts at harnessing the beauty in these discarded signs." • *„Während ich mit ausrangierten Verkehrszeichen, die im Studio umherlagen, herumexperimentierte, geriet ich in den Bann ihrer bedrohlichen, reflektierenden, grafikgeladenen, vom Wetter gezeichneten Existenz. Ich bemerkte außerdem, dass einige der Zeichen auf dem Schrottplatz vor Ort mit einem Schneidbrenner zerkleinert worden waren. Die Brandspuren und das geschmolzene Metall faszinierten mich, aber noch viel aufregender war der Effekt, der durch diese Art der Zerkleinerung bei der Beschichtung der Zeichen entstanden war: Das Glas war auf wunderbare Weise mit dem umgebenden Kunststoff verschmolzen, wodurch eine großartige organische Oberfläche entstand. Die Broschen sind Teil einer Reihe von Arbeiten, die meine ersten Versuche zeigen, mir die Schönheit dieser ausrangierten Verkehrszeichen zunutze zu machen."*

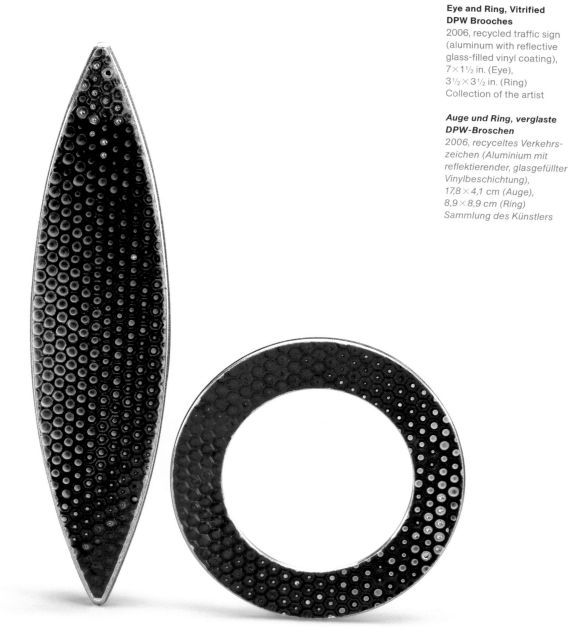

81

**Eye and Ring, Vitrified
DPW Brooches**
2006, recycled traffic sign
(aluminum with reflective
glass-filled vinyl coating),
7 × 1½ in. (Eye),
3½ × 3½ in. (Ring)
Collection of the artist

*Auge und Ring, verglaste
DPW-Broschen*
*2006, recyceltes Verkehrs-
zeichen (Aluminium mit
reflektierender, glasgefüllter
Vinylbeschichtung),
17,8 × 4,1 cm (Auge),
8,9 × 8,9 cm (Ring)
Sammlung des Künstlers*

Célio Braga
Amsterdam, The Netherlands
Born: 1965, Guimarânia, Brazil

Education · Ausbildung
Gerrit Rietveld Academie,
Amsterdam, The Netherlands,
1996–2000; School of the
Museum of Fine Arts, Boston,
Boston, Massachusetts,
1988–90

**Selected Collections ·
Sammlungen (Auswahl)**
Marie-José van den Hout
Collection, Galerie Marzee,
Nijmegen, The Netherlands;
Museu de Arte Contem-
porânea, Goiás, Goiânia,
Brazil; Stedelijk Museum,
Amsterdam, The Netherlands

"I once read that the native Brazilian Indians were fascinated by glass beads and that in order to get them, they were willing to trade gold, precious stones, and feathers from tropical birds. With that in mind, I have started collecting and buying glass beads from different places and sources. It has become a kind of obsession! Glass beads are helping me to express my fascination with the baroque, with grotesqueness, with extravagance. Bringing together 'formlessness' with bold ornamentation, and juxtaposing contrasting materials and elements of attraction and repulsion, conveys a sense of drama, movement, and tension that I like to call 'impure beauty.' Through patient labor and obsession, I am striving to transform a cheap commodity like glass beads into something precious like gold, tropical feathers, or gemstones." ▪ *„Ich habe einmal gelesen, dass die Indianer Brasiliens von Glasperlen so fasziniert waren, dass sie bereit waren, diese gegen Gold, Edelsteine und Federn tropischer Vögel zu tauschen. Mit diesem Wissen im Hinterkopf habe ich begonnen, Glasperlen von verschiedensten Orten und unterschiedlichsten Quellen zu sammeln und zu kaufen. Es ist eine Art Sucht geworden! Mit Glasperlen kann ich meine Faszination für den Barock, das Groteske und das Extravagante zum Ausdruck bringen. Indem ich ‚Formlosigkeit' mit reichhaltigen Verzierungen kombiniere und anziehende und abstoßende Materialien und Elemente einander gegenüberstelle, vermittle ich ein Gefühl von Drama, Bewegung und Spannung, das ich gerne mit ‚unreiner Schönheit' bezeichne. Durch geduldiges Arbeiten und mit Obsession will ich es schaffen, einen billigen Handelsartikel wie Glasperlen in etwas so Wertvolles wie Gold, tropische Federn oder Edelsteine zu verwandeln."*

Fourteen brooches from
the Rubros series
2002–03, glass beads, felt, silk,
cotton, hair, 3×4 in. (each)
Collection of the Stedelijk
Museum, Amsterdam

*Vierzehn Broschen der
Rubros-Serie
2002–03, Glasperlen, Filz,
Seide, Baumwolle, Haar,
jeweils 8×10 cm
Sammlung des Stedelijk
Museums, Amsterdam*

Helen Britton
Perth, Australia /
Munich, Germany
Born: 1966, Lithgow,
Australia

Education · Ausbildung
Akademie der Bildenden
Künste, Munich, Germany,
1999–2003; Curtin University
of Technology, Perth, Australia,
1999; Edith Cowan University,
Perth, Australia, 1990

**Selected Collections ·
Sammlungen (Auswahl)**
Art Gallery of Western Australia,
Perth, Australia; Curtin University
of Technology, Perth, Australia;
Die Neue Sammlung, Staatliches
Museum für Angewandte Kunst,
Design in der Pinakothek der
Moderne, on permanent loan
from the Danner Foundation,
Munich, Germany; Powerhouse
Museum, Sydney, Australia;
Schmuckmuseum Pforzheim,
Pforzheim, Germany; South
Australian Museum, Adelaide,
Australia; Stedelijk Museum,
Amsterdam, The Netherlands

"The glass that I am working with comes mainly from the postwar European costume-jewelry industry. This was a time of hope and fantasy, a time when it was dreamed that a new world would be established and that order and peace would be maintained. It was a dream that was not realized. I am using these little glass fragments in new contexts, and they have become sinister, complex, and paradoxical. They evoke what it means to be living now, while reminding us of what it might have meant to be living now." ▪ *„Das Glas, mit dem ich arbeite, stammt vorwiegend aus der Modeschmuckindustrie der Nachkriegszeit. Das war eine Zeit der Hoffnung und der großen Fantasien, eine Zeit, in der man davon träumte, eine neue Welt aufzubauen, in der Ordnung und Frieden herrschen würden. Der Traum erfüllte sich nicht. Ich verwende diese kleinen Glasstückchen in neuen Kontexten, und so erhalten sie einen unheilvollen, komplexen und widersinnigen Charakter. Sie zeigen, was es bedeutet, in der heutigen Zeit zu leben, und erinnern uns gleichzeitig daran, wie das Leben heute hätte sein können.“*

Dry Valley (brooch)
2006, found glass, silver,
paint, 3×2½×1½ in.
Collection of the artist

Ausgetrocknetes Tal (Brosche)
2006, gefundenes Glas,
Silber, Farbe, 8×6×3,5 cm
Sammlung der Künstlerin

Pierre Cavalan
Sydney, Australia
Born: 1954, Paris, France

Education · Ausbildung
BJOP–Union Française de la
Bijouterie, Joaillerie, Orfèvrerie,
des Pierres et des Perles, Paris,
France, 1975–79

**Selected Collections ·
Sammlungen (Auswahl)**
Canberra Museum and Art
Gallery, Canberra, Australia;
Musée des Arts Décoratifs de
Montréal, Montreal, Canada;
Museum of Arts & Design,
New York, New York; Museum
of Fine Arts, Houston, Houston,
Texas; National Gallery of
Australia, Canberra, Australia;
National Museum of Australia,
Canberra, Australia; National
Museum of Scotland,
Edinburgh, Scotland; Northern
Territory Museum of Art and
Sciences, Darwin, Australia;
Powerhouse Museum, Sydney,
Australia; Tasmanian Museum
and Art Gallery, Hobart,
Australia

"The inspiration for this work came from the northern beaches of Australia. By crinkling the metal of the neckpiece, I was able to emulate natural formations created by wave action on the sand. I set colored glass in bezels to signify objects washed up on the beach and left behind after the tide receded. The central glass section reflects the 'manmade,' as do the remaining soldered objects, which both give the piece rigidity and act as messengers of happiness." ▪ *„Inspiriert wurde ich zu dieser Arbeit von den Stränden im Norden Australiens. Indem ich das Metall für den Halsschmuck ‚zerknitterte' und in Falten legte, konnte ich die Struktur, wie sie in der Natur durch die Wellenbewegung am Strand entsteht, nachbilden. Darauf verteilte ich eingefasstes farbiges Glas, um Objekte darzustellen, die vom Meer an den Strand gespült wurden und nach der Flut zurückgeblieben sind. Die Glasfläche vorne in der Mitte stellt das Künstliche, vom Menschen Gemachte dar, ebenso die übrigen gelöteten Objekte. Beide Elemente geben dem Schmuck Festigkeit und sind Boten des Glücks."*

Victory (neckpiece)
1996, found glass, silver, found
objects, 9½×9½×½ in.
Collection of the Museum of
Arts & Design, New York,
gift of Helen Williams Drutt
English in honor of Barbara
Tober, 2007

Sieg (Halsschmuck)
1996, gefundenes Glas, Silber,
Fundobjekte, 24,1×24,1×1,3 cm
Sammlung des Museum of
Arts & Design, New York.
Schenkung von Helen Williams
Drutt English zu Ehren von
Barbara Tober, 2007

Simsa Cho
Amsterdam, The Netherlands
Born: 1962, Chiba, Japan

Education · Ausbildung
Gerrit Rietveld Academy,
Amsterdam, The Netherlands,
1986–89; Tama Art University,
Tokyo, Japan, 1982–86

**Selected Collections ·
Sammlungen (Auswahl)**
Design Museum Gent,
Ghent, Belgium; Nationaal
Glasmuseum Leerdam,
Leerdam, The Netherlands;
De Nederlandsche Bank,
Amsterdam, The Netherlands

"An intrinsic characteristic of glass is that it transmits light. We feel universal energy, for example the energy of sunlight, through glass. Another characteristic of glass that interests me is resonance. We know that energy waves affect our emotions and even our physical health. We also know that energy waves change if they resonate with other wave motions. These two characteristics of glass—transmission and resonance—drew me into creating objects that touch the body. I am interested in the effect that these characteristics of glass have on the body and on human life." ▪ *„Eine wesentliche Eigenschaft von Glas ist, dass es Licht überträgt. Wir fühlen die Energie des Universums, z. B. die Energie des Sonnenlichts, durch Glas hindurch. Eine weitere Eigenschaft von Glas, die ich sehr interessant finde, ist Resonanz. Wir wissen, dass Energiewellen Auswirkungen auf unsere Gefühle und sogar auf unsere körperliche Gesundheit haben. Diese beiden Eigenschaften von Glas – Lichtübertragung und Resonanz – haben mich dazu bewegt, Objekte zu schaffen, die mit dem Körper in Berührung kommen. Ich will wissen, welche Effekte diese Eigenschaften von Glas auf den Körper und das menschliche Leben haben."*

Václav Cigler
Prague, Czech Republic
Born: 1929, Vsetín,
Czech Republic

Education · Ausbildung
Vysoká škola umělecko-
průmyslová v Praze, Prague,
Czech Republic, 1951–58;
Střední prumyslová škola
sklářská, Novy Bor, Czech
Republic, 1948–52

**Selected Collections ·
Sammlungen (Auswahl)**
Corning Museum of Glass,
Corning, New York; Glasmuse-
um, Leiden, The Netherlands;
Kunstgewerbemuseum, Berlin,
Germany; Moravská galerie v
Brně, Brno, Czech Republic;
Museé des Arts Décoratifs,
Paris, France; Muzeum Kampa,
Prague, Czech Republic;
Severočeské muzeum v Liberci,
Liberec, Czech Republic;
Slovenská národná galéria,
Bratislava, Slovakia; Stedelijk
Museum, Amsterdam, The
Netherlands; Tate, London,
England

"I am not a jeweler; however, the moment I realized that jewelry does not have to be a mere fashion accessory, but is capable of 'forming' a person and enabling that person to communicate with others, I discovered the possibility of psychological as well as aesthetic experimentation through jewelry. This inspiration has given birth to a wide range of creations, among them objects that focus on the optical proper-ties of glass." ▪ *„Ich bin kein Schmuckkünstler. Aber in dem Moment, als ich erkannte, dass Schmuck nicht nur ein reines Modeaccessoire sein muss, sondern einen Menschen ‚formen' und zur Kommunikation mit anderen befähigen kann, habe ich die Möglichkeit des psychologischen und ästhetischen Experimen-tierens mit Schmuck entdeckt. Diese Erkenntnis hat mich zu zahlreichen Werken verschiedenster Art inspiriert, darunter auch Arbeiten, die die optischen Eigenschaften von Glas zum Thema haben."*

Necklace
1967, optical glass, chrome,
8¾ in. (diam.)
Collection of the artist

Halskette
1967, optisches Glas,
Chrom, 22 cm (Dm)
Sammlung des Künstlers

Patty Cokus
Seattle, Washington
Born: 1977, Syracuse,
New York

Education · Ausbildung
Massachusetts College of Art,
Boston, Massachusetts,
1996–2000, B.F.A.; Mercyhurst
College, Erie, Pennsylvania,
1995–96

"My recent Cardiovascular Brooch series attempts to highlight the relationship bodily organs have with the many 'foods' that nourish and/or weaken them. The glass in my brooches contains, isolates, magnifies, and transforms various substances for the viewer and wearer to inspect, similar to the way in which glass test tubes function in scientific laboratories. Using miniscule amounts of familiar consumable substances reduces them to the point that they can be viewed as color and texture and at the same time eliminates important experiences of food such as taste and smell. One is persuaded to see the food in a new light, without being tantalized or repulsed by its aroma and flavor." ▪ *„Mit meiner jüngsten Serie Kardiovaskularbroschen will ich die Beziehung darstellen, die zwischen Körperorganen und vielfältigen ‚Nahrungsmitteln' besteht, die diese nähren und/oder schwächen. Die Glasröhrchen enthalten, isolieren, vergrößern und verwandeln verschiedene Substanzen für den Betrachter und Träger der Broschen, ähnlich wie dies in Teströhrchen in wissenschaftlichen Labors geschieht. Indem ich nur winzige Mengen bekannter essbarer Substanzen verwende, reduziere ich diese so weit, dass man sie rein als Farbe und Struktur betrachten kann und für Nahrung so wichtige Aspekte wie Geruch und Geschmack außer Acht bleiben. Ich bringe den Betrachter dazu, Nahrung in einem neuen Licht zu sehen, ohne von ihrem Geruch oder Geschmack angezogen oder abgestoßen zu werden."*

Cardiovascular Brooch: Clogged
2006, borosilicate glass tubes, soft glass, sterling silver, salted butter, 1¾×1¾×½ in.
Collection of the artist

Cardiovascular Brooch: Pump
2006, borosilicate glass tubes, sterling silver, aspirin, 1½×1¾×1 in.
Collection of the artist

Cardiovascular Brooch: Flow
2006, borosilicate glass tubes, sterling silver, 2004 California Shiraz, cold-pressed extra virgin olive oil, 1½×2½×1 in.
Collection of the artist

Kardiovaskularbrosche: Verstopft
2006, Röhrchen aus Borosilikatglas, Weichglas, Sterlingsilber, gesalzene Butter, 4,5×4,5×1,5 cm
Sammlung der Künstlerin

Kardiovaskularbrosche: Pumpe
2006, Röhrchen aus Borosilikatglas, Sterlingsilber, Aspirin, 4×4,5×2,5 cm
Sammlung der Künstlerin

Kardiovaskularbrosche: Fluss
2006, Röhrchen aus Borosilikatglas, Sterlingsilber, kalifornischer Shiraz Jahrgang 2004, kalt gepresstes natives Olivenöl, 4×6×2,5 cm
Sammlung der Künstlerin

Giselle Courtney
Sydney, Australia
Born: 1960, Sydney, Australia

Education · Ausbildung
Sydney College of the Arts,
Sydney, Australia, 1976–80, B.A.

**Selected Collections ·
Sammlungen (Auswahl)**
City of Hobart Art Gallery,
Hobart, Tasmania, Australia;
Corning Museum of Glass,
Corning, New York; Griffith
Regional Art Gallery, Griffith,
Australia; Museum and Art
Gallery of the Northern
Territory, Darwin, Australia;
Powerhouse Museum, Sydney,
Australia; Queensland Art
Gallery, Brisbane, Australia;
Queen Victoria Museum and
Art Gallery, Launceston,
Tasmania, Australia; Toowoom-
ba Regional Art Gallery,
Toowoomba, Australia; Wagga
Wagga Art Gallery, Wagga
Wagga, Australia

"The optical clarity of glass, the way it refracts and reflects light, attracts me. The borosilicate glass I use is both strong and capable of being sculpted. It allows fine detail. Once the glass is created and light burns inside it, it is rather like a magical dimension, changing as the light changes, or as the glass moves. The tiny winged elements circling the neckpiece in *Like Moths to a Flame* have the airy, glistening, glowing qualities of glass, lightly clasped by the electro-formed gold wires. The wearer is the flame, with the weightless, effortless flight of the moths in joyous dance around the neck. There is something mesmerizing about using fire, flameworking, to create these delicate, ethereal pieces." ▪ *Die optische Klarheit von Glas, die Art, wie es Licht bricht und reflektiert, fasziniert mich. Das Borosilikatglas, das ich für meine Arbeiten verwende, ist sowohl fest als auch gut formbar und ermöglicht feine Details. Ist das Glas erst einmal geschaffen und brennt ein Licht darin, so gleicht dies einer magischen Dimension, die sich mit den Veränderungen des Lichts und den Bewegungen des Glases ebenfalls verändert. Die winzigen, geflügelten Elemente, die den Halsschmuck umschwärmen in* Wie Motten das Licht, *verkörpern das Luftige, Glitzernde und Glänzende von Glas, zart eingefasst in elektrogeformten Golddraht. Der Träger des Schmucks ist die Flamme, um dessen Hals die Motten schwerelos und ohne Anstrengung ihren Freudentanz vollführen. Es hat etwas Faszinierendes, dass diese zarte, ätherische Arbeit mit Hilfe von Feuer und über offener Flamme geschaffen wurde."*

**Like Moths to a Flame
(neckpiece)**
2006, flameworked borosilicate
glass, electro-formed metal,
gold-plating, 14×13 in.
(length×width)
Collection of the artist

*Wie Motten im Licht
(Halsschmuck)*
*2006, geflammtes, lampen-
geblasenes Borosilikatglas,
elektrogeformtes Metall,
Goldplattierung, 35,5×33 cm
(Länge×Breite)*
Sammlung der Künstlerin

Ramón Puig Cuyàs
Barcelona, Spain
Born: 1953, Mataró,
Barcelona, Spain

Education · Ausbildung
Escola Massana, Barcelona,
Spain, 1969–74

**Selected Collections ·
Sammlungen (Auswahl)**
Badisches Landesmuseum,
Karlsruhe, Germany; Espace
Solidor, Cagnes-sur-Mer,
France; Cooper-Hewitt,
National Design Museum,
Smithsonian Institution, New
York, New York; Copoteca FAD,
Foment de les Arts Decoratives,
Barcelona, Spain; Kunst-
industrimuseet, Copenhagen,
Denmark; Musée des Arts
Décoratifs de Montréal,
Montreal, Canada; Museu de les
Arts Decoratives, Barcelona,
Spain; Museum Boijmans Van
Beuningen, Rotterdam, The
Netherlands; Museum für Kunst
und Gewerbe Hamburg,
Germany; Museum of Fine
Arts, Houston, Houston, Texas;
Muzeum Českého Ráje v
Turnov, Turnov, Czech Republic;
Nordenfjeldske Kunstindustri-
museum, Trondheim, Norway;
Royal College of Art, London,
England; Schmuckmuseum
Pforzheim, Germany

"Glass does not have the nobility of crystals, which are formed by the forces of nature, but it is for just this reason that I like using bits of found glass. They reflect the value of small things; things we don't consider important. Using glass that has been rounded and polished by time and sand to make jewelry, set in a simple and spontaneous way with no artificiality, is for me a way of trying to convert jewelry into metaphor and to revive the sense of magic associated with wearing a jewel or ornament. Deep down, when I collect a piece of glass and play with it to make jewelry, it is a way for me to nourish the child that resides inside me." ▪ *„Glas ist nicht so edel wie Kristalle, die durch die Kräfte der Natur geformt werden. Aber genau das ist der Grund, warum ich gerne Glasstückchen verwende, die ich irgendwo gefunden habe. Sie zeigen, dass auch kleine Dinge einen Wert haben, Dinge, die wir als unbedeutend betrachten. Schmuck aus Glas herzustellen, das im Laufe der Zeit von Sand rund geschliffen und poliert wurde, und es einfach und spontan, ohne jegliches Gekünstelte zu gestalten, ist für mich der Versuch, Schmuck zu einer Metapher zu machen und das Gefühl von Magie teilweise wieder aufleben zu lassen, das mit dem Tragen von Schmuck und anderen Verzierungen in der Vergangenheit assoziiert wurde. Wenn ich eine Glasscherbe sammle und damit herumspiele, um ein Schmuckstück daraus zu machen, nähre ich das Kind, das ich tief in mir trage."*

Brooch (Ref. no. 601) from
the Archipelago series
1998, found glass, silver,
wood, paper, pebble, gold,
garnet, coral, 3×½ in.
Collection of the artist

*Brosche (Ref. No. 601) aus
der Archipel-Serie*
*1998, gefundenes Glas, Silber,
Holz, Papier, Kiesel, Gold,
Granat, Koralle, 7,5×1 cm*
Sammlung des Künstlers

Rian de Jong
Amsterdam, The Netherlands
Born: 1951, Zoeterwoude,
The Netherlands

Education · Ausbildung
Gerrit Rietveld Academie,
Amsterdam, The Netherlands,
1979–85

**Selected Collections ·
Sammlungen (Auswahl)**
CODA Museum (formerly Van
Reekum Museum), Apeldoorn,
The Netherlands; Gemeente-
museum Den Haag, The Hague,
The Netherlands; Kunstge-
bouw, Rijswijk, The Nether-
lands; Musée de l'Horlogerie,
Geneva, Switzerland; Musée
des Arts Décoratifs de
Montréal, Montreal, Canada;
Museum Boijmans Van
Beuningen, Rotterdam, The
Netherlands; Museum für
Kunst und Gewerbe, Hamburg,
Germany; Museum voor
Moderne Kunst, Arnhem, The
Netherlands; Schmuck-
museum Pforzheim, Pforzheim,
Germany; Sørlandets Kunst-
museum, Kristiansand, Norway;
Stedelijk Museum, Amster-
dam, The Netherlands;
Stedelijk Museum 's-Herto-
genbosch, 's-Hertogenbosch,
The Netherlands; Vydalo
Muzeum, Turnov, Czech
Republic

"I use all kinds of materials to make my jewelry, to tell my story. Glass in particular has many interesting facets to explore. It is beautiful for its transparency and color, especially when light shines through it. It is also cool and vulnerable and can appear soft, shiny, sharp, and even warm while casting. In my representational works, such as the cast portrait heads, glass allows me to develop a visual language with which to express the precariousness of human interaction—to convey social and psychological harmony or conflict." ▪ *„Ich verwende alle Arten von Materialien, um meine Schmuckstücke herzustellen, meine Geschichte zu erzählen. Insbesondere Glas bietet viele interessante Facetten, die man erforschen kann. Es ist schön, weil es transparent und farbig ist, vor allem, wenn Licht hindurchscheint. Gleichzeitig ist es kühl und empfindlich und kann weich, glänzend, scharf und während des Gießprozesses sogar warm wirken. Bei meinen gegenständlichen Arbeiten, wie den gegossenen Porträtköpfen, kann ich mit Glas eine visuelle Sprache entwickeln, die zum Ausdruck bringt, wie heikel und schwierig die zwischenmenschliche Kommunikation ist – um damit soziale und psychologische Harmonie oder einen Konflikt auszudrücken."*

Twice (brooch)
2005, cast glass, silver,
1¾×1¼×1 in.
Collection of the artist

Doppelt (Brosche)
2005, gegossenes Glas,
Silber, 4,3×3,2×2 cm
Sammlung der Künstlerin

Georg Dobler
Berlin, Germany
Born: 1952, Bayreuth,
Germany

Education · Ausbildung
Berufsfachschule für
Goldschmiede, Pforzheim,
Germany, 1969–71, 1979–85

**Selected Collections ·
Sammlungen (Auswahl)**
Cooper-Hewitt, National
Design Museum, Smithsonian
Institution, New York, New
York; Kunstindustrimuseet,
Copenhagen, Denmark; Israel
Museum, Jerusalem, Israel;
Kunstgewerbemuseum, Berlin,
Germany; Münchner Stadt-
museum, Munich, Germany;
Musée des Beaux-Arts de
Montréal, Montreal, Canada;
Museum of Fine Arts, Houston,
Houston, Texas; National
Museum of Modern Art, Kyoto,
Japan; Philadelphia Museum
of Art, Philadelphia, Pennsylva-
nia; Royal College of Art,
London, England; Schmuck-
museum Pforzheim, Pforzheim,
Germany; Stedelijk Museum,
Amsterdam, The Netherlands

"I use glass in my work because it is an intrinsically aesthetic material—transparent, hard, shining. It reminds me of an ice cube. Its worth is purely a matter of design and function. I like its differences—clear, sandblasted, colored. To me glass is interchangeable with rock crystal and other clear semiprecious stones. Mainly, I have used it as a part of larger structures rather than as a structure in itself: as a covering over flat materials or as an abstraction of petals in my flower brooches. The use of glass by Lalique and other art nouveau and art deco artists inspires me." ▪ *„Ich arbeite mit Glas, weil es ein von Natur aus ästhetisches Material ist – transparent, hart, glänzend. Es erinnert mich an einen Eiswürfel. Seinen Wert erhält es ausschließlich durch Design und Funktion. Ich mag seine Verschiedenartigkeit – klar, sandgestrahlt, koloriert. Für mich ist Glas mit Bergkristall und anderen klaren Halbedelsteinen austauschbar. Ich setze es vor allem als Teil einer größeren Struktur und weniger als eigene Struktur ein: als Abschluss über flachen Materialien oder als abstrakte Blütenblätter für meine Blumenbroschen. Die Art und Weise, wie Lalique und andere Art Noveau- und Art Déco-Künstler Glas verwenden, inspiriert mich."*

Mechanical Flower (brooch)
2005, quartz glass, silver,
4¾×2×1 in.
Collection of the artist

Mechanische Blume (Brosche)
2005, Quarzglas, Silber,
12×5×2 cm
Sammlung des Künstlers

Robert Ebendorf
Greenville, North Carolina
Born: 1938, Topeka, Kansas

Education · Ausbildung
Statens Handverks-og Kunst-
Industriskole, Oslo, Norway,
1963–64; University of Kansas,
Lawrence, Kansas, 1962,
M.F.A.; University of Kansas,
Lawrence, Kansas, 1960, B.F.A.

**Selected Collections ·
Sammlungen (Auswahl)**
Art Institute of Chicago, Chica-
go, Illinois; Brooklyn Museum of
Art, Brooklyn, New York; Cleve-
land Museum of Art, Cleveland,
Ohio; Cooper-Hewitt, National
Design Museum, Smithsonian
Institution, New York, New York;
Corning Museum of Glass,
Corning, New York; Kunst-
industrimuseet, Oslo, Norway;
Metropolitan Museum of Art,
New York, New York; Musée
des Arts Décoratifs de Montréal,
Montreal, Canada; Museum of
Arts & Design, New York, New
York; Museum of Fine Arts,
Boston, Boston, Massachu-
setts; National Gallery of Victo-
ria, Melbourne, Australia;
National Museum of Modern
Art, Seoul, South Korea; Power-
house Museum, Sydney, Aus-
tralia; Schmuckmuseum
Pforzheim, Pforzheim, Germany;
Smithsonian American Art
Museum, Renwick Gallery,
Washington, D.C.; Victoria and
Albert Museum, London,
England

"I find glass attractive to use in my work because of the unexpected forms and effects of the material. Glass presents an interesting optic quality; by placing something underneath it, I can bring imagery and patterns to the viewer. Often, glass that has been silkscreened has an interesting surface embellishment, as is the case with the black type on the Absolut Vodka bottle. When I use shards of broken car window glass, the small fragments create an active textural surface that has the appearance of ice because of the way the light interacts with the broken glass. I find that tumbled sea glass has a warm, sensual quality, so sea glass often becomes gemstones in my jewelry." ▪ *„Für mich ist Glas als Material attraktiv, weil es so unerwartete Formen und Effekte bietet. Glas hat eine interessante optische Eigenschaft: wenn ich etwas darunter lege, kann ich Bilder und Muster für den Betrachter erzeugen. Oft weist Glas, das mit Siebdruck bearbeitet wurde, eine interessante Oberfläche auf, wie z. B. die schöne schwarze Schrift auf den Absolut Vodka-Flaschen. Wenn ich mit den Scherben von Autoglas arbeite, entsteht durch die kleinen Fragmente eine aktive strukturelle Oberfläche, die durch das Licht-spiel in dem gebrochenen Glas wie Eis aussieht. Ich finde, dass Meerglas einen warmen, sinnlichen Charakter hat. Deshalb verwende ich es häufig als Schmuckstein für meine Arbeiten."*

Fragments (brooch)
2006, broken glass from Absolut Vodka bottle and
beer bottle, metal jar lid,
tintype photograph,
2×3 in. (diam.× length)
Collection of the artist

Fragmente (Brosche)
2006 , Glasscherben einer
Absolut Vodka-Flasche und
einer Bierflasche,
Metallverschluss eines Kon-
servenglases, Blechfotografie,
5×7,6 cm (Dm × Länge)
Sammlung des Künstlers

Andreas Eberharter
Vienna, Austria
Born: 1971, Schwaz, Austria

Education · Ausbildung
Politechnic, Graz, Austria,
1993–1995 (sculpture);
Politechnic, Steyr, Austria,
1989–1993 (goldsmith)

**Selected Collections ·
Sammlungen (Auswahl)**
Kunstdepot Landhaus Tirol,
Innsbruck, Austria; Museum
auf Abruf (MUSA), Vienna,
Austria; Österreichisches
Museum für Angewandte
Kunst, Vienna, Austria

"Swarovski crystals enliven and refresh the anodized aluminum base of these three bracelets. The combination is very elegant and sexy." ▪
„Bei diesen drei Armreifen wird die Grundform aus eloxiertem Aluminium von Swarovski-Kristallen belebt und erfrischt. Die Kombination wirkt sehr elegant und sexy."

Crystal Code (three bracelets)
2003, Swarovski crystals,
aluminum, 25 in.
Collection of the artist

Kristallcode (drei Armreifen)
2003, Swarovski-Kristalle,
Aluminium, 64 cm
Sammlung des Künstlers

Sandra Enterline
San Francisco, California
Born: 1960, Oil City,
Pennsylvania

Education · Ausbildung
Rhode Island School of Design,
Providence, Rhode Island, 1983,
B.F.A.; Rochester Institute
of Technology, School for
American Crafts, Rochester,
New York, 1980

**Selected Collections ·
Sammlungen (Auswahl)**
Charles A. Wustum Museum
of Fine Arts, Racine, Wisconsin;
Museum of Arts & Design,
New York, New York; Oakland
Museum of California, Oakland,
California; Smithsonian
American Art Museum, Renwick
Gallery, Washington, D.C.

"I use glass for its capacity to contain and reveal substances. I am especially drawn to lab wares such as ampoules and flasks for their unique and curious forms and for their reference to science. I have encased remnants from my personal collections, including reminders of past celebrations and personal milestones—dried petals from my wedding bouquet, snippets of hair from first haircuts, and baby teeth—as well as geological specimens from all over the world—mica, black sand, salt, borax powder, and charcoal —in ampoules that are to be worn. These souvenirs also house nostalgic substances such as Fred the cat's ashes, 'blankie' scraps, and petroleum collected from my birthplace. The beauty of the glass container is that any substance can be displayed in its pure state, however rich, gritty, or odd it is." ▪ *„Ich verwende Glas wegen seiner Eigenschaft, Substanzen aufzunehmen und zu offenbaren. Besonders faszinierend finde ich Laborgläser wie Ampullen, Kolben und Flaschen wegen ihrer einzigartigen und eigenwilligen Formen und ihres Bezugs zur Wissenschaft. Ich habe Überbleibsel aus meiner persönlichen Sammlung in Ampullen eingeschlossen, die zum Tragen gedacht sind. Dafür habe ich Erinnerungen an vergangene Feste und persönliche Meilensteine wie getrocknete Blütenblätter von meinem Hochzeitsstrauß, Haarschnipsel von den ersten Haarschnitten und Babyzähnchen gewählt, aber auch geologische Proben aus aller Welt wie Glimmererde, Schwarzsand, Salz, Boraxpulver und Holzkohle. Daneben fungieren diese Andenken auch als Behältnisse für Substanzen mit nostalgischem Wert wie die Asche der Katze Fred, Schnipsel von ‚Blankie'- Reisekatalogen und Erdöl aus meinem Geburtsort. Die Schönheit der Glasbehälter besteht darin, dass jede Substanz so gezeigt werden kann, wie sie wirklich ist, ganz gleich wie großartig, unschön oder merkwürdig das ist."*

1000 Souvenirs (section of wall installation)
1999, laboratory glass, sterling silver, steel, various found objects,
$2\frac{1}{2} \times \frac{1}{2} \times \frac{1}{2}$ in. (each)
Collection of the artist

1000 Andenken (Teil einer Wandinstallation)
1999, Laborglas, Sterlingsilber, Stahl, verschiedene Fund-objekte, je 6,4 × 1,6 × 1,6 cm
Sammlung der Künstlerin

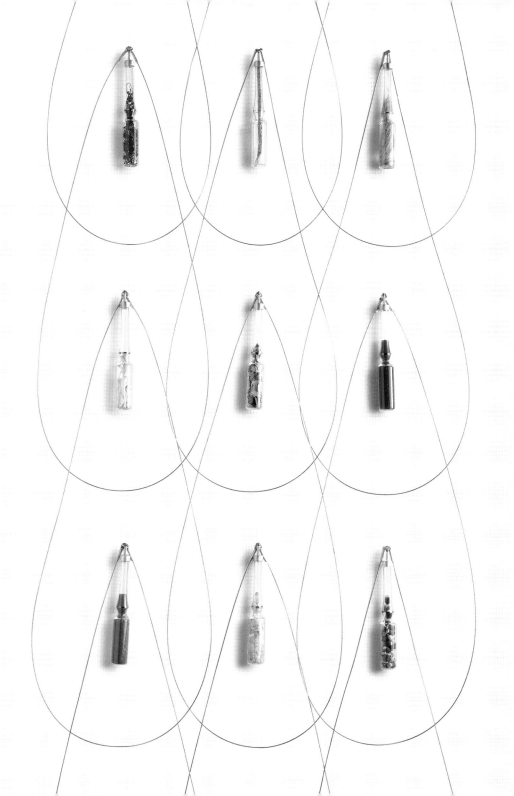

Donald Friedlich
Madison, Wisconsin
Born: 1954, Montclair,
New Jersey

Education · Ausbildung
Rhode Island School of
Design, Providence, Rhode
Island, 1979–82, B.F.A.

**Selected Collections ·
Sammlungen (Auswahl)**
Corning Museum of Glass,
Corning, New York; Mint
Museum of Craft + Design,
Charlotte, North Carolina;
Museum of Arts & Design,
New York, New York; Museum
of Fine Arts, Boston, Boston,
Massachusetts; Museum of
Fine Arts, Houston, Houston,
Texas; Samuel Dorsky Museum
of Art, New Paltz, New York;
Smithsonian American Art
Museum, Renwick Gallery,
Washington, D.C.; Victoria and
Albert Museum, London,
England

"I am drawn to glass because of the wide range of forms and colors it allows. My colored glasswork is usually the result of working with a skilled glassblower under my direction. After the initial shapes are blown, I then do extensive cutting and grinding to achieve the final form. In my colorless glasswork, I exploit the transparency, translucency, and optical qualities of the glass to magnify the weave and color of the fabric on which the brooch is worn. I think of these pieces as 'site adaptive.' I am trying to bridge three craft media: I am making jewelry made of glass with textile imagery. My biggest challenge is to find a graceful way to make the glass wearable. I do it by adding gold as both a design element and the pin mechanism." ▪ *„Ich arbeite gerne mit Glas wegen der vielfältigen Formen und Farben, die dieses Material ermöglicht. Meine farbigen Glasarbeiten entstehen in der Regel in Zusammenarbeit mit einem ausgebildeten Glasbläser unter meiner Anleitung. Wenn die Grundform geblasen ist, bearbeite ich diese intensiv durch Schneiden und Schleifen, bis das Glas seine endgültige Form hat. Bei meinen farblosen Glasarbeiten mache ich mir die Transparenz, die Licht-durchlässigkeit und die optischen Eigenschaften von Glas zunutze, um das Gewebe und die Farbe des Stoffes, auf dem die Brosche getragen wird, zu verstärken. Ich betrachte diese Schmuckstücke als ‚an den (Trage-)Ort anpassbar'. Ich versuche, eine Brücke zwischen drei handwerklichen Medien zu schlagen: Ich mache Schmuck aus Glas mit textilem Erscheinungsbild. Die größte Herausforderung ist dabei für mich, eine elegante Lösung zu finden, das Glas tragbar zu machen. Dafür füge ich Gold hinzu, einmal als Designelement und zum anderen als Nadel und Verschluss."*

**Brooch from the
Translucence series**
2004, glass, 22k gold, 18k gold,
14k gold, 3×3×1/2 in.
Collection of the artist

Brosche der Transluzenz-Serie
*2004, Glas, 22 Karat Gold, 18 Karat
Gold, 14 Karat Gold, 8×8×1 cm
Sammlung des Künstlers*

Karl Fritsch
Munich, Germany
Born: 1963, Sonthofen, Germany

Education · Ausbildung
Akademie der Bildenden Künste
München, Munich, Germany,
1987–94; Berufsfachschule
für Goldschmiede, Pforzheim,
Germany, 1982–85

**Selected Collections ·
Sammlungen (Auswahl)**
Angermuseum Erfurt, Germany;
Auckland Museum, Auckland,
New Zealand; Espace Solidor,
Cagnes-sur-Mer, France; Hiko
Mizuno College of Jewelry,
Tokyo, Japan; Museum für
Kunst und Gewerbe, Hamburg,
Germany; Museo del Gioiello
d'Autore, Padua, Italy; Die Neue
Sammlung, Staatliches Museum
für Angewandte Kunst, Design
in der Pinakothek der Moderne,
on permanent loan from the
Danner Foundation, Munich,
Germany; Royal College of Art,
London, England; Schmuck-
museum Pforzheim, Pforzheim,
Germany; Schmuck und Edel-
stein Museum, Turnov, Czech
Republic; Stedelijk Museum,
Amsterdam, The Netherlands;
Te Papa National Museum,
Wellington, New Zealand

"Moments in which I 'let go' of conventions play a major part in my work. The glass I have used in these rings came to me as a gift twenty years ago, when I was training to be a goldsmith. These cut-glass stones were a treasure that I had not touched until two years ago. Then the colors and shapes of the stones demanded that I pile them up in a specific way, and the pieces developed into autonomous forms." ▪

„Momente, in denen ich Konventionen ‚sausen lasse', spielen eine große Rolle für meine Arbeit. Das Glas, das ich für diese Ringe verwendet habe, habe ich vor 20 Jahren geschenkt bekommen, als ich die Aus-bildung zum Goldschmied machte. Es war ein Schatz, und bis vor zwei Jahren habe ich ihn nicht angerührt. Dann jedoch verlangten die Farben und Formen der Steine danach, von mir auf eine ganz bestimmte Weise aufgetürmt zu werden, und ganz von selbst entwickelten die Stücke ihre Form."

Ring
2004, cut glass, oxidized
silver,
3 ¼ × 2 ½ × 1 ½ in.
Collection of the artist

Ring
2004, geschnittenes Glas,
oxidiertes Silber, 8 × 6 × 4 cm
Sammlung des Künstlers

Thomas Gentille
New York, New York
Born: 1936, Mansfield, Ohio

Education · Ausbildung
Cleveland Institute of Art,
Cleveland, Ohio 1958

**Selected Collections ·
Sammlungen (Auswahl)**
Cleveland Museum of Art,
Cleveland, Ohio; Cooper-Hewitt,
National Design Museum,
Smithsonian Institution, New
York, New York; Musée des
Beaux-Arts de Montréal, Mon-
treal, Canada; Museum of Arts
& Design, New York, New York;
Museum of Fine Arts, Houston,
Houston, Texas; National Gallery
of Victoria, Melbourne, Australia;
Die Neue Sammlung, Staat-
liches Museum für Angewandte
Kunst, Design in der Pinakothek
der Moderne, on permanent
loan from the Danner Founda-
tion, Munich, Germany;
Panstwowa Galeria Sztuki,
Lodz, Poland; Philadelphia
Museum of Art, Philadelphia,
Pennsylvania; Victoria and
Albert Museum, London,
England

"Silica—a component of glass—is an important ingredient in concrete. It is also a protector and sealant on clay when used in the form of a glaze. It is the stuff of which beaches are made; yet processed properly, it becomes transparent glass. Thus transformed, glass has the ability to express and reveal endless qualities and effects—from quiet humility to astonishing invisibility to dazzling refraction." ▪

„Quarz – ein Bestandteil von Glas – ist eine wichtige Komponente von Beton. Außerdem dient es zum Schutz und zur Versiegelung von Ton, wenn es als Glasur verwendet wird. Es ist der Stoff, aus dem die Strände sind. Verarbeitet man es jedoch entsprechend, wird daraus transparentes Glas. Auf diese Weise verwandelt, verfügt Glas über die Fähigkeit, zahllose Eigenschaften und Effekte wiederzugeben und zu offenbaren – von ruhiger Bescheidenheit über überraschende Unsichtbarkeit bis hin zu schillernder Brechung des Lichts."

Brooch
2007, industrial glass,
aircraft plywood, maple, pigment,
3×4×½ in.
Collection of the artist

Brosche
2007, Industrieglas, Flugzeug-
sperrholz, Ahorn, Farbpigmente,
7,8×10,2×1,2 cm
Sammlung des Künstlers

Karen Gilbert
Healdsburg, California
Born: 1971, Springfield, Oregon

Education · Ausbildung
Pilchuck Glass School,
Stanwood, Washington, 1996,
1999; California College of the
Arts, Oakland, California,
1991–93; University of San
Francisco, San Francisco,
California, 1989–90

**Selected Collections ·
Sammlungen (Auswahl)**
Tacoma Art Museum,
Tacoma, Washington

"I see my work from two perspectives—the exploration of materials and the content of my ideas. The relationship between glass and silver is at the core of my exploration of materials. I am interested in the conversation between solid and transparent, hard and soft, simple and complex, color and starkness. As for the content of my work, forms in nature and science are intriguing to me. I see primal forms as road maps for everything we think and feel." ▪ *„Ich sehe meine Arbeit aus zweierlei Perspektiven – der Erforschung der Materialien und des Inhalts meiner Ideen. Die Beziehung zwischen Glas und Silber steht im Zentrum meiner Untersuchungen der Materialien. Ich interessiere mich für den Austausch zwischen massiv und transparent, hart und weich, einfach und komplex, Farbe und Kargheit. Was den Inhalt meiner Arbeit betrifft, so faszinieren mich Formen aus der Natur und der Wissenschaft. Für mich sind die Urformen die Pläne für unser Denken und Fühlen."*

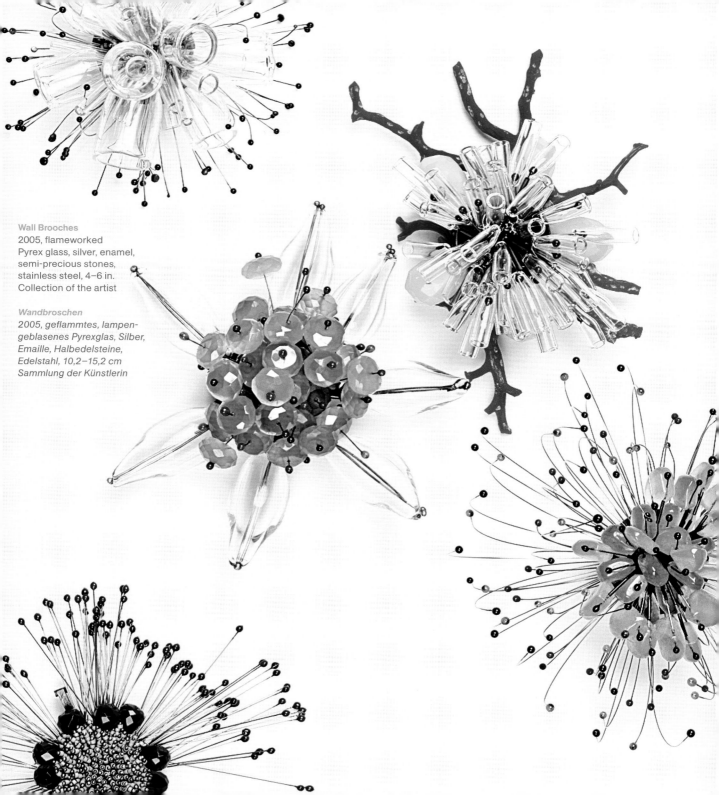

Wall Brooches
2005, flameworked
Pyrex glass, silver, enamel,
semi-precious stones,
stainless steel, 4–6 in.
Collection of the artist

Wandbroschen
2005, geflammtes, lampen-
geblasenes Pyrexglas, Silber,
Emaille, Halbedelsteine,
Edelstahl, 10,2–15,2 cm
Sammlung der Künstlerin

Mieke Groot
Amsterdam, The Netherlands
Born: 1949, Alkmaar,
The Netherlands

Education · Ausbildung
Gerrit Rietveld Academie,
Amsterdam, The Netherlands,
1969–76

**Selected Collections ·
Sammlungen (Auswahl)**
Carnegie Museum of Art, Pittsburgh, Pennsylvania; Corning Museum of Glass, Corning, New York; Frans Hals Museum, Haarlem, The Netherlands; Hokkaido Museum of Modern Art, Sapporo, Japan; Kunstindustrimuseet, Copenhagen, Denmark; Kunstmuseum Düsseldorf, Düsseldorf, Germany; Kurokabe Glass Museum, Nagahama, Japan; Musée des Arts Décoratifs, Lausanne, Switzerland; Musée des Arts Décoratifs, Paris, France; Musée du Verre, Charleroi, Belgium; Musée du Verre, Sars-Poteries, France; Museo Vetrario, Murano, Italy; Museum Boijmans Van Beuningen, Rotterdam, The Netherlands; Museum of Fine Arts, Boston, Boston, Massachusetts; Museum of Fine Arts, Houston, Houston, Texas; Museum für Angewandte Kunst, Frankfurt, Germany; Nationaal Glasmuseum Leerdam, Leerdam, The Netherlands; Pilchuck Collection, Pilchuck Glass School, Stanwood, Washington; Stedelijk Museum, Amsterdam, The Netherlands; Toledo Museum of Art, Toledo, Ohio; Victoria and Albert Museum, London, England

"For almost thirty years now I have made objects in glass that are meant to be viewed and experienced as art, independently of their being worn on the body. I am a collector of ethnic jewelry from around the world and am fascinated by its powerful shapes and symbolic values. The necklaces I make are cultural hybrids that express the many types of interactions that take place in the global community of object makers." ▪ „Seit nunmehr fast 30 Jahren mache ich Objekte aus Glas, die als Kunst gesehen und erlebt werden sollen, unabhängig davon, ob sie am Körper getragen werden. Ich sammle ethnischen Schmuck aus aller Welt und bin fasziniert von dessen ausdrucksstarken Formen und symbolischen Werten. Meine Halsketten – Kulturhybride – bringen die vielfältigen Interaktionen zum Ausdruck, die in der globalen Welt der ‚Sachenmacher' stattfinden."

Dieg Bou Diar (necklace)
2006, blown glass beads made
from tomato paste containers,
steel, silver, 9 ½ in. (diam.)
Collection of the artist

Dieg Bou Diar (Kette)
2006, geblasene Glasperlen,
Perlen aus Tomatenpasten-
Behältern, 25 cm (Dm)
Sammlung der Künstlerin

Therese Hilbert
Munich, Germany
Born: 1948, Zurich, Switzerland

Education · Ausbildung
Akademie der Bildenden
Künste München, Munich,
Germany, 1972–78;
Hochschule für Gestaltung
und Kunst Zürich, Zurich,
Switzerland, 1964–69

**Selected Collections ·
Sammlungen (Auswahl)**
Deutsches Goldschmiedehaus,
Hanau, Germany; Israel
Museum, Jerusalem, Israel;
Kunstgewerbemuseum, Berlin,
Germany; Museum für Ange-
wandte Kunst, Frankfurt,
Germany; Museum of Arts &
Design, New York, New York;
Museum of Fine Arts, Houston,
Houston, Texas; National
Gallery of Victoria, Melbourne,
Australia; Die Neue Samm-
lung, Staatliches Museum für
Angewandte Kunst, Design in
der Pinakothek der Moderne,
on permanent loan from the
Danner Foundation, Munich,
Germany; Powerhouse Muse-
um, Sydney, Australia;
Schmuckmuseum Pforzheim,
Pforzheim, Germany; Stedelijk
Museum, Amsterdam, The
Netherlands; Stadtmuseum,
Munich, Germany

"For the moment, I exist. Passions slumber in me that may explode, then be held in check again. Jets of rage or joy lie within me, ready to burst and catch fire. In myself I am energy, fire, lava. I am a volcano. Most often, I am half asleep: my craters wait for this continual boiling to rise, emerge, satisfy its instincts; for my incandescent passions to pour out, ignite, and spread forth in an assault on the world."—Eugène Ionesco, *Volcano* ▪ *„Im Moment existiere ich. Leidenschaften schlummern in mir, die explodieren und dann wieder in Schach gehalten werden können. Wellen der Wut oder der Freude warten in mir, bereit, auszubrechen und Feuer zu fangen. Ich selbst bin Energie, Feuer, Lava. Ich bin ein Vulkan. Die meiste Zeit befinde ich mich im Halbschlaf: Meine Krater warten darauf, dass das ständig Brodelnde in mir nach oben steigt, hervorbricht, seine Instinkte befriedigt; nämlich meine glühenden Leidenschaften auszuspeien, zu entzünden und im Angriff damit die Welt zu bedecken."* *–Eugène Ionesco,* Vulkan

Glow (brooch)
2005, obsidian (volcanic glass),
blackened silver, 2×½ in.
Collection of the artist

Glut (Brosche)
2005, Obsidian (vulkanisches
Glas), geschwärztes Silber,
5×1,6 cm
Sammlung der Künstlerin

Timothy Horn
Melbourne, Australia / Cape
Cod, Massachusetts
Born: 1964, Melbourne,
Australia

Education · Ausbildung
Massachusetts College of Art,
Boston, Massachusetts, 2004,
M.F.A.; Australian National
University, Canberra, Australia,
2001, B.F.A.; Victorian College
of the Arts, Melbourne,
Australia, 1988, post-graduate
diploma (Sculpture)

**Selected Collections ·
Sammlungen (Auswahl)**
National Gallery of Australia,
Canberra, Australia; Mills
College Art Museum, Oakland,
California; University of South
Australia Art Museum,
Adelaide, Australia

"I am intrigued by the ability of glass to imitate precious minerals and gems. When setting out to make these works, my studio walls were cloaked with images of jewelry in eighteenth-century portraiture. This led me to conduct research into the techniques of that era, particularly those that Diderot describes for costume jewelry in his *Encyclopédie*: counterfeit diamonds of glass paste that were cut, polished, and foiled to increase their brilliance; pearlescent glass blown to resemble pearls. I spent several months affecting an artificial baroque pearl. Translating the metal from silver to nickel-plated bronze repositions the work as quasi-industrial rather than precious. Inflating the object to near-human scale transmogrifies notions of desire and the desired, possession and the possessed. Bending the iconic significance of both jewel and gem outs their intimacy and suggests new interpretations for their longstanding relationship." ▪ *„Ich bin fasziniert davon, wie Glas wertvolle Mineralien und Edelsteine imitieren kann. Als ich mich daran begab, diese Arbeiten zu erstellen, waren die Wände meines Studios über und über mit Bildern von Schmuck aus der Porträt-malerei des 18. Jahrhunderts bedeckt. Das brachte mich dazu, Nachforschungen über die Techniken anzustellen, die man in dieser Zeit anwandte, vor allem über die Technik, die Diderot in seiner* Encyclopédie *im Zusammenhang mit Modeschmuck nennt: nachgemachte Diamanten aus Glaspaste, die geschnitten, poliert und mit Folie beschichtet wurden, um ihnen größeren Glanz zu verleihen, sowie Perlmuttglas, das so geblasen wurde, dass es wie Perlen aussah. Ich verbrachte mehrere Monate damit, eine künstliche barocke Perle hervorzubringen. Die Überführung des Metalls von Silber in vernickelte Bronze qualifiziert die Arbeit eher als quasi-industriell denn als wertvoll. Indem das Objekt fast zur Größe eines Menschen aufgebläht wird, werden die Vorstellungen von Begehren und Begehrtem, Besitz und Besessenem transformiert. Indem der Kultsymbolcharakter sowohl von Schmuck als auch von Edelstein verändert wird, wird deren Vertrautheit miteinander öffentlich gemacht und eine neue Auslegung dieser alten Beziehung nahegelegt."*

Difficult to Swallow (Boy Germs)—**wall installation**
2001, mirrored blown glass, lead crystal, nickel-plated bronze, Easter egg foil, 25 ½ × 15 ¾ × 6 in.
Private collection, San Francisco, courtesy Hosfelt Gallery, San Francisco / New York

Schwer zu schlucken (Bubenkeime) – Wandinstallation
2001, verspiegeltes, geblasenes Glas, Bleikristall, vernickelte Bronze, Folie von Ostereiern, 64 × 40 × 15 cm
Privatsammlung, San Francisco, mit freundlicher Genehmigung der Hosfelt Gallery, San Francisco / New York

Svatopluk Kasalý
Třešť, Czech Republic
Born: 1944, Pelhřimov,
Czech Republic

Education · Ausbildung
Stredni umělecko-průmyslova
škola sklarska, Železný Brod,
Czech Republic, 1961–65

**Selected Collections ·
Sammlungen (Auswahl)**
Corning Museum of Glass,
Corning, New York; Moravská
galerie v Brně, Brno, Czech
Republic; Muzeum Skla a
Bižuterie v Jablonci nad Nisou,
Jablonec nad Nisou, Czech
Republic; Schmuckmuseum
Pforzheim, Pforzheim, Ger-
many; Severčeské Muzeum v
Liberci, Liberec, Czech Repub-
lic; Slovenská národná galéria,
Bratislava, Slovakia;
Uměleckoprůmyslové
muzeum v Praze, Prague,
Czech Republic

"From the beginning of my career, I have made glass jewelry as well as monumental glass works in architecture that are inspired by the magnificent tradition of Czech glassmaking. My small jewelry creations are individually designed objects that are intended not only as ornaments to enhance the aesthetic appearance of a woman but also as individually conceived works of art. I create my jewelry for a specific type of woman, style of dress, and social atmosphere. I use a nontraditional and unique method to combine glass and metal. I am interested in exploring the different characteristics of these two materials and in joining them into one organic unit, seeking always to avoid casual, extraneous, and painterly features. I use primarily potash-glass and lead glass, materials that have to be shaped entirely by cutting. I try to choose a jewel to suit the person for whom I am making the piece." ▪ *„Seit dem Beginn meiner Karriere als Künstler habe ich sowohl Schmuck aus Glas als auch Monumentalkunst aus Glas für den architektonischen Bereich hergestellt, inspiriert von der großartigen Tradition der tschechischen Glasherstellung. Meine kleinen Schmuckkreationen sind individuell gestaltete Objekte, die nicht nur als Verzierung gedacht sind, um das ästhetische Erscheinungsbild einer Frau zu verschönern, sondern auch als individuell konzipierte Kunstwerke. Ich kreiere meinen Schmuck für einen ganz bestimmten Typ von Frau, für einen speziellen Kleidungsstil und eine bestimmte soziale Atmosphäre. Um Glas und Metall miteinander zu kombinieren, setze ich eine einzigartige, nicht auf Tradition beruhende Methode ein. Ich will die unterschiedlichen Eigenschaften dieser beiden Materialien erforschen und sie zu einer organischen Einheit zusammenfügen. Dabei versuche ich immer, zufällige, nicht wesentliche und malerische Elemente zu vermeiden. Ich verwende vorwiegend Pottascheglas und Bleikristall, die geschnitten werden müssen, um ihre Form zu erhalten. Ich bemühe mich, einen Edelstein zu wählen, der zu der Person passt, für die ich das Schmuckstück mache."*

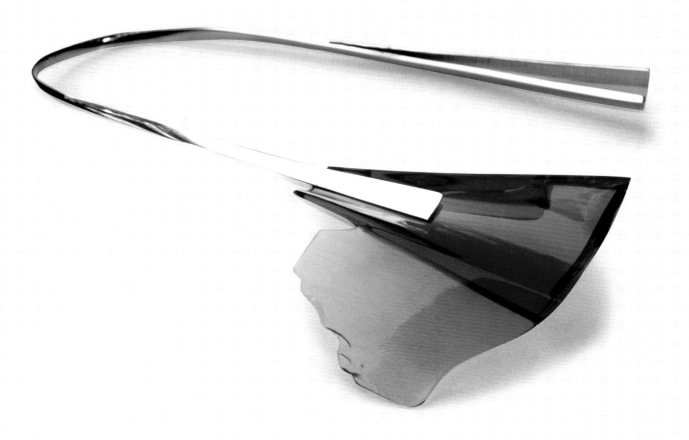

Neckpiece
2001, cut and polished glass,
brass, platinum, 9×10 in.
Collection of Eliska Stölting,
Germany

Halsschmuck
2001, geschnittenes und
poliertes Glas, Messing,
Platin, 23×25 cm
Sammlung Eliska Stölting,
Deutschland

Jaroslav Kodejš
Železný Brod, Czech Republic
Born: 1938, Radčice,
Czech Republic

Education · Ausbildung
Výtvarný Institut Pub, Jablonec
nad Nisou, Czech Republic,
1960–63

**Selected Collections ·
Sammlungen (Auswahl)**
Moravská galerie v Brně, Brno,
Czech Republic; Museum of
Contemporary Art, Sydney,
Australia; Museum of Fine Arts,
Houston, Houston, Texas;
Muzeum Českého ráje v Turnově,
Turnov, Czech Republic; Muzeum
Skla a Bižuterie v Jablonci nad
Nisou, Jablonec nad Nisou,
Czech Republic; Schmuckmu-
seum Pforzheim, Pforzheim,
Germany; Severočeské
muzeum, Liberec, Czech
Republic; Slovenská národná
galéria, Bratislava, Slovakia;
Uměleckoprůmyslové muzeum v
Praze, Prague, Czech Republic

"I use glass as a primary material when creating jewelry because it provides me with limitless possibilities for the realization of my designs. By melting and layering individual fragments of glass, I am able to achieve painterly effects evocative of moods, memories, and places. Although glass is a simple, readily available material, it lends itself to endless manipulation and reinvention." ▪

„Wenn ich Schmuck schaffe, gehört Glas zu den von mir am häufigsten verwendeten Materialien, denn für die Umsetzung meiner Entwürfe bietet es mir grenzenlose Möglichkeiten. Durch das Schmelzen und Schichten einzelner Glasfragmente vermag ich, malerische Effekte zu erzielen, die Stimmungen, Erinnerungen und Orte hervorrufen. Wenn Glas auch ein ganz gewöhnliches, leicht erhältliches Material ist, eignet es sich doch für unendlich viele Arten der Bearbeitung und Wiedererfindung."

Brooch
2000, glass, silver, gold,
1¾×1¾ in.
Collection of the artist

Brosche
2000, Glas, Silber,
Gold, 4,9×4,9 cm
Sammlung der Künstlers

Helfried Kodré
Vienna, Austria
Born: 1940, Graz, Austria

Education · Ausbildung
Self-taught in jewelry design/
making; Universität Wien,
Vienna, Austria, 1975–83, art
history; Universität Wien,
Vienna, Austria, 1984, Ph.D.

**Selected Collections ·
Sammlungen (Auswahl)**
Artothek, Vienna, Austria;
Landesmuseum Joanneum,
Graz, Austria; Museum für
Angewandte Kunst, Cologne,
Germany; Muzeum Ceského
ráje v Turnové, Turnov, Czech
Republic; Muzeum Skla a
Biżuterie v Jablonci nad Nisou,
Jablonec nad Nisou, Czech
Republic; Die Neue Sammlung,
Staatliches Museum für
Angewandte Kunst, Design
in der Pinakothek der Moderne,
on permanent loan from the
Danner Foundation, Munich,
Germany; Österreichisches
Museum für Angewandte
Kunst, Vienna, Austria;
Sammlung der Kulturabteilung
der Stadt Wien, Vienna, Austria;
Schmuckmuseum Pforzheim,
Pforzheim, Germany

"Approximately ten years ago, when vacationing on Ischia and bathing in the hot springs on the site of the Terme-Aphrodite, I was collecting the loose tesserae floating about my feet on the pool's mosaic floor. Ever since that enjoyable Ischia summer, I have safeguarded and treasured those glass pieces—in honor of 'Aphrodite'. Now, finally, they have found a new life in this brooch—my very first made with glass.—A short anecdote, not a heady theory!" ▪ *„Vor ungefähr 10 Jahren, als ich auf Ischia Urlaub machte und in den heißen Quellen der ‚Terme Aphrodite' badete, sammelte ich die losen Mosaiksteinchen auf, die am Boden des Pools meine Füße umspülten. Seit jenem vergnüglichen Sommer auf Ischia habe ich diese Glasstückchen aufbewahrt und wie einen Schatz gehütet – zu Ehren von Aphrodite. Nun endlich haben sie in dieser Brosche – meiner ersten mit Glas – eine neue Bestimmung gefunden. – Lediglich eine kleine Anekdote, keine aufregende Theorie!"*

Brooch
2005, mosaic glass,
silver, 4×3 in.
Private collection,
Germany

Brosche
2005, Mosaikglas,
Silber, 10,5×8 cm
Privatsammlung,
Deutschland

Daniel Kruger
Munich, Germany
Born: 1951, Cape Town,
South Africa

Education · Ausbildung
Akademie der Bildenden
Künste, Munich, Germany,
1974–80; Michaelis School of
Fine Art, University of Cape
Town, Cape Town, South Africa,
1973–74; University of Stennen-
bosch, Stennenbosch,
South Africa, 1971–72

**Selected Collections ·
Sammlungen (Auswahl)**
Cooper-Hewitt, National
Design Museum, Smithsonian
Institution, New York, New
York; Hiko Mizuno College of
Jewelry, Tokyo, Japan;
Kunstgewerbemuseum, Berlin,
Germany; Landesmuseum
Joanneum, Graz, Austria;
Münchner Stadtmuseum,
Munich, Germany; Musée des
Arts Décoratifs de Montréal,
Montreal, Canada; Museum
Boijmans Van Beuningen,
Rotterdam, The Netherlands;
National Gallery of Australia,
Canberra, Australia; Power-
house Museum, Sydney, Aus-
tralia; Rhode Island School of
Design Museum, Providence,
Rhode Island; Royal College of
Art, London, England;
Schmuckmuseum Pforzheim,
Pforzheim, Germany; Stedelijk
Museum 's-Hertogenbosch,
's-Hertogenbosch, The Nether-
lands; Württembergisches
Landesmuseum, Stuttgart,
Germany

"My interest in glass is associated with the fragments of broken glass that can be found in our environment: fragments of bottles, windowpanes, motorcar headlamps, or functional and decorative glass objects from the home. This is readily available material. Fragments can be found nearly everywhere, and any glass object can easily be used to obtain fragments. Glass is transparent, refracts light, and can be colorless or colored. The surface can be matte or shiny. One can look into it or through it. The surfaces of the edges show the nature of the material. The shapes of the fragments are haphazard and predetermined, as in nature. These are properties that appeal to me and for which I find a use in jewelry." ▪ *„Mein Interesse an Glas richtet sich auf Glasscherben, die man in unserer Umgebung finden kann: Scherben von Flaschen, Fensterscheiben, Autoscheinwerfern sowie von dekorativen und funktionalen Glasobjekten aus dem Haushalt. Dieses Material ist leicht verfügbar. Scherben kann man fast überall finden und man kann sie ganz einfach aus einem beliebigen Glas-objekt gewinnen. Glas ist transparent, es bricht das Licht, kann farblos oder auch farbig, die Oberfläche matt oder glänzend sein. Man kann hinein- oder hindurch-schauen. Die Bruchflächen zeigen, wie das Material beschaffen ist. Die Form der Scherben ist zufällig oder vorgegeben, wie in der Natur. Das sind Eigenschaften, die mich ansprechen und die ich mir bei der Gestaltung von Schmuck zunutze machen kann."*

Brooch
1999, glass fragments,
gold, silver, 2 ¾×2×1 in.
Collection of the artist

Brosche
1999, Glasfragmente,
Gold, Silber, 7×5×2,5 cm
Sammlung des Künstlers

Otto Künzli
Munich, Germany
Born: 1948, Zurich, Switzerland

Education · Ausbildung
Akademie der bildenden
Künste, Munich, Germany, 1978;
Hochschule für Gestaltung und
Kunst Zürich, Zurich, Switzer-
land, 1965–70

**Selected Collections ·
Sammlungen (Auswahl)**
Auckland Museum, Auckland,
New Zealand; CODA Museum
(formerly Van Reekum Museum),
Apeldoorn, The Netherlands;
Detroit Institute of Arts, Detroit,
Michigan; Deutsches Gold-
schmiedehaus, Hanau,
Germany; Israel Museum,
Jerusalem, Israel; Kunstgewerbe-
museum, Berlin, Germany;
Museum of Arts & Design, New
York, New York; Museum of
Fine Arts, Houston, Houston,
Texas; National Museum of
Modern Art, Kyoto, Japan;
Die Neue Sammlung, Staatliches
Museum für Angewandte
Kunst, Design in der Pinakothek
der Moderne, on permanent
loan from the Danner Founda-
tion, Munich, Germany; Power-
house Museum, Sydney, Aus-
tralia; Rhode Island School of
Design Museum, Providence,
Rhode Island; Royal College of
Art, London, England; Stedelijk
Museum, Amsterdam, The
Netherlands

"In the depths of the mirror the evening landscape moved by, the mirror and the reflected figures like motion pictures superimposed one on the other. The figures and the background were unrelated, and yet the figures, transparent and intangible, and the background, dim in the gathering darkness, melted together into a sort of symbolic world not of this world."—Yasunari Kawabata, *Snow Country* ▪ *„In den Tiefen des Spiegels zog die Abendlandschaft vorüber, der Spiegel und die Figuren, die sich in ihm spiegelten, schoben sich wie Zeitlupenaufnahmen übereinander. Die Figuren und der Hintergrund hatten keinen Bezug zueinander und dennoch ver-schmolzen sie – die Figuren, transparent und nicht greifbar, und der Hintergrund, schummerig in der zunehmenden Dunkelheit – zu einer Art symbolischen Welt, die nicht von dieser Welt war."* – Yasunari Kawabata, Schneeland

Ring
1988, mirror, gold,
1½×1×½ in.
Collection of the
artist

Ring
1988, Spiegel, Gold,
4,1×2,8×1,6 cm
Sammlung des Künstlers

Stanley Lechtzin
(in collaboration with Daniella Kerner)
Elkins Park, Pennsylvania
Born: 1936, Detroit, Michigan

Education · Ausbildung
Cranbrook Academy of Art,
Bloomfield Hills, Michigan,
1962, M.F.A.; Wayne State University, Detroit, Michigan,
1960, B.F.A.

**Selected Collections ·
Sammlungen (Auswahl)**
Cooper-Hewitt, National
Design Museum, Smithsonian
Institution, New York, New
York; Cranbrook Academy of
Art, Bloomfield Hills, Michigan;
Detroit Institute of Arts,
Detroit, Michigan; Museum of
Arts & Design, New York, New
York; Museum of Fine Arts,
Houston, Houston, Texas;
Philadelphia Museum of Art,
Philadelphia, Pennsylvania;
Schmuckmuseum Pforzheim,
Pforzheim, Germany; Smithsonian American Art Museum,
Renwick Gallery, Washington,
D.C.; Tokyo National University
of Fine Arts and Music,
Tokyo, Japan; Yale University
Art Gallery, New Haven,
Connecticut

"I use industrial materials and processes, techniques that are unknown to the public, to express personal values. The forms I create evolve as they do because of my regard for the body. That my art is worn is a point of departure. I hope to compel both the wearer and the viewer to interact with the jewelry. My intent is to act as an interpreter of today's technology and to demonstrate human values through the control of the new medium of CAD/RP (Computer-Aided-Design/Rapid Prototyping). I begin with a concept that I take to the computer. Working within the solids modeling program, I create the form. When all aspects of the work are defined, the piece is complete. All that remains is to materialize the object. At this point I choose my materials. When I desire purity of surface and when the suppleness of the form is important, I use glass-filled polyamide, which offers great strength and flexibility. I am intrigued by the fact that glass, which is normally considered rigid and fragile, is paradoxically strong and flexible. Glass used in this manner achieves a unique, granular, crystalline surface. These heretofore unrealized qualities of glass expand the potential of the new medium of CAD/RP." ▪ *„Ich setze Materialien, Verfahren und Techniken aus der Industrie ein, die der Öffentlichkeit nicht bekannt sind, um damit persönliche Werte zum Ausdruck zu bringen. Die Formen, die ich schaffe, entstehen aus meiner Achtung für den Körper. Dass meine Kunst getragen wird, ist ein Ausgangspunkt. Ich hoffe, sowohl den Träger des Schmucks als auch den Betrachter dazu zu zwingen, in Interaktion mit dem Schmuck zu treten. Ich will als Übersetzer für die moderne Technologie fungieren und durch die Kontrolle neuer Medien wie CAD/RP (Computer-Aided-Design/Rapid Prototyping; rechnergestützte Konstruktion/schneller Prototypenbau) menschliche Werte demonstrieren. Ich beginne mit einem Entwurf, den ich in den Computer eingebe. Mit Hilfe des Gestaltungsprogramms für Feststoffe kreiere ich die Form. Wenn alle Aspekte der Arbeit definiert sind, ist das Werkstück fertig. Es bleibt lediglich noch die Realisierung des Objekts. An diesem Punkt wähle ich meine Materialien aus. Wenn ich eine reine Oberfläche haben möchte und die Geschmeidigkeit der Form von Bedeutung ist, verwende ich mit Glas gefülltes Polyamid, das gleichzeitig hohe Stabilität und Flexibilität bietet. Mich fasziniert, dass Glas, das üblicherweise als so starr und zerbrechlich gilt, so erstaunlich stark und flexibel ist. Glas, das in dieser Weise verarbeitet wird, erhält eine einzigartige, körnige, kristalline Oberfläche. Diese bis dahin nicht bekannten Eigenschaften von Glas schaffen ein völlig neues Potential für das innovative Medium CAD/RP."*

PusHere Bracelet
2006, Selective-Laser-Sintered
(SLS) glass-filled nylon,
rubber O-rings, 7 in. (diam.)
Collection of the artist

Armreif Hier drücken
2006, ausgewähltes und
lasergesintertes (SLS) mit Glas
gefülltes Nylon, Dichtungsringe
aus Gummi, 17,7 cm (Dm)
Sammlung des Künstlers

Tarja Lehtinen
Lappeenranta, Finland
Born: 1983, Tampere,
Finland

Education · Ausbildung
Lappeenrannan Ammatti-
korkeakoulu, Taiteen yksikkö
(South Karelia Polytechnic
School of Fine Arts and
Design), Lappeenranta, Finland,
2002–06; Kouvolan Käsi- ja
Taideteollisuusoppilaitos
(School of Arts and Crafts),
Kouvola, Finland, 1998–2002

**Selected Collections ·
Sammlungen (Auswahl)**
Marie-José van den Hout
Collection, Galerie Marzee,
Nijmegen, The Netherlands

"I have always liked to work with hard materials like stone and glass. These materials are strong and resistant and offer an endless variety of colors. Glass is fascinating because it never disappears; it can be melted down and molded again. Recycled bottle glass is intriguing because it is at once old and new, valuable and waste. I wanted to give recycled bottle glass a new form and a different use. Cameos are a very old form of jewelry. They have changed over the years, but some elements have always remained. They tell a story of their time, what was dreamed, desired, or honored. Studying the history of cameos gave me an idea of what a cameo might be today. I realized it could combine old and traditional aspects with new techniques and design. I decided to use sandblasting to create cameos in the bottoms of glass bottles, and I used the same subject for my cameos that has been in common use for a long time: a silhouette portrait of a woman." ▪ *„Ich habe schon immer gerne mit harten Materialien wie Stein oder Glas gearbeitet. Diese Materialien sind stark und beständig und bieten endlose Farb-variationen. Glas ist faszinierend, weil es nie verschwindet; man kann es schmelzen und neu formen. Recyceltes Glas ist verblüffend, weil es gleichzeitig alt und neu, wertvoll und Abfall ist. Ich wollte recyceltem Flaschenglas eine neue Form und einen neuen Verwendungszweck geben. Kameen sind eine sehr alte Form von Schmuck. Sie haben sich im Laufe der Jahre verändert, aber einige Elemente sind immer gleich geblieben. Sie erzählen die Geschichte ihrer Zeit, wovon die Menschen träumen, was sie begehren und was sie ehren. Die Auseinandersetzung mit der Geschichte der Kameen hat mir eine Vorstellung davon vermittelt, wie Kameen heute aussehen könnten. Ich erkannte die Möglichkeit, darin alte und traditionelle Aspekte mit neuen Techniken und einem neuen Design zu kombinieren. Und ich entschied mich, Kameen mittels Sandstrahltechnik aus den Böden von Glasflaschen herzustellen. Dabei blieb das Thema meiner Kameen das gleiche wie schon seit langer, langer Zeit: die Silhouette eines Frauenporträts."*

Cameo Brooches
2006, recycled and
sandblasted glass, silver,
stainless steel, 3×1½ in.
Collection of the artist

Kameebroschen
2006, recyceltes und
sandgestrahltes Glas, Silber,
Edelstahl, 8×4 cm
Sammlung der Künstlerin

Jacqueline I. Lillie
Vienna, Austria
Born: 1941, Marseilles, France

Education · Ausbildung
Akademie für Angewandte
Kunst Wien, Vienna, Austria,
1962–1965

**Selected Collections ·
Sammlungen (Auswahl)**
Cooper-Hewitt, National Design
Museum, Smithsonian Institution,
New York, New York; Corning
Museum of Glass, Corning, New
York; Metropolitan Museum of
Art, New York, New York;
Museum of Arts & Design, New
York, New York; Österreichisches
Museum für Angewandte Kunst,
Vienna, Austria; Powerhouse
Museum, Sydney, Australia;
Württembergisches Landes-
museum, Stuttgart, Germany

"Serendipity prompted my initial decision to work with glass: a hatbox full of minute antique glass beads in a Viennese junk-shop set things in motion. Fascinated by the range and subtlety of the hues that the miniscule beads offered, I realized that singularity was a matter of range, not size. The artistic challenge lay in achieving uniqueness through a matching of color and material: blending the visual agility of the minute Bohemian beads with their intrinsic durability. All of the other features of my work are subordinate to the many thousands of beads used in the creation of my pieces. Glass jewelry is not an expression of status, but a reflection of the wearer's attitudes towards life and the environment. Each piece should adapt to and be an extension of the wearer's persona. The techniques I use and the patterns I devise represent an endeavor to reconcile imagination with the practical demands of personal adornment." ▪

„Ein glücklicher Zufall brachte mich dazu, mich für den Werkstoff Glas zu entscheiden: Eine Hutschachtel voller winziger antiker Glasperlen in einem Wiener Trödelladen setzte die Dinge in Bewegung. Fasziniert von der breiten Palette und den feinen Farb- nuancierungen, die diese winzigen Perlen zu bieten hatten, erkannte ich, dass Einzigartigkeit eine Frage des Spielraums und nicht der Größe ist. Die künstlerische Herausforderung lag darin, Einzigartigkeit durch die richtige Kombination von Farbe und Material zu schaffen: die visuelle Lebendigkeit der winzigen böhmischen Perlen mit der ihnen eigenen Beständigkeit zusammenzubringen. Alle anderen Aspekte meiner Arbeit sind den vielen tausend Glasperlen untergeordnet, die ich für meine Schmuckstücke verwende. Glasschmuck ist kein Statussymbol, sondern bringt die Haltung der Trägerin gegenüber dem Leben und der Umwelt zum Ausdruck. Jedes Stück sollte der Person, die den Schmuck trägt, angepasst und eine Fortsetzung dieser Person sein. Die Technik, die ich verwende, und die Muster, die ich erfinde, verkörpern mein Streben, die Sprache der Fantasie mit dem Anspruch in Einklang zu bringen, andere zu schmücken."

Combined Necklace and Bracelet
2006, individually knotted glass beads, silk thread, titanium magnetic closures, 35½×1¾ in.
Courtesy of the artist and Rosanne Raab Associates

Kombinierter Hals- und Armschmuck
2006, einzeln geknotete Glasperlen, Seidenfaden, Titanmagnetverschlüsse, 90×4,5 cm
Mit freundlicher Genehmigung der Künstlerin und Rosanne Raab Associates

Linda MacNeil
Kensington, New Hampshire
Born: 1954, Framingham,
Massachusetts

Education · Ausbildung
Rhode Island School of
Design, Providence, Rhode
Island, 1976, B.F.A.

**Selected Collections ·
Sammlungen (Auswahl)**
Les Archives de la Cristallerie
Daum, Nancy and Paris,
France; Cleveland Museum of
Art, Cleveland, Ohio; Corning
Museum of Glass, Corning,
New York; Detroit Institute of
Arts, Detroit, Michigan; Metro-
politan Museum of Art, New
York, New York; Mint Museum
of Craft + Design, Charlotte,
North Carolina; Museum of
Arts & Design, New York, New
York; Museum of Fine Arts,
Boston, Boston, Massachusetts;
Museum of Fine Arts, Houston,
Houston, Texas; Racine Art
Museum, Racine, Wisconsin;
Rhode Island School of Design
Museum, Providence, Rhode
Island; Smithsonian American
Art Museum, Renwick Gallery,
Washington, D.C.; Toledo
Museum of Art, Toledo, Ohio;
Victoria and Albert Museum,
London, England

"Glass intrigues me because it offers me the creative freedom to make my own forms, which are unique to each piece of jewelry. In some works, plate glass is cut, polished, and mirrored to emphasize the illusion of depth. In others, I have used cast glass filled with hundreds of bubbles to soften the forms visually. These and other glass qualities are distinctly different from the diamonds and rubies within the composition of a necklace. The designs are similar to my previous work in style and method, but the combination of glass and precious stones in my recent work has inspired me to explore classic traditions in jewelry." ▪ *„Glas fasziniert mich, weil es mir die schöpferische Freiheit gibt, meine eigenen Formen zu schaffen, die für jedes Schmuckstück einzigartig sind. Für manche Arbeiten wird Flachglas geschnitten, poliert und gespiegelt, um den Eindruck von Tiefe zu verstärken. Für andere Arbeiten habe ich gegossenes Glas verwendet, das mit Hunderten von Blasen gefüllt ist, um optisch weichere Formen zu erzielen. In diesen und anderen Eigenschaften unterscheidet sich Glas in der Komposition eines Halsschmucks beträchtlich von Diamanten und Rubinen. In Bezug auf Stil und Methode ist das Design dem früherer Arbeiten von mir ähnlich, aber die Kombination von Glas und Edelsteinen in meiner jüngsten Arbeit hat mich dazu inspiriert, mich mit den klassischen Traditionen von Schmuck zu beschäftigen.“*

**Necklace from the
Elements series**
2006, polished clear glass,
polished 19k white gold,
white diamonds, 6 in. (diam.)
Private collection, United
States

*Halsschmuck der
Elemente-Serie*
*2006, poliertes Klarglas,
poliertes 19 Karat Weißgold,
weiße Diamanten, 15,2 cm (Dm)
Privatsammlung, USA*

Stefano Marchetti
Padua, Italy
Born: 1970, Padua, Italy

Education · Ausbildung
Accademia di Belle Arti di
Venezia, Venice, Italy,
1990–94; Istituto Statale
d'Arte Pietro Selvatico, Padua,
Italy, 1984–89

**Selected Collections ·
Sammlungen (Auswahl)**
Fonds national d'art contem-
porain, Paris, France; Marie-
José van den Hout Collection,
Galerie Marzee, Nijmegen,
The Netherlands; Landes-
museum Joanneum, Graz,
Austria; Musée des Arts Déco-
ratifs, Paris, France; Museum
für Kunst und Gewerbe,
Hamburg, Germany; Museum
of Arts & Design, New York,
New York; Museum voor
Moderne Kunst, Arnhem, The
Netherlands; National Museums
of Scotland, Edinburgh,
Scotland

"Giving shape to a piece of jewelry is quite simple: first a dialogue needs to be established between fire and material and then the conversation must be informed with personal insights. I choose to use 'fire techniques' as the tool, and glass and precious metals as the material. My first contact with glass was indirect, an attempt to 'translate' metal manufacturing techniques into work with glass. The result of this research, represented here by a necklace, is the incorporation of metal mosaic into the process for creating Venetian *murrina*." ▪ „Einem Schmuckstück eine Form zu geben, ist ganz einfach: Zunächst muss ein Dialog zwischen Feuer und dem Material aufgebaut werden, und dann muss die Konversation zwischen den beiden mit persönlichen Erkenntnissen angereichert werden. Ich habe mich für die ‚Feuertechnik' als Werkzeug und für Glas und Edelmetalle als Materialien entschieden. Mein erster Kontakt mit Glas war indirekter Natur, der Versuch, eine Methode der Metallverarbeitung auf die Arbeit mit Glas zu übertragen. Das Ergebnis dieser Forschungen, das hier in Form eines Halsschmucks vorgestellt wird, ist die Eingliederung von Metallmosaik in das Verfahren zur Herstellung einer Murrina Veneziana."

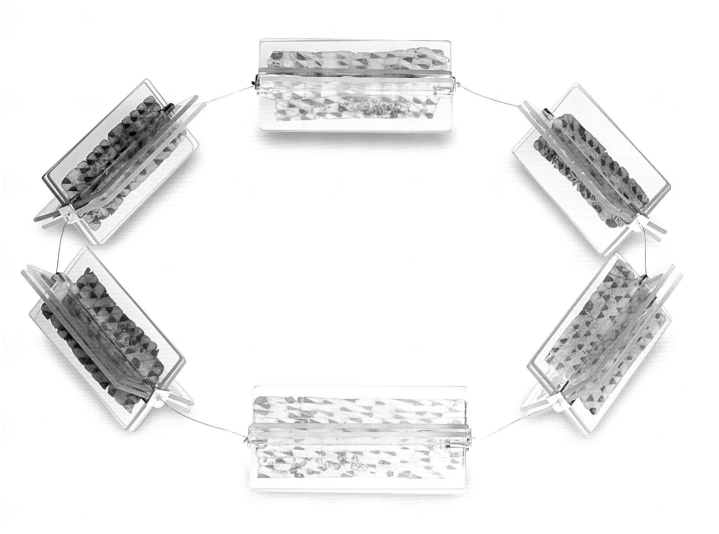

Necklace
2006, plate glass, yellow gold,
silver, 8¾ in. (diam.)
Collection of the artist

Halskette
2006, Flachglas, Gelbgold,
Silber, 22 cm (Dm)
Sammlung des Künstlers

Nanna Melland
Munich, Germany
Born: 1969, Oslo, Norway

Education · Ausbildung
Akademie der Bildenden
Künste München, Munich,
Germany, 2001–06; Institut
for Ædelmetal Copenhagen,
Denmark, 2000–01; Elve-
bakken videregående skole,
Oslo, Norway, 1993–1995;
Universitetet i Oslo, Norway,
1989–1997

**Selected Collections ·
Sammlungen (Auswahl)**
Marie-José van den Hout
Collection, Galerie Marzee,
Nijmegen, The Netherlands;
Hiko Mizuno College of
Jewelry, Tokyo, Japan

"I was inspired to use glass while studying at the Anatomical Institute in Munich, where I saw rows of glass jars containing organs suspended in formaldehyde. I was fascinated by the way in which the glass containers gave the repulsive and perhaps even brutal body fragments a poetic beauty and life of their own. I had already cast the insides of a pig heart in epoxy resin and decided I wanted to enclose some remains within a glass sphere. When I put the sphere over the remains, the glass gave the piece a special kind of space and presence. Gone was the dullness of the organ's surface; the fragment became almost magical, as if it existed in a little world of its own." ▪ *„Die Inspiration, Glas als Material zu verwenden, erhielt ich während meines Studiums am Anatomischen Institut in München, wo ich Reihen von Glasbehältern mit Organen in Formaldehyd sah. Ich war fasziniert davon, wie die Glasbehälter den abstoßenden, teilweise fast brutal wirkenden Körperfragmenten eine poetische Schönheit und ein eigenes Leben gaben. Ich hatte bereits das Innere eines Schweineherzens in Epoxydharz gegossen und beschloss, einige Reste davon in eine Glaskugel einzuschließen. Als ich die Kugel über die Reste stülpte, gab das Glas dem Objekt eine ganz besondere Raum-wirkung und eine ganz besondere Gegenwart. Verschwunden war die Eintönigkeit der Oberfläche des Organs; das Fragment wirkte fast märchenhaft, als ob es in einer eigenen kleinen Welt existieren würde."*

Fragment of Life (necklace)
2004, blown glass, silver,
epoxy, steel, 3×2 in. (glass
piece), 14 in. (chain)
Collection of Hiko Mizuno,
Japan

*Fragment des Lebens
(Halskette)*
*2004, geblasenes Glas, Silber,
Epoxid, Stahl, Glaselement:
8×5,6 cm, Kette: 36 cm
Sammlung Hiko Mizuno, Japan*

Martina Mináriková
Dvur Králové nad Labem,
Czech Republic
Born: 1968, Bratislava, Slovakia

Education · Ausbildung
Stredná umelecko-priemyselná
škola, Bratislava, Slovakia
Vysoká škola umělecko-
průmyslová v Praze, Prague,
Czech Republic, 1993, M.A.

**Selected Collections ·
Sammlungen (Auswahl)**
Muzeum Skla a Bižuterie v
Jablonci nad Nisou, Jablonec
nad Nisou, Czech Republic;
Slovenská národná galéria,
Bratislava, Slovakia;
Severočeské muzeum v Liberci,
Liberec, Czech Republic;
Uměleckoprůmyslové museum
v Praze, Prague, Czech
Republic

"I admire pure, massive glass for its transparency and brightness, but in my work I use a different type of glass—glass that has come to me by accident, as a gift or as a found object. I have glass balls of different colors, some of them beaten up on the surface. These look especially majestic and mysterious to me. I discovered a big pot of old glass beads of various shapes in the loft of our house. These are things that cannot be found in shops today. My jewelry pieces represent the processes that occur day by day in the micro-world of the human body. With these little beads, full of light, my pieces come alive." ▪ *Ich bewundere reines massives Glas wegen seiner Transparenz und seinem Glanz. Für meine Arbeit verwende ich allerdings eine andere Art von Glas – Glas, das durch Zufall den Weg zu mir gefunden hat, als Geschenk oder als Fundobjekt. Ich habe Glaskugeln von verschiedenen Farben, einige haben angeschlagene Stellen an der Oberfläche. Diese sehen für mich besonders majestätisch und geheimnisvoll aus. Auf dem Speicher unseres Hauses habe ich einen großen Topf alter Glasperlen verschiedenster Formen gefunden. So etwas findet man heute nicht mehr in Geschäften. Meine Schmuckstücke stellen die Prozesse dar, die tagtäglich in der Mikrowelt des menschlichen Körpers ablaufen. Mit diesen kleinen Perlen voller Licht erwachen meine Schmuckstücke zum Leben."*

**Atom (brooch) from the
Creation series**
2000, pressed glass, silver,
Czech garnet,
3 ½×3½×1½ in.
Collection of the artist

*Atom (Brosche) der
Schöpfungs-Serie*
2000, Pressglas, Silber,
tschechischer Granat,
9×9×4 cm
Sammlung der Künstlerin

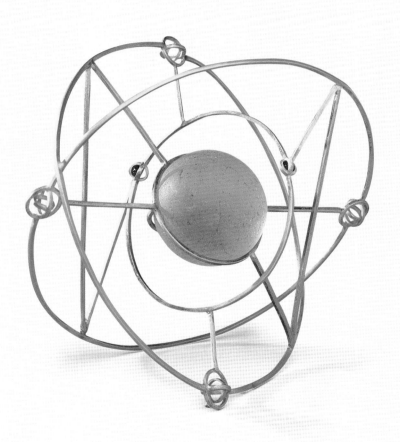

Kazuko Mitsushima
Osaka, Japan
Born: 1946, Hyogo
Prefecture, Japan

Education · Ausbildung
Konan University, Kobe,
Japan, 1968

**Selected Collections ·
Sammlungen (Auswahl)**
Corning Museum of Glass,
Corning, New York; Hiko
Mizuno College of Jewelry,
Tokyo, Japan; National
Museums of Scotland,
Edinburgh, Scotland; Shouha
Museum, Ise, Japan

"When molten glass swirls and flows wildly with a will of its own, the beauty of the movement excites me and inspires my ideas for jewelry. I am also enchanted by the sharp brilliance of broken glass. I do not like to add much else to the glass when I make a piece of glass jewelry. I approach my jewelry as art, and I try to show the individuality of the glass. I finish the piece naturally and simply. I believe that jewelry never completely comes to life until it is worn, so I am happy when the wearer says that my jewelry gives her energy. The energy I draw from molten glass has sustained me for over thirty years." ▪ *„Wenn geschmolzenes Glas wild herumwirbelt und fließt, ganz nach eigenem Willen, erregt mich die Schönheit der Bewegung und inspiriert mich zu Ideen für meinen Schmuck. Ich liebe auch die scharfe Brillanz von zerbrochenem Glas. Wenn ich ein Schmuckstück aus Glas herstelle, möchte ich zu dem Glas nicht mehr viel hinzufügen. Ich betrachte meinen Schmuck als Kunst und versuche damit, die Individualität des Glases darzustellen. Das fertige Stück ist natürlich und einfach. Ich bin der Meinung, dass Schmuck erst dann wirklich zum Leben erweckt wird, wenn er getragen wird. Deshalb bin ich froh, wenn die Trägerin sagt, dass mein Schmuck ihr Energie gibt. Die Energie, die ich aus geschmolzenem Glas gewinne, hat mich über dreißig Jahre genährt."*

Will of Glass (neckpiece)
2006, blown, cut, and etched
glass, 14×12×4 in.
Collection of the artist

Wille aus Glas (Halsschmuck)
2006, geblasenes, geschnittenes
und geätztes Glas, 36×30×10 cm
Sammlung der Künstlerin

Evert Nijland
Amsterdam, The Netherlands
Born: 1971, Oldenzaal,
The Netherlands

Education · Ausbildung
Sandberg Institute, Amsterdam, The Netherlands,
1996–97; Gerrit Rietveld
Academie, Amsterdam,
The Netherlands, 1989–95

**Selected Collections ·
Sammlungen (Auswahl)**
Nederlands Textielmuseum,
Tilburg, The Netherlands;
Schmuckmuseum Pforzheim,
Pforzheim, Germany; Stedelijk
Museum, Amsterdam, The
Netherlands; Victoria and
Albert Museum, London,
England

"Glass has become the most important material in my work. I started using glass five years ago when I embroidered small glass beads in different sizes and colors onto fabric. This enabled me to 'paint' with glass and to create a lively surface that could capture the reflection of light. During a recent stay in Venice, I was struck by that city's elusive atmosphere, its almost musical scenery, sometimes dazzlingly illuminated, at other times emerging from the shadows, but always closely connected to the sound, rhythm, and movement of the omnipresent water. I also became enthralled by antique Venetian glass beads. In the series of large lamp-blown neckpieces I created in Venice, I developed my own fresh interpretation of the traditional techniques of Venice's artisans." ▪ *„Glas ist zum wichtigsten Material in meiner Arbeit geworden. Ich habe vor etwa fünf Jahren begonnen, mit Glas zu arbeiten, als ich kleine Glasperlen verschiedener Größe und Farbe auf Stoff stickte. So konnte ich mit Glas ‚malen' und eine lebendige Oberfläche schaffen, in der sich das Licht spiegelte. Vor kurzem war ich in Venedig. Ich war beeindruckt von der schwer fassbaren Atmosphäre der Stadt, ihrer fast musikalischen Kulisse, manchmal strahlend erleuchtet, dann wieder aus dem Schatten hervortretend, aber immer eng verbunden mit dem Klang, dem Rhythmus und der Bewegung des allgegenwärtigen Wassers. Was mich auch faszinierte, waren die antiken venezianischen Glasperlen. Mit der Serie großen Halsschmucks aus vor der Lampe geblasenem Glas, die ich in Venedig kreierte, habe ich meine eigene neue Interpretation der traditionellen Technik venezianischer Künstler entwickelt."*

Fiori (necklace) from
the Venezia series
2006, flameworked glass,
glass beads, silk thread, gold,
24 in. (length)
Collection of the artist

*Fiori (Halsschmuck) aus
der Venedig-Serie
2006, geflammtes Glas,
Glasperlen, Seidenfaden, Gold,
60 cm (Länge)
Sammlung des Künstlers*

Ted Noten
Amsterdam, The Netherlands
Born: 1956, Tegelen,
The Netherlands

Education · Ausbildung
Gerrit Rietveld Academie,
Amsterdam, The Netherlands,
1986–90; Stadsakademie voor
de Beeldende Kunsten
Maastricht, Maastricht,
The Netherlands, 1983–86

**Selected Collections ·
Sammlungen (Auswahl)**
ARCO, Lisbon, Portugal; CODA
Museum (formerly Van Reekum
Museum), Apeldoorn, The
Netherlands; European Ceramic
Work Centre, 's-Hertogen-
bosch, The Netherlands; Fonds
national d'art contemporain,
Paris, France; Hiko Mizuno
College of Jewelry, Tokyo,
Japan; Musée des Arts Déco-
ratifs de Montréal, Montreal,
Canada; Espace Solidor,
Cagnes-sur-Mer, France;
Museum voor Moderne Kunst,
Arnhem, The Netherlands;
Nederlands Textielmuseum,
Tilburg, The Netherlands;
Rhode Island School of Design
Museum, Providence, Rhode
Island; Royal College of Art,
London, England; Schmuck-
museum Pforzheim, Pforzheim,
Germany; Stedelijk Museum,
Amsterdam, The Netherlands;
Stedelijk Museum 's-Hertogen-
bosch, 's-Hertogenbosch, The
Netherlands

"*The Real Love Bracelet* focuses on the theme of marriage: the longing for marriage and actual marriage. The bracelet is in two parts: the silver bracelet and the glass ball. Within the glass ball, there are two wedding rings waiting to be worn. When a couple marries, the glass is broken so the wedding rings can be put on. With every passing year, the rings shine more brilliantly." ▪ „Der Armreif der wahren Liebe *behandelt das Thema Ehe: das Sehnen nach der Ehe und die tatsächliche Ehe. Der Armreif besteht aus zwei Teilen: dem Silberreif und der Glaskugel. In der Glaskugel befinden sich zwei Eheringe, die darauf warten, getragen zu werden. Wenn ein Paar heiratet, wird das Glas zerbrochen, so dass die Ringe getragen werden können. Mit jedem Jahr, das vergeht, bekom-men die Ringe einen größeren Glanz.*"

The Real Love Bracelet
2005, blown glass, gold wedding
rings, silver, 4 in. (diam., glass),
2 ¼ in. (diam., bracelet)
Collection of the artist

Der Armreif der wahren Liebe
2005, geblasenes Glas,
goldene Eheringe, Silber,
Glaskugel: 10 cm (Dm),
Armreifs: 5,5 cm (Dm)
Sammlung des Künstlers

Emiko Oye
San Francisco, California
Born: 1974, Parma, Ohio

Education · Ausbildung
Syracuse University, Syracuse,
New York, 1992–97, B.F.A.

**Selected Collections ·
Sammlungen (Auswahl)**
Oakland Museum of California,
Oakland, California; National
Ornamental Metal Museum,
Memphis, Tennessee; Ohio
Craft Museum, Columbus, Ohio;
Society for Contemporary Craft,
Pittsburgh, Pennsylvania

"As an artist who works primarily with salvaged materials, I was egged on by the challenge of incorporating found glass into my jewelry. Glass presents itself as having the same alluring attributes—the possibility of color and transparency—as the found plastics I was using, but it also gives an immediate air of strength and elegance that plastics do not. The 'in the red: fashion*craft*art' tiara series utilizes recycled lab pipettes of Pyrex glass in an unforgiving, fragile, and difficult-to-alter form, requiring the precision and delicacy of a surgeon's hand to execute." ▪ *„Als Künstlerin, die vorwiegend mit aufgelesenen Materialien arbeitet, wurde ich von dem Ehrgeiz getrieben, auch gefundenes Glas in meinen Schmuck zu integrieren. Glas stellt sich mit den gleichen verführerischen Eigenschaften – der Möglichkeit von Farbe und Transparenz – dar, wie die gefundenen Kunststoffe, die ich verwendete, aber es vermittelt auch sofort eine Aura von Stärke und Eleganz, was Kunststoff nicht kann. Bei der ‚Im Roten: Mode*Handwerk* Kunst'- Diademserie werden recycelte Laborpinzetten aus Pyrexglas in kompromisslos fragiler und schwer zu ändernder Form verwendet, für deren Bearbeitung die Präzision und das Feingefühl einer Chirurgenhand erforderlich ist."*

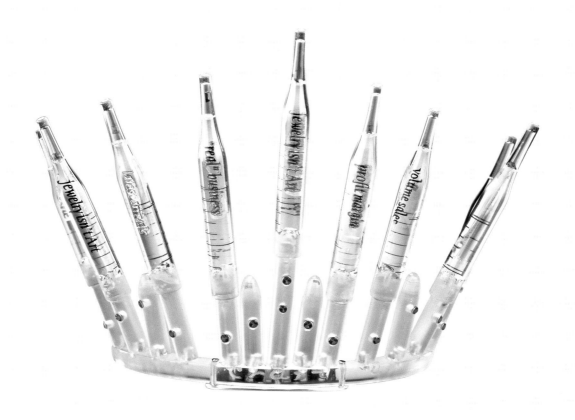

Craft Tiara from the "in the red: fashion*craft*art" series
2006, recycled glass, acrylic, silver, resin, transparency film, rubies, sapphires, synthetic ruby, gold, 4 1/2 × 2 1/2 × 4 in.
Collection of the artist

Handwerks-Diadem aus der „Im Roten: Mode*Handwerk* Kunst"-Serie
2006, recyceltes Glas, Acryl, Silber, Harz, transparente Folie, Rubine, Saphire, synthetischer Rubin, Gold, 11,4 × 6,4 × 10,2 cm
Sammlung der Künstlerin

Martin Papcún
Prague, Czech Republic
Born: 1979, Levice, Slovakia

Education · Ausbildung
Vysoká škola umělecko-
průmyslová v Praze, Prague,
Czech Republic, 2000–06;
SUPŠ, Turnov, Czech Repub-
lic, 1995–99; Integrovaná
Střední Škola, Turnov, Czech
Republic, 1994–95

**Selected Collections ·
Sammlungen (Auswahl)**
SUPŠ, Turnov, Czech Republic

"Glass is simultaneously tangible and intangible, reality and illusion. It leads us to awareness through its ability to create the 'in,' 'behind,' 'beyond'—it knows no boundaries or limits of purpose. Its being revolves more around the way it is perceived than around the matter that constitutes it. The possibility of balancing the perception of material certainly in time and in illusion is the reason behind my use of glass." ▪ *„Glas ist gleichzeitig greifbar und nicht greifbar, Realität und Illusion. Es schafft Erkenntnis durch seine Fähigkeit, das ‚Drinnen', ‚Dahinter' und ‚Darüber-Hinaus' zu schaffen – es kennt keine Grenzen oder Einschränkungen beim Verwendungszweck. Seine Existenz dreht sich mehr um seine Wahrnehmung als um die Materie, die es darstellt. Die Möglichkeit, die Wahrnehmung des Materials zwischen Zeit und Illusion auszubalancieren, ist der Grund, warum ich Glas verwende."*

Brooch
1999, borosilicate glass,
silver, brass, iron, PVC,
4 5/16×4 3/4×3/4 in.
Collection of the artist

Brosche
1999, Borosilikatglas, Silber,
Messing, Eisen, PVC,
11×12×2 cm
Sammlung des Künstlers

Joan Parcher
Providence, Rhode Island
Born: 1956, Pittsburgh,
Pennsylvania

Education · Ausbildung
Rhode Island School of
Design, Providence, Rhode
Island, 1986; Kent State University, Kent, Ohio, 1979, B.F.A.

**Selected Collections ·
Sammlungen (Auswahl)**
Cooper-Hewitt, National
Design Museum, Smithsonian
Institution, New York, New
York; Detroit Institute of Arts,
Detroit, Michigan; Musée des
Arts Décoratifs de Montréal,
Montreal, Canada; Museum of
Arts & Design, New York, New
York

"I grew up near a surreal and brilliant landscape. This was a wide, open area where many millions of rejected lenses from a glass factory were left. The earth sparkled with all these vitreous pieces. I still see the sparkles. They are like the phosphenes that glitter when I close my eyes tightly and rub them. I enjoy making jewelry and trying to capture and make sense of these sparkles, these floating bits of light. Jewelry gives pleasure. I appreciate the wonderful fun that I have in being able to make something that gives so much pleasure." ▪ *„Ich bin in der Nähe einer herrlichen, surrealen Landschaft aufgewachsen. Es war ein weites, offenes Gelände, auf dem viele Millionen Linsen, die Ausschussware einer Glasfabrik, zurückgeblieben waren. Die Erde glitzerte von all diesen Glasstückchen. Ich sehe immer noch das Funkeln vor mir. Es ist wie die Lichterscheinungen im Auge, die auftreten, wenn ich meine Augen ganz fest schließe und sie dann reibe. Es macht mir Spaß, Schmuckstücke zu kreieren und zu versuchen, dieses Funkeln, diese fließenden Fetzen Licht einzufangen und ihnen einen Sinn zu geben. Schmuck bringt Freude. Ich schätze das wunderbare Vergnügen, das ich darüber empfinde, in der Lage zu sein, etwas zu schaffen, das Freude bereitet."*

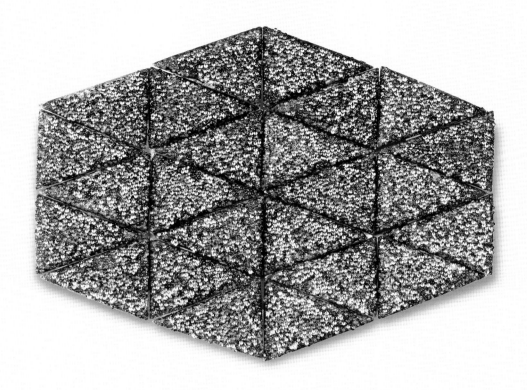

Phosphene Brooch
2006, reflective glass, enamel,
copper, silver, 3½×2½×¼ in.
Collection of the artist

Lichterscheinungsbrosche
2006, Spiegelglas, Emaille, Kupfer,
Silber, 9×6,4×1 cm
Sammlung der Künstlerin

Francesco Pavan
Padua, Italy
Born: 1937, Padua, Italy

Education · Ausbildung
Istituto Statale d'Arte Pietro
Selvatico, Padua, Italy, 1955

**Selected Collections ·
Sammlungen (Auswahl)**
Inge Asenbaum Collection,
Vienna, Austria; Kunstgewerbe-
museum, Berlin, Germany;
Landesmuseum Joanneum,
Graz, Austria; Musée des Arts
Décoratifs, Paris, France;
Museum of Fine Arts, Houston,
Houston, Texas; National
Museums of Scotland, Edin-
burgh, Scotland; Die Neue
Sammlung, Staatliches
Museum für Angewandte
Kunst, Design in der Pinakothek
der Moderne, on permanent
loan from the Danner Founda-
tion, Munich, Germany;
Schmuckmuseum Pforzheim,
Pforzheim, Germany

"Unlike freestanding sculpture that can be viewed from all sides, jewelry, as a result of its relationship with the body, can be seen only from limited perspectives. I have tried to get around this limitation on perspectives by working with primary shapes that are recognizable at once—such as the cube and the cylinder—and by using glass to create transparent and, consequently, open shapes that can be read from multiple perspectives and that allow a glimpse of the interior of the object. Each piece starts with an acknowledgment of its knowable, basic shape, but freely moves on to seemingly limitless transformations of form and space." ▪ *„Im Gegensatz zu frei stehenden Skulpturen, die man von allen Seiten anschauen kann, kann man Schmuck aufgrund seiner Beziehung zum Körper nur aus einer begrenzten Perspektive betrachten. Ich habe versucht, diese Einschränkung der Perspektive zu überwinden, indem ich mit Urformen arbeite, die sofort zu erkennen sind – wie z.B. Würfel und Zylinder – und indem ich Glas verwende, um transparente und somit offene Formen zu schaffen, die von verschiedensten Perspektiven aus betrachtet werden können und zudem noch einen Blick ins Innere des Objekts gewähren. Jedes Stück beginnt mit der Anerkennung seiner bekannten Grundform, bewegt sich dann aber frei hin zu scheinbar grenzenlosen Veränderungen von Form und Raum."*

Trasparenze 1 (brooch)
2000, plate glass, white gold,
2³/₄×4¹/₂×1 in.
Collection of Nancy Olnick,
New York

Trasparenze 1 (Brosche)
2000, Flachglas, Weißgold,
7,1×11,5×2,6 cm
Sammlung Nancy Olnick,
New York

Ruudt Peters
Amsterdam, The Netherlands /
Stockholm, Sweden
Born: 1950, Naaldwijk,
The Netherlands

Education · Ausbildung
Gerrit Rietveld Academie,
Amsterdam, The Netherlands,
1970–74

**Selected Collections ·
Sammlungen (Auswahl)**
CODA (formerly Van Reekum
Museum), Apeldoorn, The
Netherlands; Cooper-Hewitt
National Design Museum,
Smithsonian Institution, New
York, New York; Gemeente-
museum, Arnhem, The Nether-
lands; Hiko Mizuno College
of Jewelry, Tokyo, Japan;
Stedelijk Museum 's-Herto-
genbosch, 's-Hertogenbosch,
The Netherlands; Musée des
Arts Décoratifs, Paris, France;
Museum für Angewandte
Kunst, Vienna, Austria; Museum
of Arts & Design, New York,
New York; Philadelphia Museum
of Modern Art, Philadelphia,
Pennsylvania; Schmuck-
museum Pforzheim,
Pforzheim, Germany; Stedelijk
Museum, Amsterdam, The
Netherlands

"Glass, to me, represents a physical and philosophical void." ▪ *„Glas ist für mich ein physikalischer und philosophischer Hohlraum.“*

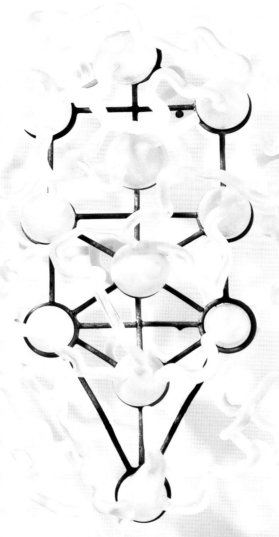

Sefiroth Metatron (brooch)
2006, blown laboratory glass,
silver, 5½×4×2 in.
Collection of the artist

Sefiroth Metatron (Brosche)
2006, geblasenes Laborglas,
Silber, 14×10×5 cm
Sammlung des Künstlers

Michael Petry
London, England
Born: 1960, El Paso, Texas

Education · Ausbildung
Middlesex University, London,
England, 2004–present;
London Guildhall University,
London, England, 1999, M.A.;
Rice University, Houston,
Texas, 1981, B.A.

**Selected Collections ·
Sammlungen (Auswahl)**
British Museum, London,
England; Kunst- und Ausstel-
lungshalle der Bundesrepublik
Deutschland, Bonn, Germany;
Leopold-Hoesch-Museum,
Düren, Germany; Museum
Bellerive, Zurich, Switzerland;
Museum of Arts & Design,
New York, New York; Museum
of Fine Arts, Houston, Houston,
Texas; New Art Gallery Walsall,
Walsall, England; Rogaland
Kunstmuseum, Stavanger,
Norway

"At the start of this millennium I began working with blown glass in a number of site-specific projects. Therefore, I have come to glass with a very particular and demanding point of view; I want it to look a certain way, to do certain things, to hang in a certain way. Since I collaborate with the hot workers, I usually insist we try something even if they think it won't work—unless they say it is dangerous, and then I listen. Smash! Crunch! Ouch! Ideas can also shatter...." ▪ *„Zu Beginn dieses Jahrtausends habe ich begonnen, bei einigen standortspezifischen Projekten mit geblasenem Glas zu arbeiten. Daher bin ich mit einer ganz besonderen und sehr anspruchsvollen Einstellung an das Material Glas herangegangen; ich will, dass es ein ganz bestimmtes Aussehen hat, ganz bestimmte Dinge tut, in einer ganz bestimmten Weise hängt. Seit ich mit den Hitzearbeitern zusammenarbeite, bestehe ich in der Regel darauf, etwas Neues zu probieren, auch wenn sie der Meinung sind, dass es nicht funktioniert – außer sie sagen, dass es gefährlich ist, und dann horche ich auf das ‚Brechen. ... Blasen. ... Bersten. ... Ups!' Auch Ideen können zerplatzen. ..."*

The Treasure of Memory
2000, blown glass beads,
yachting rope, aluminum wall
mounts, approx. 50 feet
Collection of the Museum of
Arts & Design, New York,
donated by Devin Borden,
Hiram Butler Gallery, Houston

Der Schatz der Erinnerung
2000, geblasene Glaskugeln,
Schiffstau, Wandaufhängung
aus Aluminium, ca.15,25 m
Sammlung des Museum of
Arts & Design, New York,
gestiftet von Devin Borden,
Hiram Butler Gallery, Houston

Katja Prins
Amsterdam, The Netherlands
Born: 1970, Haarlem,
The Netherlands

Education · Ausbildung
Gerrit Rietveld Academie,
Amsterdam, The Netherlands,
1993–97; M.T.S. Vakschool,
Schoonhoven, The Netherlands,
1989–93

**Selected Collections ·
Sammlungen (Auswahl)**
CODA Museum (formerly Van
Reekum Museum), Apeldoorn,
The Netherlands; European
Ceramic Workcentre,
's-Hertogenbosch, The
Netherlands; Glasmuseum
Alter Hof Herding, Coesfeld-
Lette, Germany; Museum voor
Moderne Kunst Arnhem,
Arnhem, The Netherlands;
Nationaal Glasmuseum
Leerdam, Leerdam, The
Netherlands; Nederlands
Textielmuseum, Tilburg,
The Netherlands

"With these works I want to tell a story about the body—the body as an instrument/ machine and instruments/machines as extensions of the body. These works are also about my fascination with the way we manipulate our bodies, the fact that these days we can change them, sculpt them—our bodies as extensions of our minds. In my jewelry, the glass parts are abstractions of human body parts. In some I have also used sealing wax. Sealing wax has some of the same properties as glass: for one, it freezes in the midst of movement. Because of its color and history, it has other references, as well. My hope is that the viewer can discover his own stories in my work. Therefore I try to steer clear of too many explanations. My shapes and materials are never unequivocal. They can be interpreted in different ways." ▪ *„Mit diesen Arbeiten möchte ich eine Geschichte über den Körper erzählen – der Körper als Instrument/Maschine, Instrumente/ Maschinen als Fortsetzungen des Körpers. Diese Arbeiten handeln aber auch davon, wie fasziniert ich von der Art bin, wie wir unsere Körper manipulieren, von der Tatsache, dass wir sie heutzutage verändern, formen können – unsere Körper sind Fortsetzungen unseres Denkens. Bei meinen Schmuckstücken sind die Teile aus Glas abstrakte Ausführungen menschlicher Körperteile. Bei manchen habe ich auch Siegellack verwendet. Siegellack hat einige Eigenschaften mit Glas gemeinsam: Zum einen erstarrt es in der Bewegung. Aufgrund seiner Farbe und seiner Geschichte hat es auch andere Bezüge. Meine Hoffnung ist, dass der Betrachter seine eigene Geschichte in meiner Arbeit wiederfindet. Deshalb versuche ich, möglichst wenig zu erklären. Die Formen und Materialien, die ich verwende, sind niemals eindeutig. Sie können auf unterschiedliche Weise verstanden werden.“*

Brooch
2005, blown glass, silver,
sealing wax, 2 ¾ in. (width)
Collection of the artist

Brosche
2005, geblasenes Glas, Silber,
Siegellack, 7 cm (Breite)
Sammlung der Künstlerin

Wendy Ramshaw
London, England
Born: 1939, Sunderland,
England

Education · Ausbildung

Central School of Art and
Design, London, England,
1969–70; University of Reading,
Reading, England, 1960–61;
College of Art and Industrial
Design, Newcastle-upon-Tyne,
England, 1956–60

**Selected Collections ·
Sammlungen (Auswahl)**

Art Gallery of South Australia,
Adelaide, Australia; British
Museum, London, England;
Cooper-Hewitt, National
Design Museum, Smithsonian
Institution, New York, New
York; Corning Museum of
Glass, Corning, New York;
Kundstindustrimuseet, Oslo,
Norway; Musée des Arts
Décoratifs, Paris, France;
Museum für Kunst und
Gewerbe, Hamburg, Germany;
Museum of Arts & Design,
New York, New York; Museum
of Fine Arts, Boston, Boston,
Massachusetts; Museum of
Fine Arts, Houston, Houston,
Texas; National Gallery of
Victoria, Melbourne, Australia;
National Museum of Modern
Art, Kyoto, Japan; Die Neue
Sammlung, Staatliches Muse-
um für Angewandte Kunst,
Design in der Pinakothek der
Moderne, on permanent loan
from the Danner Foundation,
Munich, Germany; Philadel-
phia Museum of Art, Philadel-
phia, Pennsylvania; Royal
Museum, Edinburgh, Scotland;
Schmuckmuseum Pforzheim,
Pforzheim, Germany; Stedelijk
Museum, Amsterdam, The
Netherlands; Victoria and
Albert Museum, London,
England

"The inspiration for the shape of the tears in this necklace came from a segment of mauve glass with a droplet-like shape that was once part of a Victorian chandelier. This water-shaped form was recreated in luminous glass in shades of blue and green. The double-stranded necklace is strung to appear like a cascade of water drops. Over one hundred of these glass droplets are hung on the steel of the necklace, achieving an apparently random effect. The necklace expresses my feelings for the beautiful Dora Maar, who, according to the visual records of Picasso, wept many tears. The beauty of the colors may detract from her sadness and crying. Dora Maar's tears are lifted into another realm, as one might find in a fairy tale, that does not necessarily have a happy ending." ▪ *„Inspiriert wurde ich zu der Form der Tränen für diese Hals-kette von einem Segment aus malvefarbigem Glas in Tropfenform, das einmal Teil eines viktorianischen Kronleuchters war. Diese vom Wasser bestimmte Form wurde in leuchtendem Glas in verschiedenen Grün- und Blauschattierungen nachgebildet. Die doppelreihige Halskette ist so aufgezogen, dass sie wie eine Kaskade von Wassertropfen wirkt. Mehr als hundert dieser Glastropfen hängen am Stahldraht der Kette, wodurch ein Effekt der Zufälligkeit erreicht wird. Mit der Halskette bringe ich meine Gefühle für die schöne Dora Maar zum Ausdruck, die Picassos Bildern zufolge viele, viele Tränen vergossen hat. Die Schönheit der Farben mag von ihrer Traurigkeit und ihrem Weinen ablenken. Dora Maars Tränen werden in ein anderes Reich gehoben, wie in einem Märchen, aber das muss nicht unbedingt ein gutes Ende bedeuten."*

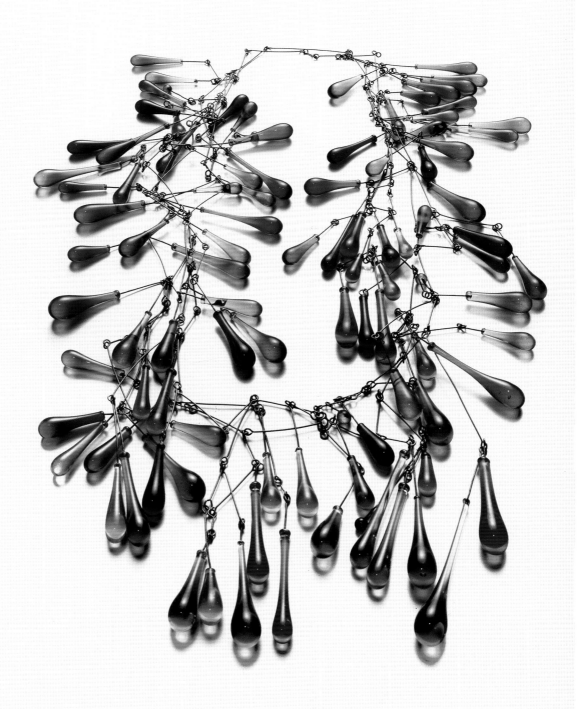

Chain of Glass Tears for
Weeping Woman (necklace)
from the Picasso's
Ladies series
1989/1998, lamp-worked
glass, blackened steel,
16⅛×3½×¼ in.
Collection of the Museum of
Arts & Design, New York,
gift of Barbara Tober, 2005

*Kette aus Glastränen der
weinenden Frau (Halskette)
aus der Serie „Picasso's
Ladies"
1989/1998, vor der Lampe
geblasenes Glas,
geschwärzter Stahl,
41×8,9×0,6 cm
Sammlung des Museum
of Arts & Design, New York.
Schenkung von Barbara
Tober, 2005*

Piergiuliano Reveane
Venice, Italy
Born: 1943, Venice, Italy

Education · Ausbildung
L'Istituto d'Arte di Venezia,
Venice, Italy, 1960–64

**Selected Collections ·
Sammlungen (Auswahl)**
Inge Asenbaum Collection,
Vienna, Austria; Museum
Boijmans Van Beuningen,
Rotterdam, The Netherlands;
Schmuckmuseum Pforzheim,
Pforzheim, Germany

"Geometry appears to me to be 'the inspiration' for all forms and even for the underlying structure of the figure and of nature. It might seem, then, that my imaginative world would be limited by a rigorous and precisely defined 'Euclidean' order. However, within this order, I conduct personal research into form—or better—into forms, without becoming imprisoned in 'ideological or aesthetic cages.' Realizing that 'forms come from forms,' I am involved in never-ending research that continually yields astonishing and unpredictable results." ▪ „Geometrie ist für mich die ‚Inspiration' für jede Form und sogar die der Figur und der Natur zugrunde liegende Struktur. Dies mag den Eindruck erwecken, dass meine Vorstellungswelt durch eine strenge, genau definierte ‚euklidische' Ordnung begrenzt ist. Aber innerhalb dieser Ordnung führe ich persönliche Untersuchen der Form oder besser der Formen durch, ohne mich durch einen ‚ideologischen oder ästhetischen Käfig' einengen zu lassen. Mit der Erkenntnis, dass ‚Formen aus Formen entstehen', befinde ich mich in nie endenden Forschungen, die immer wieder neue erstaunliche und unvorhersehbare Resultate hervorbringen."

Vetrata I (bracelet)
2004, antique window glass,
gold, diamonds, zinc, 6 ¾ in.
Collection of the artist

Vetrata I (Armschmuck)
2004, antikes Fensterglas,
Gold, Diamanten, Zink, 17 cm
Sammlung des Künstlers

Marianne Schliwinski
Munich, Germany
Born: 1944, St. Peter-Ording,
Germany

Education · Ausbildung
Schule für Bau und Gestaltung, Munich, Germany,
1972–74

**Selected Collections ·
Sammlungen (Auswahl)**
Corning Museum of Glass,
Corning, New York; Kunstgewerbemuseum, Berlin,
Germany; Münchner Stadtmuseum, Munich, Germany;
Museum für Angewandte
Kunst, Frankfurt, Germany; Die
Neue Sammlung, Staatliches
Museum für Angewandte
Kunst, Design in der Pinakothek
der Moderne, on permanent
loan from the Danner Foundation, Munich, Germany;
Schmuckmuseum Pforzheim,
Pforzheim, Germany;
Württembergisches Landesmuseum, Stuttgart, Germany

"Glass is more than just a chemical formula. It is a fascinating substance that has often inspired the artistic avant-garde to flights of fancy. It has a mystique capable of conveying knowledge, truth, and, of course, lucidity. This can be experienced in my jewelry. My pieces emerge like elusive visions that are consigned to recollection—to the past, which I invoke and which safeguards my images." ▪ *„Glas ist mehr als eine chemische Formel. Es ist eine faszinierende Substanz, die die Avantgarde der Künstler schon häufig zu Höhenflügen der Fantasie inspiriert hat. Es hat etwas Geheimnisvolles, wodurch es Wissen, Wahrheit und natürlich Klarheit vermitteln kann. Das kann man auch an meinen Schmuckstücken erfahren. Meine Arbeiten erscheinen als schwer fassbare Visionen, die auf Erinnerung ausgerichtet sind – auf die Vergangenheit, die ich heraufbeschwöre und die meine Bilder schützt."*

Brooch
2002, found beach glass,
silver, plastic, printed tin,
2 ¾ × 1 ¾ × ¼ in.
Private collection, Germany

Brosche
2002, gefundenes Strandglas,
Silber, Plastik, bedruckte Dose,
6,8 × 4,7 × 0,6 cm
Privatsammlung, Deutschland

Bernhard Schobinger
Richterswil, Switzerland
Born: 1946, Zurich, Switzerland

Education · Ausbildung
Goldsmith apprenticeship,
Zurich, Switzerland, 1963–67;
Johannes Itten Vorkurs,
Kunstgewerbeschule, Zurich,
Switzerland, 1962–63

Collections · Sammlungen
Aargauer Kunsthaus, Aarau,
Switzerland; Art Collection of
H. M. Queen Beatrix of Holland,
Gemeentemuseum Den Haag,
The Hague, The Netherlands;
Grassimuseum, Leipzig,
Germany; Hiko Mizuno College
of Jewelry, Tokyo, Japan;
Kunstsammlung des Bundes
der Schweizerischen Eidge-
nossenschaft, Bern, Switzer-
land; Musée des Arts Décoratifs,
Paris, France; Museum Bellerive,
Zurich, Switzerland; Museum
Boijmans Van Beuningen,
Rotterdam, The Netherlands;
Museum of Fine Arts, Boston,
Boston, Massachusetts;
Museum of Fine Arts, Houston,
Houston, Texas; Die Neue
Sammlung, Staatliches Museum
für Angewandte Kunst, Design
in der Pinakothek der Moderne,
on permanent loan from the
Danner Foundation, Munich,
Germany; Rhode Island
School of Design Museum,
Providence, Rhode Island;
Royal College of Art, London,
England; Schweizerisches
Landesmuseum, Zurich,
Switzerland; Stedelijk Museum,
Amsterdam, The Netherlands;
Württembergisches Landes-
museum, Stuttgart, Germany;
Zuger Kunsthaus, Zug,
Switzerland

"Probably (given that early childhood memory tends to turn into a nebulous 'fog') this was my first encounter with glass: as my tiny fingertip glided across the edge of a cracked window, I suddenly felt a stabbing pain. Moments later, blood oozed from my wounded skin. From that time on, I was aware of glass's hidden danger. The wonder in glass came to me through the colorful church windows that I saw when I was growing up. Equally miraculous were the stained glass windows in my parents' house. As the sun rose over Lake Zurich, its rays would penetrate the colorful windows and cast lively, kaleidoscopic patterns onto the walls, floors, and ceilings throughout the house. This beauty was not tangible; it was ephemeral and immaterial. Still later, in the summer of 1980, I saw West Broadway, at that time the strip for Punk and New Wave advocates in New York City, ablaze under the mid-day sun. Embedded in the almost molten black tar were myriads of glittering splinters of glass—diamonds of a different kind—things considered to be without value revealing their hidden beauty." ▪ *„Es wird meine erste Erfahrung mit Glas gewesen sein, denn die Erinnerung verliert sich im Dunstkreis der frühesten Kindheit, aber ich weiß noch genau, wie ich erschrocken war von einem heftigen Stich, als die kleine Fingerkuppe über die Kante des gesprungenen Fensters glitt. Kurz darauf trat Blut aus der geschlitzten Oberfläche der Haut. Von diesem Moment an war mir die unsichtbare Gefahr bewusst. Dieses geheimnisvolle Material besaß eine seltsame Ambivalenz zwischen Gefahr und Wunderbar. Das Wunderbare zeigte sich mir in den farbigen Fenstern der Kirchen, die ich später zu sehen bekam. Denselben Zauber vollbrachten die Wappenscheiben in der Wohnung des Elternhauses. Wenn jeweils die Sonne über dem Zürichsee aufging, wurde das Licht durch die farbigen Scheiben auf Wände, Böden und Decken geworfen, und bunte, leuchtende Flecken wanderten in der Folge durch die Räume wie in einem riesigen Kaleidoskop. Das Wesen jener Schönheit war nicht greifbar, sondern ephemerer und immaterieller Natur. Zwei Dekaden später, im Sommer 1980, NYC. Der West Broadway, die damalige Meile von Punk und New Wave, glüht in der Mittagshitze. Eingewalzt in den aufgeweichten, schwarzen Straßenbelag, glitzern Myriaden Splitter von Glas und Rückspiegeln wie Diamanten einer Gegenwelt. Die geheime Schönheit des Wertlosen."*

Poison-bottle Bracelet
2003, glass from Swiss poison
bottle, paper label, gold urushi
lacquer, 2⅝×3⅛ in.
Collection of the artist

Giftflaschen-Armreif
2003, Glas von Schweizer
Giftflasche mit Papieretikette,
Urushi-Streugoldlack,
6,6×7,9 cm
Sammlung des Künstlers

Joyce Scott
Baltimore, Maryland
Born: 1948, Baltimore,
Maryland

Education · Ausbildung
Instituto Allende, San Miguel
de Allende, Mexico, 1971;
Maryland Institute College of
Art, Baltimore, Maryland, 1970

**Selected Collections ·
Sammlungen (Auswahl)**
Baltimore Museum of Art,
Baltimore, Maryland; Brooklyn
Museum of Art, Brooklyn, New
York; Corning Museum of
Glass, Corning, New York;
Detroit Institute of Arts, Detroit,
Michigan; Mint Museum of Art,
Charlotte, North Carolina;
Musée des Beaux-Arts de
Montréal, Canada; Museum of
Fine Arts, Houston, Houston,
Texas; Museum of Arts &
Design, New York, New York;
Newark Museum, Newark,
New Jersey; Philadelphia
Museum of Art, Philadelphia,
Pennsylvania; Racine Art
Museum, Racine, Wisconsin;
Rhode Island School of Design
Museum, Providence, Rhode
Island; Smithsonian American
Art Museum, Renwick Gallery,
Washington, D.C.; Stedelijk
Museum 's-Hertogenbosch,
's-Hertogenbosch, The
Netherlands

"The creation of art is my testimony to life. I am addicted to the desire to luxuriate in beauty, to take pride in making it and looking at it. Glass affords me this submission. As an old hippy still searching for translucency in mind and deed, working with blown/manipulated glass and beads is bringing me closer to my goal." ▪ *„Kunstwerke zu schaffen, ist mein Zeugnis des Lebens. Ich bin dem Verlangen verfallen, in Schönheit zu baden, stolz darauf zu sein, Schönheit zu kreieren und sie anzuschauen. Glas ermöglicht mir dies. Als alter Hippie, der immer noch nach der Durchsichtigkeit von Gedanken und Taten sucht, bringt mich die Arbeit mit geblasenem/bearbeitetem Glas und Perlen meinem Ziel näher."*

Water Coral (neckpiece)
2006, flameworked glass,
glass beads, coral,
8 ½×12×3 in.
Collection of the artist

Wasserkoralle (Halsschmuck)
2006, lampengeblasenes
Glas, Glasperlen, Koralle,
21,5×30,5×7,6 cm
Sammlung der Künstlerin

Sondra Sherman
San Diego, California
Born: 1958, Philadelphia,
Pennsylvania

Education · Ausbildung
Akademie der Bildenden
Künste München, Munich,
Germany, 1990; Tyler School
of Art, Temple University,
Philadelphia, Pennsylvania,
1980

**Selected Collections ·
Sammlungen (Auswahl)**
Museum of Fine Arts, Boston,
Boston, Massachusetts; Myers
School of Art, The University
of Akron, Ohio; Philadelphia
Museum of Art, Philadelphia,
Pennsylvania; Rhode Island
School of Design Museum,
Providence, Rhode Island;
Smithsonian American Art
Museum, Washington, D.C.

"The visual qualities of transparency and reflection give an energy and presence to jewelry that transcends its small scale. These qualities are traditionally incorporated in jewelry in the form of precious gemstones. I frequently choose to use glass rather than gemstones in order to assert the artistic value of the piece rather than the intrinsic value of its materials. *Gertrude and Alice* utilizes antique crystal chandelier pendants as gender symbols in an abstract form of portraiture. The chandelier crystals are faceted to multiply reflections similar to the way gemstones are, and they also have an air of elegance because of their association with chandeliers, while their shapes function as a reference to sexuality. The relative lightness of glass allowed me to give emphasis to the symbolic role of the shapes and materials." ▪ *„Die visuellen Qualitäten von Lichtdurchlässigkeit und Reflektion geben Schmuck eine Energie und eine Präsenz, die über seinen begrenzten Rahmen hinausgehen. Diese Qualitäten werden im Schmuck traditionell durch wertvolle Edelsteine verkörpert. Ich wähle häufig Glas statt Edelsteine, um den künstlerischen Wert des Schmuckstücks anstelle des eigentlichen Wertes des Materials geltend zu machen. Bei* Gertrude und Alice *verwende ich Anhänger von einem antiken Kristallkronleuchter als Geschlechtssymbole in Form abstrakter Porträts. Die Kristalle des Kronleuchters haben einen Facettenschliff, so dass sie das Licht mehrfach reflektieren, ähnlich wie Edelsteine. Außerdem gibt ihnen die Verbindung zum Kronleuchter eine elegante Aura, während ihre Form einen Bezug zur Sexualität herstellt. Das relative geringe Gewicht von Glas hat es mir ermöglicht, die Bedeutung von Form und Material zu betonen."*

**Gertrude and Alice
("hers-n-hers" pendant set
with presentation box)**
2000, chandelier crystal,
mirror, silver, gold, tourma-
lines, 8×12×1⁵/₁₆ in.
Collection of Sharon M.
Campbell, United States

*Gertrude und Alice
(„Für sie und sie"-Anhängerset
in Präsentationsbox)*
*2000, Kronleuchterkristall,
Spiegel, Silber, Gold,
Turmaline, 20,3×30,5×3,2 cm
Sammlung Sharon M.
Campbell, USA*

Jiří Šibor
Brno, Czech Republic
Born: 1966, Brno,
Czech Republic

Education · Ausbildung
Střední škola pro zpracování
kovu, Kuřim, Czech Republic,
1989–91; Střední odborné
učiliště pro zpracování kovu,
Kuřim, Czech Republic,
1981–84

**Selected Collections ·
Sammlungen (Auswahl)**
Moravská galerie v Brně, Brno,
Czech Republic; Umělecko-
průmyslové muzeum v Praze,
Prague, Czech Republic;
Muzeum Skla a Bižuterie v
Jablonci nad Nisou, Jablonec
nad Nisou, Czech Republic;
Severočeské muzeum v
Liberci, Liberec, Czech
Republic

"I have always felt challenged to try different approaches to exploiting glass's fundamental properties—its fragility and its reflectiveness. To make my brooches, I use rods of lead glass in a broad range of colors, fashioning smaller pieces from these rods with the help of rotary diamond tools. The stainless steel structure that I use to hold the glass components in my brooches protects those components and, at the same time, subtly reflects light." ▪ *„Ich wollte schon immer verschiedene Ansätze ausprobieren, um die grundlegenden Eigenschaften von Glas zu ergründen – seine Zerbrechlichkeit und sein Reflexionsvermögen. Für meine Broschen habe ich Stäbchen aus Bleiglas in verschiedensten Farben verwendet und aus diesen mit Hilfe von Diamantwerkzeugen kleinere Stücke hergestellt. Die Edelstahlkonstruktion, mit der die Glaskomponenten in meinen Broschen zusammen-gehalten werden, schützt diese Komponenten und reflektiert gleichzeitig ganz zart das Licht."*

Brooch
2004, cut glass, stainless steel,
2 ³/₈ × 1 ½ × ¾ in.
Collection of the artist

Brosche
2004, Schnittglas, Edelstahl,
6 × 3,8 × 2 cm
Sammlung des Künstlers

Markéta Šílená
Turnov, Czech Republic
Born: 1957, Semily,
Czech Republic

Education · Ausbildung
Vysoká škola umělecko-
průmyslová, Prague, Czech
Republic, 1976–82;
Střední uměleckoprůmyslová
škola sklářská, Železný Brod,
Czech Republic, 1972–76

**Selected Collections ·
Sammlungen (Auswahl)**
Moravská galerie v Brně, Brno,
Czech Republic; Le Musée
du Verre, Sars-Poteries, France;
Muzeum Českého ráje v
Turnově, Turnov, Czech Repub-
lic; Muzeum Skla a
Bižuterie v Jablonci nad Nisou,
Jablonec nad Nisou, Czech
Republic; National Liberty
Museum, Philadelphia, Pennsyl-
vania; Severočeské muzeum v
Liberci, Liberec, Czech Republic;
Uměleckoprůmyslové muzeum
v Praze, Prague, Czech Republic

"I think of my jewelry as sculpture, yet its relationship with the viewer is more immediate than is sculpture's, and the person wearing my jewelry becomes a co-creator of my art. The combination of glass and metal—two totally different types of physical matter—intrigues me. Sometimes this combination results in an equilibrium or balance between the two materials, sometimes in a duel, or confrontation. The oscillation between glass—with its translucence, insinuation, and mysteriousness—and metal—with its cold brightness, rigidity, and precision—is my constant source of inspiration." ▪

„Ich betrachte meinen Schmuck als Skulptur, aber seine Beziehung zum Betrachter ist eine unmittelbarere als bei einer Skulptur, und die Person, die meinen Schmuck trägt, wird zum Mitschöpfer meiner Kunst. Die Kombination von Glas und Metall – zwei völlig verschiedenen physikalischen Materien – fasziniert mich. Manchmal führt diese Kombination zu einem Gleichgewicht oder Ausgleich zwischen den beiden Materialien, manchmal zu einem Duell oder zur Konfrontation. Die Schwingung zwischen Glas – mit seiner Lichtdurchlässigkeit, versteckten Andeutungen und Rätsel-haftigkeit – und Metall – mit seiner kalten Helligkeit, Starrheit und Genauigkeit – ist für mich eine ständige Quelle der Inspiration."

Brooch
2005, cast glass,
white brass, 4 1/4 in.
Collection of the artist

Brosche
2005, gegossenes Glas,
weißes Messing, 10,8 cm
Sammlung der Künstlerin

Peter Skubic
St. Michael, Austria
Born: 1935, Gornji-
Milanovac, Serbia

Education · Ausbildung
Akademie für Angewandte
Kunst in Wien, Vienna, Austria,
1954–1958; Fachschule für
Metallkunstgewerbe in Steyr,
Steyr, Austria, 1952–1954

**Selected Collections ·
Sammlungen (Auswahl)**
Badisches Landesmuseum,
Karlsruhe, Germany; Kunst-
gewerbemuseum, Berlin,
Germany; Museum Boijmans
Van Beuningen Rotterdam,
The Netherlands; Museum des
20. Jahrhunderts, Vienna,
Austria; National Museum of
Modern Art, Kyoto, Japan;
Neue Galerie der Stadt Linz,
Linz, Austria; Die Neue
Sammlung, Staatliches Muse-
um für Angewandte Kunst,
Design in der Pinakothek der
Moderne, on permanent loan
from the Danner Foundation,
Munich, Germany; Öster-
reichisches Museum für Ange-
wandte Kunst, Vienna, Austria;
Schmuckmuseum Pforzheim,
Pforzheim, Germany

"I made this brooch during a jewelry symposium in Vitorial, Spain. It is made from broken glass from an exhibition vitrine. I dug out the pyrite with my own hands from a mine in the Basque country. Both glass and steel are synthetic, or manmade, materials, and they bear testimony to man's creativity. Consequently, I am more interested in them than in naturally occurring precious gems. For me, selection of an appropriate material and the related technical process for working it is the starting point for decisions about form and content. It is my personal, psychological, and philosophical attitude that has to emanate from the materials I use." ▪ *„Ich habe diese Brosche während eines Schmucksymposiums in Vitorial, Spanien, gemacht. Sie ist aus dem zerbrochenen Glas einer Ausstellungsvitrine hergestellt. Das Pyrit habe ich mit eigenen Händen aus einem Bergwerk im Baskenland ausgegraben. Sowohl das Glas als auch der Stahl sind synthetische bzw. von Menschen hergestellte Materialien, sind Zeugnis der Kreativität des Menschen. Deshalb interessieren sie mich mehr als die in der Natur vorkommenden Edelsteine. Für mich ist die Wahl des geeigneten Materials und des entsprechenden Bearbeitungsverfahrens der Ausgangspunkt für Form und Inhalt. Es ist meine persönliche, psychologische und philosophische Haltung, die das von mir verwendete Material ausstrahlen muss."*

Brooch
2004, window-glass frag-
ments, gold leaf, pyrite, stainless steel, 3 3/4 × 2 × 1/2 in.
Collection of the artist

Brosche
*2004, Scherben von Fenster-
glas, Blattgold, Pyrit, Edelstahl,
9,6×5,2×1,6 cm*
Sammlung des Künstlers

Kiff Slemmons

Chicago, Illinois
Born: 1944, Maxton,
North Carolina

Education · Ausbildung
Self-taught as a jeweler and
metalsmith; University of Iowa,
Iowa City, Iowa, 1963–68, B.A.

**Selected Collections ·
Sammlungen (Auswahl)**
Château Musée, Cagnes-sur-
Mer, France; Contemporary
Museum, Honolulu, Hawaii;
Mint Museum of Craft +
Design, Charlotte, North
Carolina; Museum of Arts &
Design, New York, New York;
Museum of Fine Arts, Houston,
Houston, Texas; Racine Art
Museum, Racine, Wisconsin;
Smithsonian American Art
Museum, Renwick Gallery,
Washington, D.C.; Tacoma Art
Museum, Tacoma, Washington;
Victoria and Albert Museum,
London, England

"Materials are often chosen to serve an idea. Their metaphoric possibilities can be released through their context. As an artist making jewelry, I often think about scale and how perception works close up. In *Circumspect,* I wanted to use glass in the context of lenses for seeing clearly and for seeing close up. I am always after clarity in my work— clarity without abandoning mystery. Lenses provide clarity. Mirrors provide another kind of clarity. Both types of glass serve my intentions. They surround the wearer with a number of analytical and optical possibilities for self-examination and for scrutiny by others. In a culture obsessed with self-indulgence and appearance, as ours is, such 'self-reflection' is revealing." ▪ *„Materialien werden oft ausgesucht, um einer Idee zu dienen. Ihre metaphorischen Möglichkeiten können durch ihren Kontext freigesetzt werden. Als Schmuckkünstlerin denke ich oft über Maßstäbe nach und darüber, wie Wahrnehmung aus der Nähe funktioniert. Bei* Circumspect *wollte ich Glas im Zusammenhang mit Linsen verwenden, um klar und um nah zu sehen. Bei all meinen Arbeiten will ich Klarheit erzielen – ohne den Verlust von Rätselhaftigkeit. Linsen schaffen Klarheit. Spiegel schaffen eine andere Form der Klarheit. Beide Glassorten erfüllen meine Absichten. Sie umgeben den Betrachter mit mehreren analytischen und optischen Möglichkeiten der Selbstprüfung und der genauen Prüfung durch andere. In einer Kultur, die so der Genusssucht und dem äußeren Erscheinungsbild verfallen ist wie die unsere, ist solch eine ‚Selbstreflexion' aufschlussreich. "*

Circumspect (neckpiece)
2003, mirrors, lenses, silver,
brass, 14 × 13 × ½ in.
Collection of the Museum of
Arts & Design, New York,
Museum purchase with funds
provided by Ann Kaplan, 2004

Circumspect (Halsschmuck)
2003, Spiegel, Linsen, Silber,
Messing, 35,6 × 33 × 1,3 cm
Sammlung des Museum
of Arts & Design, New York.
Museumserwerb mit
finanziellen Mitteln zur
Verfügung gestellt von
Anne Kaplan, 2004

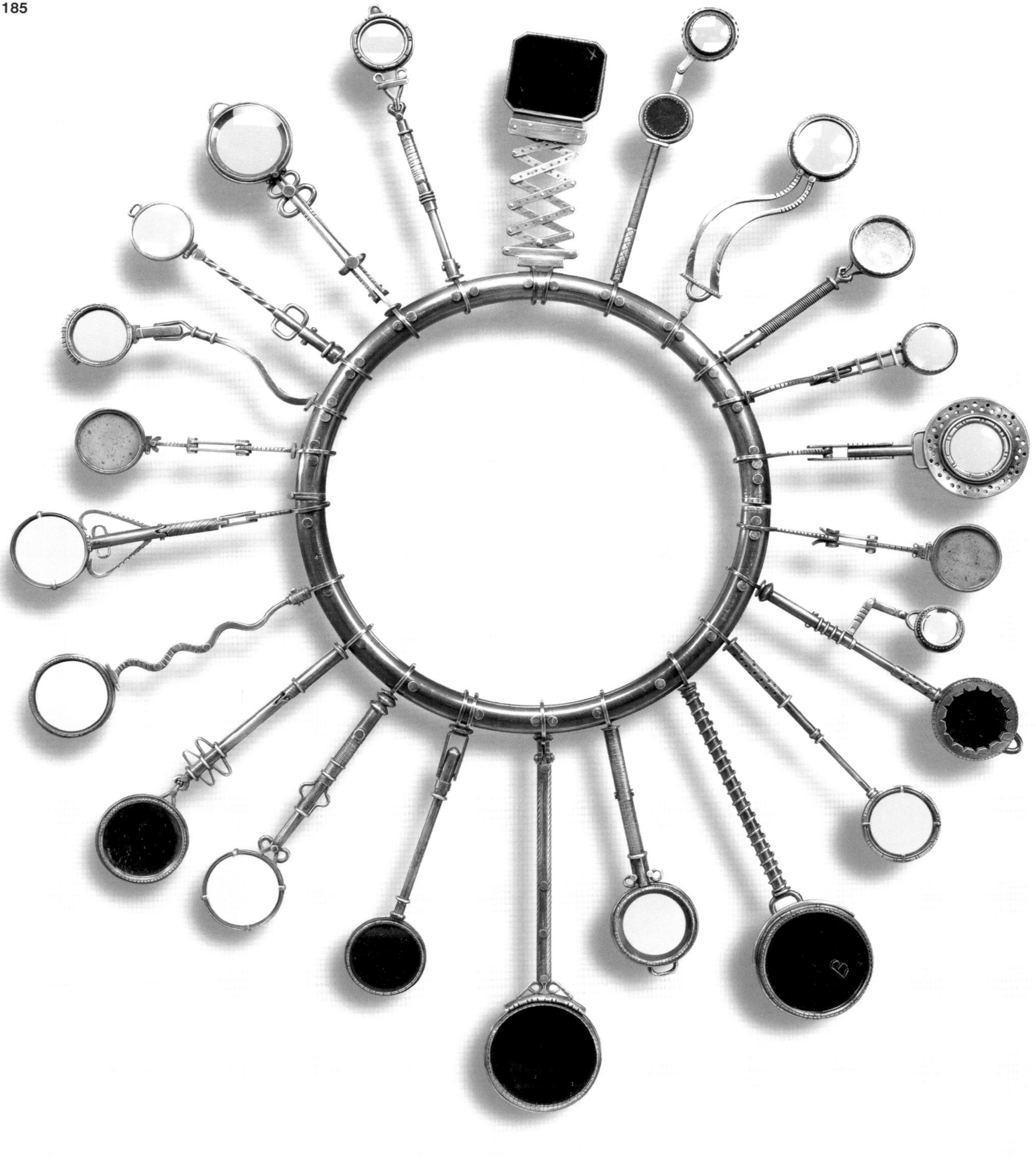

Terhi Tolvanen
Amsterdam, The Netherlands
Born: 1968, Helsinki, Finland

Education · Ausbildung
Gerrit Rietveld Academie,
Amsterdam, The Netherlands,
1993–99; Muotoiluinstituutti,
Lahti University of Applied
Sciences, Lahti, Finland,
1989–93

**Selected Collections ·
Sammlungen (Auswahl)**
Gintaro Galerija-Muziejus,
Vilnius, Lithuania; Françoise
van den Bosch Foundation,
Stedelijk Museum, Amsterdam,
The Netherlands

"My work is about human intervention in nature, which is unavoidable because nature grows and changes ceaselessly. In choosing materials, I search for those that can illustrate the borders between the natural and the artificial. Glass itself is ambivalent, but the irregular shapes of the droplets of melted glass that I use in my jewelry refer to organic forms. I combine glass with all kinds of different materials. The textures and colors shine through the glass and the glass alters the intensity of the color and creates depth in the pieces, an effect that can only be achieved with glass." ▪ *„Das Thema meiner Arbeit ist das Eingreifen des Menschen in die Natur, das unvermeidlich ist, da die Natur unaufhörlich wächst und sich verändert. Wenn ich Materialien auswähle, suche ich nach solchen, die die Grenzen zwischen dem Natürlichen und dem Künstlichen vor Augen führen. Glas an sich ist ambivalent, aber die unregelmäßigen Formen der Tropfen von geschmolzenem Glas, die ich für meinen Schmuck verwende, verweisen auf organische Formen. Ich kombiniere Glas mit den verschiedensten Materialien. Die Strukturen und Farben scheinen durch das Glas hindurch und das Glas verändert die Intensität der Farben und gibt den Schmuckstücken Tiefe, ein Effekt, den man nur mit Glas erzielen kann."*

Fungus Vitreus Caerulens (brooch)
from the Substralia series
2004, cast glass, tourmaline, silk,
hazelnut wood, grape wood,
4¾×2¼×1¼ in.
Private collection, The Netherlands

*Fungus Vitreus Caerulens
(Brosche) der Substralia-Serie*
*2004, gegossenes Glas, Turmalin,
Seide, Haselnussholz, Holz vom
Weinstock, 12×5,5×3,5 cm
Privatsammlung, Niederlande*

Giorgio Vigna
Milan, Italy
Born: 1955, Verona, Italy

Education · Ausbildung
Liceo Artistico di Verona,
Verona, Italy, 1970; C.E.A.
Centro Educazione Artistica,
Verona, Italy, 1964

**Selected Collections ·
Sammlungen (Auswahl)**
Museo Internazionale delle
Arti Applicate Oggi, Turin, Italy

"Glass is like water that has been captured, its unstoppable flow suspended for a moment in time. Simple, primordial, molded by the soft power of fire, transparent, a constant play of light and its infinite possibilities, substantial yet insubstantial, glass plays out its existence in an eternal dialogue with its own form. Sculptures and jewels are born out of the inner energy of glass, out of the evocative forms and patterns that emerge as glass is worked. Fluid forms bring the genealogy of the physical material to life, re-evoking the gestures and work tools of ancient history, as does pairing the material with members of the family of metals. Glass is precious, its mysterious force is alluring; it demands intimacy, to be touched, to be worn in an extraordinary adventure of discovery and experience." ▪ *„Glas ist wie gefangenes Wasser, dessen unaufhörlicher Fluss für einen Moment ausgesetzt hat. Einfach, ursprünglich, geformt durch die sanfte Kraft des Feuers, transparent, ein konstantes Spiel von Licht und seinen unbegrenzten Möglichkeiten, wesenhaft und dennoch unwesenhaft spielt Glas seine Existenz in einem ewigen Dialog seiner eigenen Form aus. Skulpturen und Juwelen werden aus der inneren Energie des Glases heraus geboren, heraus aus bewegenden Formen und Mustern, die sich bilden, wenn Glas bearbeitet wird. Flüssige Formen erwecken – wie das Paaren des Materials mit Stoffen aus der Familie der Metalle – die Genealogie des physikalischen Materials zum Leben, indem es Ausdrucksformen und Werkzeuge der antiken Geschichte wieder wachruft. Glas ist edel, seine geheimnisvolle Kraft verlangt nach Intimität, danach, berührt zu werden, in einem außergewöhnlichen Abenteuer von Entdeckung und Erfahrung getragen zu werden."*

Gorgoglio (necklace)
2002, blown glass, copper,
silver, 15¾×6 in.
Collection of the artist

Gorgoglio (Halsschmuck)
2002, geblasenes Glas, Kupfer,
Silber, 40×15 cm
Sammlung des Künstlers

Nancy Worden
Seattle, Washington
Born: 1954, Boston,
Massachusetts

Education · Ausbildung
University of Georgia, Athens,
Georgia, 1980, M.F.A.; Central
Washington University,
Ellensburg, Washington,
1977, B.A.

**Selected Collections ·
Sammlungen (Auswahl)**
Museum of Arts & Design,
New York, New York; Museum
of Fine Arts, Boston, Boston,
Massachusetts; Museum of
Fine Arts, Houston, Houston,
Texas; Racine Art Museum,
Racine, Wisconsin; Seattle
Art Museum, Seattle,
Washington; Stedelijk Museum
's-Hertogenbosch, 's-Herto-
genbosch, The Netherlands;
Tacoma Art Museum, Tacoma,
Washington; University of
Georgia, Athens, Georgia

"The first jewelry I made with glass was in 1988. I often refer to older jewelry traditions in my work and a long tradition exists for putting hair or a photo or some other keepsake behind glass in jewelry. Recently, I hired James Minson to make specific shapes for me in Pyrex because it is more resilient than ordinary glass. I wanted the preciousness of glass, but with less breakage. In *Prudence*, I used glass mirrors and the vials James made. I electro-formed on the glass to hold it in place and to imply age, such as that of an old church reliquary. The glass vials convey fragility in keeping with the frailty of the dried roses." ▪ *„Mein erstes Schmuckstück mit Glas kreierte ich 1988. Ich nehme in meinen Arbeiten oft Bezug auf alte Schmucktraditionen. Eine sehr alte Tradition besteht darin, Haare oder ein Foto oder ein anderes Andenken in Schmuck hinter Glas einzuschließen. Kürzlich habe ich James Minson beauftragt, um für mich ganz spezielle Formen aus Pyrex herzustellen, weil Pyrex elastischer ist als normales Glas. Ich wollte die Kostbarkeit von Glas, aber in weniger zerbrechlicher Form. Bei* Umsicht *habe ich Glasspiegel und die Ampullen verwendet, die James für mich gemacht hat. Ich habe das Glas durch elektrogeformtes Kupfer in Form gehalten und ihm damit auch eine Art Patina verliehen wie z.B. eine alte Kirchenreliquie. Die Glasampullen vermitteln den Eindruck von Zerbrechlichkeit, die zu der Fragilität der getrockneten Rosen passt."*

Prudence (necklace)
2006, lamp-worked Pyrex
glass, mirrors, silver, copper,
dried roses, 13×12×1½ in.
Collection of the artist

Umsicht (Halsschmuck)
*2006, vor der Lampe
geblasenes Pyrexglas, Spiegel,
Silber, Kupfer, getrocknete
Rosen, 33×30,5×3,8 cm
Sammlung der Künstlerin*

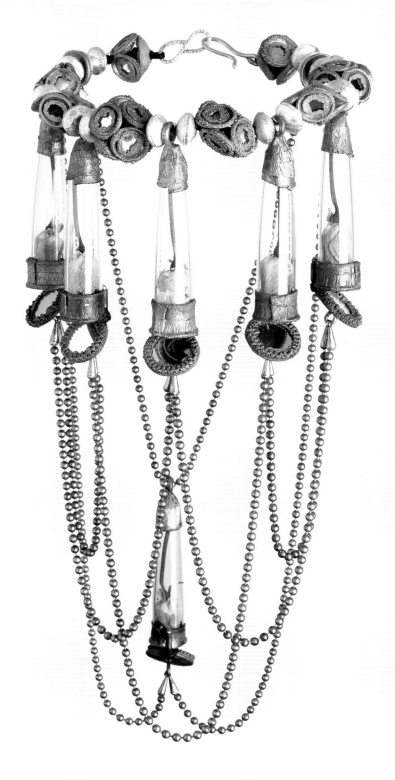

Annamaria Zanella
Padua, Italy
Born: 1966, S. Angelo di
Piove, Padua, Italy

Education · Ausbildung
Accademia di Belle
Arti, Venice, Italy, 1988–92;
Istituto Statale d'Arte Pietro
Selvatico, Padua, Italy,
1980–85

**Selected Collections ·
Sammlungen (Auswahl)**
Kunstgewerbemuseum, Berlin,
Germany; Landesmuseum
Joanneum, Graz, Austria;
Musée Bijou Contemporain,
Cagnes-sur-Mer, France;
Musée des Arts Décoratifs,
Paris, France; Museum of Arts
& Design, New York, New York;
Museo d'Arte Moderna Ca'
Pesaro, Venice, Italy; National
Museums of Scotland, Edin-
burgh, Scotland; Die Neue
Sammlung, Staatliches Muse-
um für Angewandte Kunst,
Design in der Pinakothek der
Moderne, on permanent loan
from the Danner Foundation,
Munich, Germany; Schmuck-
museum Pforzheim, Pforz-
heim, Germany

"I use glass for its force, its colors, and its capacity to be cut into compositions of perfect line and shape. Glass is strong and imprisons incredible colors. I often use glass as a precious stone; for me there is no difference." ▪ *„Ich verwende Glas wegen seiner Stärke, seinen Farben und der Möglichkeit, die es bietet, in perfekte Kombinationen von Form und Linie geschnitten zu werden. Glas ist stark und birgt unglaubliche Farben in sich. Ich benutze Glas oft als Edelstein; für mich gibt es da keinen Unterschied."*

Ring
1996, plate glass, iron,
gold, 3×2×¾ in.
Collection of the artist

Ring
1996, Flachglas, Eisen,
Gold, 8×5×2 cm
Sammlung der Künstlerin

Petra Zimmermann
Vienna, Austria
Born: 1975, Graz, Austria

Education · Ausbildung
Universität für angewandte
Kunst, Vienna, Austria,
1997–2002; Vysoká Skola
Výtvarných Umení, Bratislava,
Slovakia, 1996–98

**Selected Collections ·
Sammlungen (Auswahl)**
Bundeskanzleramt Kunst-
sektion, Vienna, Austria;
Muzeum Ceského ráje v
Turnové, Turnov, Czech
Republic; Österreichisches
Museum für Angewandte
Kunst, Vienna, Austria;
Schmuckmuseum Pforzheim,
Pforzheim, Germany

"Glass appears in my work in the form of old rhine-stones, which are often taken from jewelry from the 1950s. In my brooches, the 'authentic glitter' of the stones and the synthetic surfaces of dental plastics are on a par. In the 1930s, glass stones were used extensively in jewelry and became associated with a new type of woman—the Hollywood diva, the female star, surrounded by, and ultimately defined by, glitter." ▪ *„Glas findet sich in meinen Werken in Form von Strass, der oft von Schmuck aus den 1950er Jahren stammt. In meinen Broschen sind der 'echte Glanz' der Steine und die synthetische Oberfläche von Zahnplastiken ebenbürtig. In den 1930er Jahren wurden Glassteine sehr viel für Schmuck verwendet und standen für einen neuen Typ von Frau – die Hollywood-Diva, der weibliche Star, umgeben und letztendlich definiert durch Glimmer und Glamour."*

Pin-up VI (brooch)
2004, rhinestones, recycled
glass crystals, onyx, pyrite, gold
leaf, dental plastic, blackened
silver, gold, 5×3¼×½ in.
Collection of the artist

Pin-up VI (Brosche)
2004, Strass, recycelte
Glaskristalle, Onyx, Pyrit,
Blattgold, Dental-Kunststoff,
geschwärztes Silber,
Gold, 13×8×1,5 cm
Sammlung der Künstlerin

Bibliography · *Literaturverzeichnis*

General References

Aldred, Cyril. *Jewels of the Pharaohs: Egyptian Jewellery of the Dynastic Period*. London: Thames & Hudson, 1971.

Anderson, Patricia. *Contemporary Jewellery in Australia and New Zealand*. Sydney: Craftsman House, 1998.

Andrews, Carol A. R. *Ancient Egyptian Jewellery*. London: British Museum Publications, 1990.

Coarelli, Filippo. *Greek and Roman Jewellery*. Translated by D. Strong. Feltham: Hamlyn, 1970.

Drutt, Helen Williams, and Peter Dormer. *Jewelry of Our Time: Art, Ornament and Obsession*. London: Thames & Hudson, 1995.

Evans, Joan. *A History of Jewellery, 1100–1870*, 2nd ed. London: Faber & Faber, 1970.

Falk, Fritz, and Cornelie Holzach. *Schmuck der Moderne: Bestandskatalog der modernen Sammlung des Schmuckmuseums Pforzheim / Modern Jewellery 1960–1998: Catalogue of the Modern Collection in the Schmuckmuseum Pforzheim*. Stuttgart: Arnoldsche, 1999.

Frantz, Susanne K. *Contemporary Glass: A World Survey from the Corning Museum of Glass*. New York: Harry N. Abrams, 1989.

Gregorietti, Guido. *Jewelry: History & Technique from the Egyptians to the Present*. Secaucus, N.J.: Chartwell, 1979.

Ilse-Neuman, Ursula. *Radiant Geometries: Fifteen International Jewelers*. New York: American Craft Museum, 2001.

Ilse-Neuman, Ursula, and David Revere McFadden. *Zero Karat: The Donna Schneier Gift to the American Craft Museum*. New York: American Craft Museum, 2002.

Klein, Dan. *Artists in Glass: Late Twentieth-Century Masters in Glass*. London: Mitchell Beazley, 2001.

Lewin, Susan. *One of a Kind: American Art Jewelry Today*. New York: Harry N. Abrams, 1994.

Lightbown, Ronald W. *Mediaeval European Jewellery: With a Catalogue of the Collection in the Victoria & Albert Museum*. London: Victoria & Albert Museum, 1992.

Phillips, Clare. *Jewelry: From Antiquity to the Present*. New York: Thames & Hudson, 1996.

Ricke, Helmut, ed. *Czech Glass 1945–1980: Design in an Age of Adversity*. Düsseldorf: museum kunst palast; Stuttgart: Arnoldsche, 2005.

Strauss, Cindi, and Helen Williams Drutt English. *Ornament as Art. Avant-Garde Jewelry from the Helen Williams Drutt Collection, the Museum of Fine Arts, Houston*. Stuttgart: Arnoldsche, 2007.

Turner, Ralph. *Jewelry in Europe and America: New Times, New Thinking*. London: Thames & Hudson, 1996.

Victoria and Albert Museum. *Princely Magnificence: Court Jewels of the Renaissance, 1500–1630*. London: Debrett's Peerage in association with the Victoria and Albert Museum, 1980.

Giampaolo Babetto

Bibliography

Celant, Germano. *Giampaolo Babetto*. Milan: Skira, 1996.

Museo Correr. *Babetto, 1996–2000: Geometrie di Gioielli*. Venice: Cicero, 2000.

Folchini Grassetto, Graziella. *Contemporary Jewellery: The Padua School*. Stuttgart: Arnoldsche, 2005.

Monica Backström

Bibliography

Litell, Richard. "Monica Backström: Elegance in Glass." *Glass 83* (summer 2001): 28–33.

Gura, Judith. "Monica Backström: Forty Years of Innovation in Swedish Glass." *Modernism Magazine* 8, no. 4 (winter 2005–2006): 70–9.

Boris Bally

Bibliography

Backer, Noelle. "Transcending Garbage: Metalsmith Boris Bally Found His Sanity in a Scrap Yard." *Crafts Report* 24 (April 1998): 18–21.

Lefteri, Chris. *Metals. Materials for Inspirational Design*. Beverly, Mass.: Rockport Publishers, 2004.

Harris, Patricia, and David Lyon. "Boris Bally: Urban Enamels." *Metalsmith* 25, no. 2 (spring 2005): 52.

Célio Braga

Bibliography

Hammer, Melle, Peter van Kester, and Renée C. Hoogland. *Loss*. Amsterdam: Nieuwsbrief, 2004.

Alphen, E. J. van. "Sharing a Common Skin: Cutting, Perforating, Sewing, and Stringing in the Work of Célio Braga." In *Célio Braga: Deliriously*. Staphorst: Hein Elferink, 2006.

Helen Britton

Bibliography

Ewington, Julie. *Second Nature*. Perth: FORM: Contemporary Craft & Design, 2004.

Rosolowski, Tacey A. "Helen Britton and David Bielander: Silk Purse from a Sow's Ear / Uus Schyssdagg Angge Mache." *Metalsmith* 24, no. 3 (summer 2004): 47.

Cunningham, Jack. *Maker, Wearer, Viewer: Contemporary Narrative European Jewellery*. Edinburgh: Scottish Arts Council, 2005.

Pierre Cavalan

Bibliography

Game, Amanda. *Pierre Cavalan*. Ruthin, Wales: Ruthin Craft Centre, 1999.

Swann, Philippa. "Ephemeral Gems." *Crafts*, no. 163 (March– April 2000): 16.

Le Van, Marthe, ed. *Five Hundred Necklaces: Contemporary Interpretations of a Timeless Form*. New York: Lark Books, 2006.

Simsa Cho

Bibliography

Besten, Liesbeth den. "Amsterdam Glass." *Neues Glas / New Glass*, no. 4 (1996): 30–9.

Meitner, Richard, and Jan Verschoor. *Nieuwe Garde & Jonge Gasten / New Guard & Young Fellows*. Amstelveen: Museum Jan van der Togt, 2006.

Václav Cigler

Bibliography

Sindelová, Jana, and Michal Motycka. *Václav Cigler: Kresby*. Olomouc: Galerie Caesar, 2004.

Balgavá, Beáta, and Titus M. Eliëns. *Gedachten in Glas: Václav Cigler en Zijn School / Thinking in Glass: Václav Cigler and His School*. Zwolle: Waanders; The Hague: Gemeentemuseum, 2005.

Patty Cokus

Bibliography

Le Van, Marthe, ed. *One Thousand Rings: Inspiring Adornments for the Hand*. New York: Lark Books, 2004.

Harris, Patricia, and David Lyon. "Jewelry Hard and Soft: Plastic, Fiber, and Glass." *Metalsmith* 24, no. 1 (winter 2004): 57.

Le Van, Marthe, ed. *Five Hundred Necklaces: Contemporary Interpretations of a Timeless Form*. New York: Lark Books, 2006.

Giselle Courtney

Bibliography

Liu, Robert K., and James Minson. "Contemporary Glass Jewelry: A Continuing Tradition." *Ornament* 24, no. 3 (spring 2001): 40–5.

"Giselle Courtney—In Her Element." *Poloxygen: The International Design Art Architecture Quarterly* 18 (2006): 40–8.

199

Ramón Puig Cuyàs

Bibliography

Dibuixos de Taller/ Workshop Drawings. Contemporary Jewellery Issues. Barcelona: Renart Edicions, 1995.

Possamai Vita, Alessandra. *Pensieri Preziosi 3: Assemblaggi, Geometrie, Mito e Memoria Nei Lavori di Kruger, Peters, Puig Cuyàs e Visintin / Precious Thoughts 3, Assemblies, Geometries, Myth and Memory.* Curated by Mirella Cisotto Nalon. Oratorio San Rocco. Padua: Comune di Padova, 2006.

Victoria and Albert Museum, and Crafts Council. *Collect: The International Art Fair for Contemporary Objects.* London: Scala, 2007.

Rian de Jong

Bibliography

Unger, Marjan, and Victor Joseph. *Rian de Jong: Reisgenoten.* Amsterdam: Galerie Ra, 1999.

Wanderungen. Munich: Galerie Spektrum, 2005.

Georg Dobler

Bibliography

Eickhoff, Jürgen, and Marianne Schliwinski. *Georg Dobler: Schmuckarbeiten, 1980–2000.* Munich: Galerie Spektrum, 2000.

Maas, Barbara. "Lampionblume, Strauchtomate, Sternanis und Wilder Wein: Versuch über die Naturbroschen von Georg Dobler." *Kunsthandwerk & Design* 4 (July–August 2002): 36–41.

Steiner, Wendy. *Georg Dobler: Falsche Freunde/ False Friends.* Munich: Galerie Spektrum, 2003.

Bell, Robert. *Transformations: The Language of Craft.* Canberra: National Gallery of Australia, 2005.

Aav, Marianne, and Helen Williams Drutt. *Challenging the Châtelaine!* Helsinki: Designmuseo, 2006.

Robert Ebendorf

Bibliography

Backer, Noelle. "Robert Ebendorf: Astonishing Adornment." *Crafts Report* 25, no. 278 (June 1999): 24–7, 62.

Summers, Ruth, and Bruce Pepich. *Ebendorf: The Jewelry of Robert Ebendorf: A Retrospective of Forty Years.* Raleigh, N.C.: Gallery of Art & Design, North Carolina State University, 2002.

Tanguy, Sarah. "The Jewelry of Robert Ebendorf." *American Craft* 64, no. 1 (February–March 2004): 56–9.

Andreas Eberharter

Bibliography

Bohwongprasert, Yvonne. "Changing Tack." Review in *Bangkok Post*, 23 June 2005.

"Andi and I." *GM Magazine* (July 2005): 116.

Sandra Enterline

Bibliography

Phillips, Maria, et al. *Transformation 3: Contemporary Works in Jewelry and Small Metals: The Elizabeth R. Raphael Founder's Prize Exhibition*. Pittsburgh: Society for Contemporary Craft, 2002.

Bonansinga, Kate, and Ursula Ilse-Neuman. *Hanging in Balance: Forty-two Contemporary Necklaces*. El Paso: Stanlee and Gerald Rubin Center for the Visual Arts, University of Texas, 2004.

Harris, Patricia, and David Lyon. "Mystery and Memory: The Jewelry of Sandra Enterline." *Metalsmith* 24, no. 2 (spring 2004): 30–9.

Donald Friedlich

Bibliography

Dinsmore, Claire. "The Visual Articulations of Donald Friedlich." *Metalsmith* 16, no. 1 (winter 1996): 23–9.

Friedlich, Donald. *Donald Friedlich: A Retrospective, Jewelry 1986–98*. Iowa City: University of Iowa Museum of Art, 1998.

Brown, Glen R. "Donald Friedlich: A Reductive Art." *Ornament* 22, no. 1 (fall 1998): 44–7.

Jacquard, Nicole. "Duality and Contrast." *Craft Arts International* 62 (2004): 35–9.

"Donald Friedlich: A Jeweler Explores His Vision in Glass." *The Gather / The Corning Museum of Glass*, winter/spring 2004, 4.

Karl Fritsch

Bibliography

Baines, Robert, et al. *Karl Fritsch, Schmuck / The Jewelry of Karl Fritsch*. Amsterdam: O Book Publisher, 2001.

Lim, Andy, ed. *Karl Fritsch: Metrosideros Robusta*. Cologne: Darling Publications, 2006.

Lim, Andy, ed. *The Baby Brick*. Cologne: Darling Publications, 2007.

Thomas Gentille

Bibliography

Lynn, Vanessa S. "Thomas Gentille: The Permanence of the Ephemeral." *Metalsmith* 11, no. 4 (fall 1991): 14–9.

Ilse-Neuman, Ursula. "Thomas Gentille." In *Schmuck 2006*, 14. Munich: GHM-Gesellschaft für Handwerksmessen, 2006.

DiNoto, Andrea. "Thomas Gentille." *Metalsmith* 27, no. 1 (2007): 43.

Karen Gilbert

Bibliography

Modena, Charlene M. "Karen Gilbert: Material for Reasoning." *Metalsmith* 17, no. 5 (fall 1997): 49.

Carley, Michal Ann. "Observations: The Work of Karen Gilbert." *Metalsmith* 20, no. 3 (summer 2000): 44–5.

Mieke Groot

Therese Hilbert

Timothy Horn

Svatopluk Kasalý

Jaroslav Kodejš

Bibliography

Glasmuseum Alter Hof Herding. *Mieke Groot—Retrospective*. Coesfeld-Lette, Germany: Ernsting Foundation, 1999.

Opie, Jennifer Hawkins. *Contemporary International Glass: Sixty Artists in the V&A*. London: Victoria and Albert Museum, 2004.

Groot, Mieke, Daniel Klein, and Marjan Unger. *Mieke Groot*. Leerdam: Glas Galerie Leerdam, 2007.

Bibliography

Jünger, Hermann. "Familiar yet Totally New." *Art Aurea*, no. 3 (1989): 76–8.

Königer, Maribel. *Weiss und Schwarz: Krater-wanderung, zu den Schmuckarbeiten von Therese Hilbert*. Munich: Galerie für angewandte Kunst, Bayerischer Kunst-gewerbe-Verein, 1996.

Bibliography

Porges, Maria. "Timothy Horn." *American Craft* 65, no. 4 (August–September 2005): 60–1.

Rapture: Arngunnur Yr, Timothy Horn. San Francisco: Mills College Art Museum, 2006.

Gans, J. C. "Timothy Horn: Difficult to Swallow." *Metalsmith* 26, no. 1 (spring 2006): 50.

Bibliography

Svatopluk Kasalý: Šperky a Objekty ze Skla, 1968–1972. Brno: Moravská galerie v Brně, 1972.

Bibliography

Heigl, Curt, and Barbara Bredow. *Gold und Silber, Schmuck und Gerät von Albrecht Dürer bis zur Gegenwart: Ausstellung der Stadt Nürnberg in Verbindung mit der Landesgewerbeanstalt Bayern in der Norishalle Nürnberg, zum 500. Geburtstag Albrecht Dürers, 19. März bis 22. August 1971*. Munich: Lipp, 1971.

Schollmayer, Karl. *Neuer Schmuck: Ornamentum Humanum*. Tübingen: Wasmuth, 1974.

Krechlová, Daniela. *Jaroslav Kodejš: výtvarný sperk*. Prague: Úřad městské části Praha 20 Horní Počernice, Infocentrum Horní Počernice, 2006.

Helfried Kodré

Bibliography

Folchini Grassetto, Graziella. "Padua— Vienna, Four Stations." *Craft Arts International* 58 (2003): 98–103.

Folchini Grassetto, Graziella. *Gioielleria Contemporanea: Minimal Art*. Padua: Studio Gr. 20, 2005.

Maurer Zilioli, Ellen, Wolfgang Prohaska, and Karl Bollmann. *Helfried Kodré: Vedere l'invisibile*. Stuttgart: Arnoldsche, 2006.

Daniel Kruger

Bibliography

Staal, Gert. *Daniel Kruger: beeldende Kunst*. 's Hertogenbosch: Museum Het Kruithuis, 1994.

Jensen, Jan. "New Forms—New Materials— New Values: The Emergence of Modern Jewelry, from 1960 through 1998." *Goldschmiede Zeitung Art + Design 3* (autumn 2003).

Blauensteiner, Charlotte. "Aus der Schatztruhe: Neuer Schmuck von Daniel Kruger." *Kunsthandwerk & Design* 5 (September–October 2004): 18–23.

Bell, Robert. *Transformations: The Language of Craft*. Canberra: National Gallery of Australia, 2005.

Otto Künzli

Bibliography

Künzli, Otto. *Das dritte Auge / The Third Eye / Het Derde Oog*. Amsterdam: Stedelijk Museum, 1991.

Hufnagl, Florian. *Goldschmiede Silberschmiede. Drei Generationen von der Weimarer Zeit bis heute*. Munich: Die Neue Sammlung, 1993.

Künzli, Otto. *Gold oder Leben / Gold or Life*. Munich: Akademie der Bildenden Künste Munich, 1994.

Riklin-Schelbert, Antoinette. *Schmuckzeichen Schweiz: 20. Jahrhundert / 20th Century Swiss Art Jewelry*. St. Gallen: VGS Verlagsgemeinschaft, 1999.

Hartmann, Serge. "Le Bijou de Otto Künzli Nous Parle." *Dernières Nouvelles d'Alsace*, 2004: 25–6.

Stanley Lechtzin

Bibliography

Dormer, Peter, ed. *The Culture of Craft: Status and Future*. Manchester, England: Manchester University Press, 1997.

Falk, Fritz, and Cornelie Holzach. *Schmuck der Moderne: Bestandskatalog der modernen Sammlung des Schmuckmuseums Pforzheim / Modern Jewellery 1960–1998: Catalogue of the Modern Collection in the Schmuckmuseum Pforzheim*. Stuttgart: Arnoldsche, 1999.

McFadden, David Revere, and Ursula Ilse-Neuman. *Defining Craft 1, Collecting for the New Millennium*. New York: American Craft Museum, 2000.

Lechtzin, Stanley. *Craft in the Digital Age*. Concord, N.H.: League of New Hampshire Craftsman, 2004.

Tarja Lehtinen

Bibliography

Böck, Angela, and Titus Kockel. *Talente 2007*. Munich: Verein zur Förderung des Handwerks e.V., 2007.

"Gallery Norsu: Jewelry Designer of the Month." *Watch and Gold Magazine*, March 2007, 40.

Jacqueline I. Lillie

Bibliography

Liu, Robert K., and Elisabeth Schmuttermeier. *Jacqueline I. Lillie: Works / Arbeiten / Oeuvres, 1990–97.* New York: Rosanne Raab Associates, 1998.

Porges, Maria. "Making Rime: Jacqueline Lillie." *American Craft* 60, no. 5 (October–November 2000): 80–3.

Linda MacNeil

Bibliography

The Art Center at Hargate. *Dan Dailey and Linda MacNeil: Art in Glass and Metal.* Concord, N.H.: Exeter Press, 1999.

Ramljak, Suzanne. *United in Beauty: The Jewelry and Collectors of Linda MacNeil.* Atglen, Pa.: Schiffer Publishing, 2002.

Juan, Lee. "Linda MacNeil." *Art of Glass* 18 (2005): 26–31.

Stefano Marchetti

Bibliography

Van Berkum, Ans. *Stefano Marchetti: Longing for Shape.* Padua: n.p., 1999.

Folchini Grassetto, Graziella. "Contemporary Jewellery: An Alternative to Precious Stones and Metals." *Craft Arts International* 55 (2002): 100–2.

Folchini Grassetto, Graziella. *Oreficeria Contemporanea: Stefano Marchetti: mostra antologica.* Padua: Studio Gr. 20, 2003.

Nanna Melland

Bibliography

Le Van, Marthe, ed. *Five Hundred Brooches: Inspiring Adornments for the Body.* New York: Lark Books, 2005.

"Aslaug Juliussen; Anna Stina Naess; Nanna Melland." *Norske Kunsthåndverkere*, no. 99 (2006): 36–7.

Martina Mináriková

Bibliography

Vyskočil, Libor, Roman Tomášek, and Michal Eben. *Martina Mináriková: Kosmická Hra / Cosmic Game.* Prague: Galerie Kotelna, 2000.

Skalský, Vladimír. *Martina Mináriková: Stvoření / Stvorenie / Creation.* Dvůr Králové nad Labem: Martina Mináriková, 2004.

Kazuko Mitsushima

Bibliography

"Rings: Praying the Glaciers on the Earth Won't Melt: Cold-worked Glass, Silver, by Kazuko Mitsushima." *New Glass Review 19, Corning Magazine of Glass* (supplement to *Neues Glas/New Glass 2* [1998]): 90.

Mitsushima, Kazuko. *Glass Jewellery*. N.p.: BeeBooks, 2003.

Evert Nijland

Bibliography

Folchini Grassetto, Graziella. *Gioielli Contemporanei: L'alternativa al prezioso*. Padua: Studio Gr. 20, 1999.

Guirlandes. Amsterdam: Galerie Louise Smit, 2004.

Venezia. Amsterdam: Galerie Louise Smit, 2006.

Ted Noten

Bibliography

Staal, Gert. *Ted Noten: CH_2=C (CH_3) C (=0) OCH_3 Enclosures and Other TN's*. Rotterdam: 010 Publishers, 2006.

Folchini Grassetto, Graziella. *Plastic: Contemporary Gold*. Milan: Entratalibera, 2007.

Emiko Oye

Bibliography

Le Van, Marthe, ed. *Fabulous Jewelry from Found Objects: Creative Projects, Simple Techniques*. New York: Lark Books, 2005.

Le Van, Marthe, ed. *Five Hundred Necklaces: Contemporary Interpretations of a Timeless Form*. New York: Lark Books, 2006.

Gans, Jennifer Cross. "California Metals Now." *Metalsmith* 26, no. 2 (summer 2006): 57.

Le Van, Marthe, ed. *Five Hundred Earrings: New Directions in Contemporary Jewelry*. New York: Lark Books, 2007.

Martin Papcún

Bibliography

Oldknow, Tina. "Between Enchantment and Disillusionment." In *Coburg Glaspreis für zeitgenössische Glaskunst in Europa, 2006*. Coburg: Kunstsammlungen der Veste Coburg, 2006.

Ricke, Helmut. "Coburg Glass Prize for Contemporary Glass in Europe 2006." *Neues Glas/New Glass*, no. 2 (summer 2006): 14–23.

Joan Parcher

Francesco Pavan

Ruudt Peters

Michael Petry

Katja Prins

Bibliography

Pachikara, Cynthia. "Intimate Parallels between Installation and Wearable Art." *Metalsmith* 15 (summer 1995): 32–7.

Metcalf, Bruce. "Joan Parcher." *Metalsmith* 17, no. 4 (1997): 45.

Bibliography

14 B: Biennale Internazionale del Comune di Padova: Nove Artisti Orafi di Scuola Padovana. Padua: Comune di Padova, 1986.

Ilse-Neuman, Ursula. *Radiant Geometries: Fifteen International Jewelers.* New York: American Craft Museum, 2001.

Gioielleria Contemporanea: Padova—Vienna/ Quattro Stazioni/Francesco Pavan, Annamaria Zanella, Helfried Kodré, Peter Skubic. Padua: Studio Gr. 20, 2002.

Bibliography

Besten, Liesbeth den. *Change.* Amsterdam: Voetnoot, 2002.

Jönsson, Love. "Ruudt Peters." *Kunsthåndverk* 2, no. 96 (2005): 28–31.

Sefiroth: Ruudt Peters. Nijmegen: Galerie Marzee, 2006.

Ilse-Neuman, Ursula. "Ruudt Peters." *American Craft* 66, no. 2 (April–May 2006): 60–1.

Bibliography

The Trouble with Michael. London: ArtMedia, 2001.

De Oliveira, Nicola, and Nicola Oxley. *Installation Art in the New Millennium: The Empire of the Senses.* London: Thames & Hudson, 2003.

Bibliography

Katja Prins: Machines Are Us. Amsterdam: Galerie Louise Smit, 2004.

Katja Prins & Terhi Tolvanen. Munich: Galerie Spektrum, 2006.

Cheung, Lin, Indigo Clarke, and Beccy Clarke. *New Directions in Jewellery II.* London: Black Dog Publishing, 2006.

Wendy Ramshaw

Bibliography

Bury, Shirley. *Wendy Ramshaw: A Retrospective Survey, 1969–1981*. London: Faber & Faber, 1984.

Ramshaw, Wendy, ed. *Picasso's Ladies: Jewellery by Wendy Ramshaw*. Stuttgart: Arnoldsche, 1998.

Glenn, Virginia. "Wendy Ramshaw: Room of Dreams." *Crafts*, no. 180 (January–February 2003): 52–3.

Piergiuliano Reveane

Bibliography

14 B: Biennale Internazionale del Comune di Padova: Nove Artisti Orafi di Scuola Padovana. Padua: Comune di Padova, 1986.

Arbeiten auf Papier: Schmuck. Berlin: Galerie Stühler, 2004.

Folchini Grassetto, Graziella. *Contemporary Jewellery: The Padua School*. Stuttgart: Arnoldsche, 2005.

Marianne Schliwinski

Bibliography

Marianne Schliwinski: Verde Enigma. Munich: Galerie Spektrum, 2002.

Inside-Outside. Munich: Galerie Spektrum, 2005.

Reflexion. Munich: Galerie Spektrum, 2005.

Diven hinter Glas: Broschen von Marianne Schliwinski. Munich: Galerie Spektrum, 2007.

Bernhard Schobinger

Bibliography

Brinkmann, Esther, Sigrid Pallmert, Claire Stoullig and Fabienne Xavière Sturm. *Le bijou en Suisse au 20ᵉ siècle / Art Jewellery in Switzerland in the 20th Century / Schweizer Schmuck im 20. Jahrhundert / Gioielli d'arte in Svizzera nel 20o secolo*. Lausanne: Bibliothèque des Arts, 2002.

Fayet, Roger, and Florian Hufnagl. *Bernhard Schobinger—Jewels Now!* Stuttgart: Arnoldsche, 2003.

Joyce Scott

Bibliography

Ciscle, George. *Joyce J. Scott: Kickin' It with the Old Masters*. Baltimore: Baltimore Museum of Art, Maryland Institute College of Art, 2000.

Blessed: The Work of Joyce Scott. Milwaukee: University of Wisconsin–Milwaukee, 2006.

Sondra Sherman

Jiří Šibor

Markéta Šílená

Peter Skubic

Kiff Slemmons

Bibliography

Lieberman, Elizabeth Broadrup. "Commissions." *Metalsmith* 25, no. 3 (summer 2005): 57.

Sherman, Sondra. "Jewelers on Jewelry." *Metalsmith* 26, no. 5 (2006): 20–3.

DiNoto, Andrea. "Sondra Sherman: Seven Types of Ambiguity." *Metalsmith* 26, no. 3 (fall 2006): 52.

Bibliography

Křížová, Alena. *Metamorphoses of Czech Jewellery at the End of the 20th Century*. Prague: Academia, 2002.

Joppien, Rüdiger, Peter Pinnau, and Olga Zobel-Biró. *Zehn Jahre Galerie Biró*. Munich: Galerie Biró, 2002.

Bibliography

Křížová, Alena. *Metamorphoses of Czech Jewellery at the End of the 20th Century*. Prague: Academia, 2002.

Nováková, Kateřina. *Markéta Šílená: šperk*. Prague: Markéta Šílená, 2006.

Bibliography

Drutt, Helen Williams, Petra Zimmermann, Florian Hufnagl, and Karl Bollmann. *Peter Skubic: Between. Schmuck/Jewellery*. Stuttgart: Arnoldsche, 2001.

Unsichtbar. Munich: Galerie Spektrum, 2001.

Spiegelverkehrt. Munich: Galerie Spektrum, 2005.

Bibliography

Mayfield, Signe. *The Thought of Things: Jewelry by Kiff Slemmons, January 23–April 30, 2000*. Palo Alto, Calif.: Palo Alto Art Center, 2000.

Rosolowski, Tacey A. *Re:pair & Imperfection*. Chicago: Chicago Cultural Center, 2006.

Terhi Tolvanen

Bibliography

Katja Prins & Terhi Tolvanen. Munich: Galerie Spektrum, 2006.

Woodland. Amsterdam: Galerie Louise Smit, 2007.

Giorgio Vigna

Bibliography

Vigna, Giorgio. *Talismani*. Milan: Venini, 1998.

Metallo, Paula. "Giorgio Vigna: Fuochi d'acqua." *Glass*, no. 91 (summer 2003): 56.

Nancy Worden

Bibliography

Updike, Robin. "Multi-generational Themes: Nancy Worden." *Ornament* 24, no. 3 (spring 2001): 50–5.

Kangas, Matthew. "Nancy Worden: Excavations." *Metalsmith* 26, no. 1 (spring 2006): 26–33.

Annamaria Zanella

Bibliography

Segato, Giorgio. *Annamaria Zanella: Il Senso della Gioia / Sense of Joy*. Padua: Ed. La Matita, 1999.

Annamaria Zanella: Opere 1993–2004 / Constructive Works. Piombino Dese, Italy: Ed. Ditre Arti Grafiche, 2004.

Aav, Marianne, and Helen Williams Drutt. *Challenging the Châtelaine!* Helsinki: Designmuseo, 2006.

Collect: The International Art Fair for Contemporary Objects. London: Victoria and Albert Museum, Scala Publisher Ltd., 2007.

Petra Zimmermann

Bibliography

Blauensteiner, Charlotte. "Kunst & Künstlichkeit: Schmuck von Petra Zimmermann." *Kunsthandwerk & Design* 3 (May–June 2000): 40–3.